A COMPLETE GUIDE

MONTREAL & QUEBEC CITY

A COMPLETE GUIDE

1ST EDITION

MONTREAL
& QUEBEC CITY

Steven Howell

The Countryman Press
Woodstock, Vermont

To Lévi, it really was *coup de foudre*!

First Edition

ISBN 978-1-58157-088-5

Cover and interior photos by the author unless otherwise specified
Frontispiece photo: *View of Château Frontenac and the Old Port from the Québec-Lévis ferry*
Book design by Bodenweber Design
Composition by Opaque Design & Print Production
Maps by Mapping Specialists Ltd., Madison, WI, © The Countryman Press

Published by The Countryman Press, P.O. Box 748, Woodstock, Vermont 05091

Distributed by W. W. Norton & Company, Inc., 500 Fifth Avenue, New York, NY 10110

Manufactured in the United States of America

10 9 8 7 6 5 4 3 2 1

GREAT DESTINATIONS TRAVEL GUIDEBOOK SERIES

Recommended by *National Geographic Traveler* and *Travel + Leisure* magazines.

[A] CRISP AND CRITICAL APPROACH, FOR TRAVELERS WHO WANT TO LIVE LIKE LOCALS.
— *USA Today*

Great Destinations™ guidebooks are known for their comprehensive, critical coverage of regions of extraordinary cultural interest and natural beauty. The authors in this series are professional travel writers who have lived for many years in the regions they describe. Each title in this series is continuously updated with each printing to insure accurate and timely information. All the books contain more than one hundred photographs and maps.

Current titles available:

THE ADIRONDACK BOOK

ATLANTA

AUSTIN, SAN ANTONIO
  & THE TEXAS HILL COUNTRY

THE BERKSHIRE BOOK

BERMUDA

BIG SUR, MONTEREY BAY
  & GOLD COAST WINE COUNTRY

CAPE CANAVERAL, COCOA BEACH
  & FLORIDA'S SPACE COAST

THE CHARLESTON, SAVANNAH
  & COASTAL ISLANDS BOOK

THE CHESAPEAKE BAY BOOK

THE COAST OF MAINE BOOK

COLORADO'S CLASSIC MOUNTAIN TOWNS:
  GREAT DESTINATIONS

THE FINGER LAKES BOOK

THE FOUR CORNERS REGION

GALVESTON, SOUTH PADRE ISLAND
  & THE TEXAS GULF COAST

THE HAMPTONS BOOK

HONOLULU & OAHU:
  GREAT DESTINATIONS HAWAII

THE HUDSON VALLEY BOOK

THE JERSEY SHORE: ATLANTIC CITY TO
  CAPE MAY (INCLUDES THE WILDWOODS)

LOS CABOS & BAJA CALIFORNIA SUR:
  GREAT DESTINATIONS MEXICO

MICHIGAN'S UPPER PENINSULA

MONTREAL & QUEBEC CITY:
  GREAT DESTINATIONS CANADA

THE NANTUCKET BOOK

THE NAPA & SONOMA BOOK

NORTH CAROLINA'S OUTER BANKS
  & THE CRYSTAL COAST

PALM BEACH, MIAMI & THE FLORIDA KEYS

PHOENIX, SCOTTSDALE, SEDONA
  & CENTRAL ARIZONA

PLAYA DEL CARMEN, TULUM & THE RIVIERA
  MAYA: GREAT DESTINATIONS MEXICO

SALT LAKE CITY, PARK CITY, PROVO
  & UTAH'S HIGH COUNTRY RESORTS

SAN DIEGO & TIJUANA

SAN JUAN, VIEQUES & CULEBRA:
  GREAT DESTINATIONS PUERTO RICO

THE SANTA FE & TAOS BOOK

THE SARASOTA, SANIBEL ISLAND
  & NAPLES BOOK

THE SEATTLE & VANCOUVER BOOK: INCLUDES
  THE OLYMPIC PENINSULA, VICTORIA & MORE

THE SHENANDOAH VALLEY BOOK

TOURING EAST COAST WINE COUNTRY

WASHINGTON D.C., AND NORTHERN VIRGINIA

YELLOWSTONE & GRAND TETON NATIONAL PARKS
  AND JACKSON HOLE

YOSEMITE & THE SOUTHERN SIERRA NEVADA

If you are traveling to, moving to, residing in, or just interested in any (or all!) of these enchanting regions, a Great Destinations guidebook is a superior companion. Honest and painstakingly critical, full of information only a local can provide, Great Destinations guidebooks give you all the practical knowledge you need to enjoy the best of each region. Why not own them all?

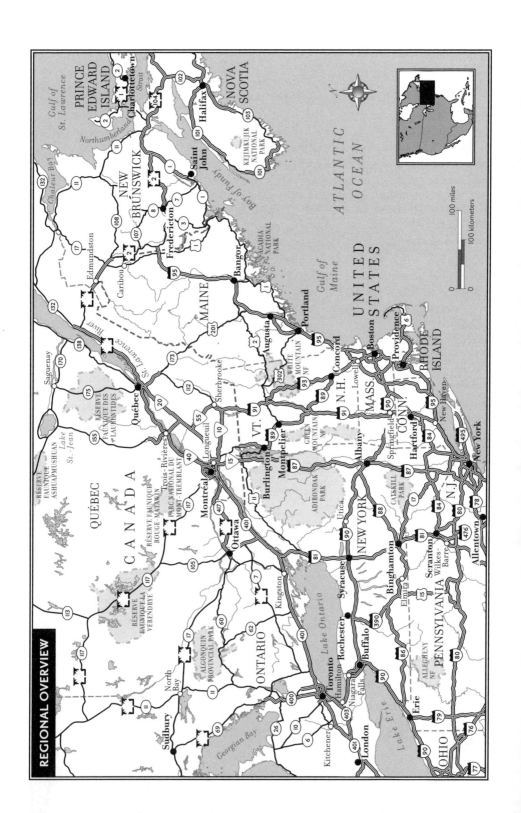

REGIONAL OVERVIEW

Contents

ACKNOWLEDGMENTS:

Gregory Gallagher—the most generous fellow scribe I know and a talent to which this writer can only aspire—most sincere thanks!

Gilles Bengle of Tourisme Montréal and Paule Bergeron of Quebec City Tourism—*merci beaucoup* for all your suggestions, assistance, and pointing me in the right direction.

Claude Chiasson and Jill Craig—thanks for the extra set of eyes and your encouragement along the way.

Thanks to Kim Grant, Jennifer Thompson, Kermit Hummel, and my new friends at The Countryman Press.

Thanks to Glenn E. Novak—I am indebted to your copyediting prowess.

Claudette Dionne—my best PR pal in town—thanks for the restaurant suggestions.

Merci to all of the museum, hotel, and restaurant staff I have met along the way—you are travel industry professionals one and all.

To the fine folks of Montreal and Quebec City—visitors may come for one reason or another, but you are the reason why they come back.

Robin Caudell—thanks for the power lunches and writing pep talks.

Plattsburgh Press-Republican and *Montreal Gazette* friends who have inspired and edited me along the way.

Montreal and Canadian friends tried and true (and the reason why you stay)—Rick, Billy, Murray, Gerald, Tony, and a whole other cast of characters. And to Paul and Rick B.— thanks for watching the house.

Chère Olive, merci pour la chaise de bureau! Et à ma famille Bérubé et Labrie—j'taime beau-coup!

To my Long Island family and friends—not a day goes by when you're not in my thoughts.

Neal and Jen—my best buds forever—I love you both more than you will ever know.

And to my dear Betty—thanks for teaching me how to laugh!!! Write on, Betty!

INTRODUCTION

Where does life—and travel—take you? Here's how I got to Montreal.

I grew up in the shadows of New York City in the suburbs of Long Island. My parents occasionally took my brothers and me into "the city"—Manhattan—for field trips about town. Every summer the '66 silver Dodge Monaco would be loaded up and off we'd go for a glorious one-week adventure to the Catskill Mountains. I was four years old when I purchased my first souvenir—a vinyl wallet of a fisherman with the words "Catskill Mountains" colorfully emblazoned across the front. My grandmother gave me the money for that treat. I still own that wallet today.

Fast forward a dozen years later during senior year at Mineola High School. One very smart curriculum move created an innovative class called New York City: Myth or Reality. Its purpose: learn as much about New York City as possible. Why? As suburban Long Islanders, it was a good chance that many of us students would live or work there in the near future.

Imagine three dozen or so high school seniors hopping on the Long Island Railroad for fun and frolic in New York City. We learned all about the city on a number of trips and explored themes like geography, the arts, neighborhoods, and architecture. We even took tests that quizzed us on the subway system!

Throughout these adventures, and as the tallest member of the class—I measure a towering 6-foot-6—I was designated the human landmark. If any student got temporarily lost, they were instructed to simply look for me. It was all in good fun, but it actually worked on a few occasions! So there I was—a tour guide/beacon leading the way. Perhaps a bit of destiny for what was to come.

The travel bug continued during my 20s. I joined friends on itineraries that included eastern Long Island, Boston, Maine, Pennsylvania, and Florida. Working for the airlines on two separate occasions helped, too. Discount employee travel led to places like Mexico, and business trips meant venturing to some great all-American cities like Pittsburgh, Houston, and Charlotte, among others.

But my most fateful trip was a car ride with no particular destination in mind. I hopped on the New York Thruway and drove north. Seven hours and one country later, I found myself in Montreal. I didn't even have a hotel reservation—something I don't recommend today.

I found a hotel, took a short nap, and ventured out for some Montreal nightlife. And there it was—I turned a street corner and stumbled upon the Montreal Jazz Festival, circa 1989, when the festival was centered along Rue St-Denis in the Latin Quarter. A party! A fantastic energetic colorful display of music, food, fun—and some of the most genuinely friendly folks you ever met in your life. I thought: Was this all for me? It was. It was for everyone. And it was *coup de foudre*—love at first sight!

Eventually I moved north to Plattsburgh, New York, an unofficial suburb of Montreal about an hour's drive south. I soon began writing for the *Press-Republican*, the local daily newspaper covering Montreal museums, restaurants, festivals—you name it (and not to inject any politics here, but the newspaper name has nothing currently to do with any political party affiliation. I mention it because it's something I've had to explain on more than one occasion to many Montreal public relations folks). That first article appeared in 1995, and I've been writing for them ever since. In addition, I currently write for the *Montreal Gazette* as well.

You've picked a great destination for your vacation in Montreal and Quebec City. These folks truly know how to have fun—and it's infectious. Summer in the city means festival season in Montreal—there are dozens from which to choose. The big three—the Grand Prix of Canada, the Montreal International Jazz Festival, and Montreal's gay pride celebration— attract hundreds of thousands of visitors from all over the world each year. And don't forget some winter fun, too. The Quebec Winter Carnival has been embracing Old Man Winter since 1955.

Arts, culture, and attractions abound. In Montreal there are dozens of museums, large and small, and hundreds of art galleries, too. In Quebec City, museums devoted to history and religious themes abound. The region also boasts the rich heritage of a nation, found at dozens of Canadian National Historic Sites. And you're just in time for plenty of special events as Quebec City celebrates its 400th anniversary in 2008.

The province is a superb spot for enjoying the great outdoors. The Montreal Botanical Garden is considered one of the best in the world, and Mount Royal Park is Montreal's all-season playground. Do bring or rent a bicycle—there are hundreds of miles of bike paths and routes throughout the region. Near Quebec City, the magnificent Montmorency Falls is the backdrop for a spectacular summer fireworks show, and a St. Lawrence River sea cruise is never far away. And if you really love the great outdoors, stay overnight in a hotel—made of ice!

Next, bring your appetite. There are thousands of restaurants in both Montreal and Quebec City that offer everything from poutine—an indigenous concoction of fries, farmer's cheese, and gravy—to inventive haute cuisine, and everything in between. It's a gourmand's dream come true.

The price is right, too. While the exchange rate is not as advantageous as it once was— the U.S. dollar is about par with the Canadian dollar—hotels, restaurants, and attractions are all reasonably priced.

I guarantee you a great time in Montreal and Quebec City and sincerely thank you for letting me be your Montreal and Quebec City travel guide and perhaps human landmark. If you see a tall guy walking along Rue Ste-Catherine, say hello, it could be me.

I wish you a bon voyage.

How to Use This Book

As demonstrated in the table of contents, this book follows an easy-to-use format. Montreal listings come first, then Quebec City. In addition, when I mention Quebec, it will stand for the province, while Quebec City will refer to the metropolis.

First up, I'll explore a brief time-line of history of the area. It's always good to know a bit about how a place is born. Next, the nitty gritty, beginning with passport requirements and what to expect at the border, plus taxes, currency, weather, and everything from area codes to taxicab telephone numbers to how to decipher a parking or street sign.

If you haven't already selected accommodations, there will be a few suggestions on where to stay. Then it's time to grab a bite to eat and some tips on how to play like a local— everything from museums for history buffs to gay nightlife, from where to bring the kids to a quick glance at festivals. Most restaurant and sightseeing entries will include suggestions of "what's nearby" that particular listing.

This is not an all-inclusive book of hotels and restaurants, rather a well-balanced selection in terms of taste, location, and a variety of budgets. The beauty of Montreal and

Quebec City is that you'll stumble upon an innovative art gallery or a little corner café that will capture your heart—one that you can call all your own. There are lots of listings of things to do. For all of the listings I'll do my best to tell you what's where and what to expect, but nothing too overly critical. Why? Critiquing is so subjective. I can stand on my head and rave about a local sushi place, but if you don't like sushi, you're not going, no matter what I say. So I'll let you know what's where and why I liked it, and you go make up your own mind.

Most important, I've arranged the book geographically. I think this is the most logical way to approach both cities. You'll be here a few days to a week at most, so I'm suggesting the most popular neighborhoods and places to visit. There are additional chapters on side trips if you want to venture outside the main city core or have extra time to explore.

Prices are listed in Canadian dollars. When I say something costs "about $10," that means the price was at or near that amount at time of publication and may have increased by the time you bought this book.

Finally, remember that prices and exchange rates fluctuate, wait staffs change, and businesses move or close. So act like a Quebecer and just go with the flow.

ACCENT ON FRENCH: A NOTE ABOUT LANGUAGE

I have incorporated a number of language and grammar styles to help you read, think, and speak like a local—specifically in French.

Plaque in Quebec City's Old Port sign commemorates the founding of Quebec by Samuel de Champlain in 1608. French is the official language of Quebec Province.

For example, family names will reflect the person's language of origin and will be written the way the person spells it, in English or French, with accents when present.

Place names will generally use the French spelling (what you'll see on signs and maps) or use an English spelling when the reference is interchangeable in both languages. For example, Montreal is often written with an accent, as in the French Montréal, and often without. Other good examples are museum references. Musée des Beaux-Arts is equally referred to as the Museum of Fine Arts—in Montreal, but not in Quebec City. Sometimes the French reference will be used. For example, Musée d'Art Contemporain de Montréal is rarely mentioned as the Museum of Contemporary Arts. You'll see the French reference more often for Quebec City listings, but I'll include both when applicable.

On the other hand, addresses will be written in French. For example, the address for the Museum of Fine Arts in Montreal is listed as 1379 Rue Sherbrooke and not as 1379 Sherbrooke St. Why? Street signs and maps are in French. Another good example is Avenue des Pins, which means Pine Avenue. People say both, but I don't want you getting lost when the street sign is written as Pins, you're looking for Pine, and you don't speak French. Another example is Rue de l'Église. It means Church Street, but people rarely say the English translation, and once again, the street sign is in French.

1

History and Practical Information—Federal and Provincial

History

The earliest known inhabitants of present-day Quebec were the native Amerindian ancestors of the current Algonquian, Iroquoian, and Micmac nations. These Indians lived all along the St. Lawrence River—as far north as the Gaspé Peninsula to as far south as the mouth of Lake Ontario. The cultivation of corn in the region dates to about the year 1000, which meant these once nomadic peoples could now stay put with enough food to last through the harsh Quebec winter. Also around the year 1000, Leif Eriksson became the first European to arrive in North America, landing in present-day Newfoundland. Half a millennium later, John Cabot reached the shores of Newfoundland in 1497.

A few decades later, in search of a passage to China, French explorer Jacques Cartier set sail as an envoy under the King of France. Instead of finding China, he arrived in present-day Prince Edward Island in June 1534. A few weeks later Cartier landed on the Gaspé Peninsula, planted a wooden cross, and claimed the new North American digs in honor of France.

By autumn 1535 Cartier made his way up the St. Lawrence River to Hochelaga—an Iroquoian settlement near present-day Montreal. He became the first European to encounter Quebec's indigenous peoples. Two main goals became the mission for the visit— export some nice furs and import the fear of God. A trading post was soon established— beaver being the pelt *du jour*, and the conversion of the native peoples to Catholicism began.

More than a half century later, in 1603, Samuel de Champlain charted the same area. But the Hochelaga of Cartier's time no longer existed. What became of these native Iroquoians remains a mystery to archaeologists today. Champlain, after more adventures on the northern North American coast, returned to the St. Lawrence five years later and on July 3, 1608, founded Quebec City as a permanent settlement and not just a trading post. Harsh winters and less-than-thrilled native peoples threatened to wipe out the small community, but the new inhabitants of the French settlement stayed put and persevered.

Sometime around 1627 King Louis XIII created a seigneurial system of land ownership. And, oh Lord, that meant only Roman Catholics could settle in New France. Missionaries soon sprang up. In 1642 new arrivals Paul Chomedey de Maisonneuve and Jeanne Mance founded Ville Marie, now Montreal. Mance established Montreal's first hospital. And in 1643 Chomedey planted a cross atop Mount Royal to thank God—and his lucky stars, which were now visible after a flood threatened to wash away the settlement. A modern-day version of the cross remains atop Mount Royal to this day. It's perhaps the most iconic landmark of the city.

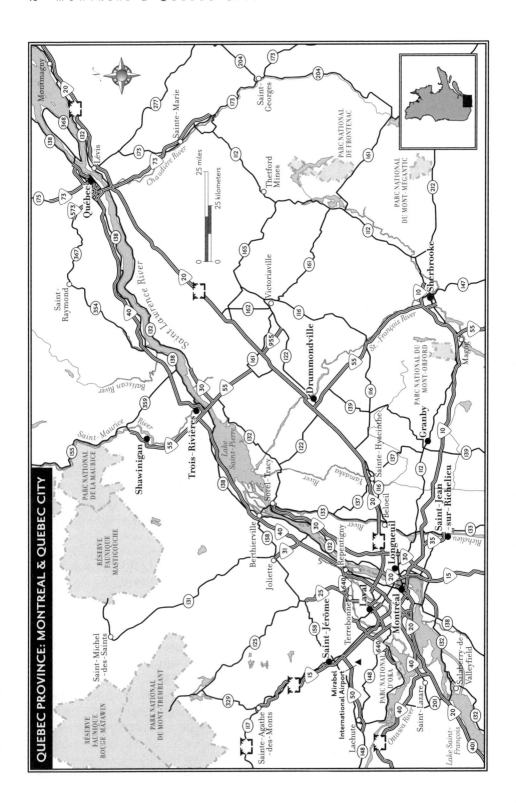

QUEBEC PROVINCE: MONTREAL & QUEBEC CITY

Things really got under way when Louis XIV officially decreed New France a province in 1663. The *filles du roi*, young orphan girls, were sent to New France to meet and marry the new settlers and help build the population. But the French were always outnumbered—first by the native Indians, and years later by their British counterparts who settled the 13 original colonies to the south. Embracing the art of diplomacy, French settler and then governor Louis-Hector de Callière brokered the Great Peace of 1701, an accord that meant a hospitable co-existence between the New France settlers and some 39 First Nations.

Fast forward a half century later when British and French troops were engaged in the Seven Years War worldwide, and its North American counterpart, the French and Indian War between 1754 and 1763, which is known to French Canadians as the War of the Conquest.

The beginning of the end of New France took place during the Battle of the Plains of Abraham in 1759. Under the command of General James Wolfe, and after an immense buildup, the British managed to gain a foothold outside the French stronghold of Quebec City, where the French commander, Louis-Joseph de Montcalm, came out to meet them. The battle lasted about 20 minutes.

The French army didn't fare so well. Although the French almost managed to recapture Quebec City the following year, by 1763 New France was ceded to England with the signing of the Treaty of Paris. Nonetheless, some 50,000 French-speaking settlers remained. To avoid any further conflict, the British passed the Quebec Act in 1774, which officially recognized the Roman Catholic French-speaking inhabitants.

Next, the American colonists entered the picture when the American Revolution broke out in 1775. The Americans did win Montreal and held it for some seven months between the autumn of 1775 and the summer of 1776, but the British repulsed the Americans at Quebec City and eventually pushed them out of Canada. France, still fuming from its defeat, helped the Americans with money and munitions and in 1778 entered the war as an ally, turning the tide against the British, who ceded the American colonies with the Treaty of Paris of 1783.

Both during and after the war, tens of thousands of Loyalists, American colonists who remained loyal to the crown, fled north to Canada and joined the French-speaking residents. This land, British North America, remained under the British crown. From 1791 to 1841 present-day southern Ontario was known as Upper Canada, while present-day southern Quebec was known as Lower Canada.

Stifling British rule led the French-speaking majority, along with many working-class English speakers, to rebel. The result was the Patriotes Rebellions of 1837–38. The British solution to the uproar was an attempt to assimilate the two cultures by passing the Act of Union in 1840, which joined Upper and Lower Canada into one province to be known as Canada. Further appeasement came in 1842, when Parliament granted amnesty to the Patriotes, abolished the seigneurial system, and legalized the French language.

The birth of this nation started in the 1860s when the British North American colonies of Canada (Upper and Lower Canada) and the Atlantic Maritime provinces of Nova Scotia, New Brunswick, Prince Edward Island, and Newfoundland sought to self-govern. In 1867 the British parliament passed the British North America Act, which created the Dominion of Canada. The new country consisted of the provinces of Ontario, Quebec, New Brunswick, and Nova Scotia. Prince Edward Island joined the confederation in 1873 and Newfoundland followed much later, in 1949.

Canada joined the war efforts in the First and Second World Wars, but did so by conscription, basically a draft. This was met by strong opposition, specifically by the French inhabi-

Quebec City was for centuries a stronghold for the French in North America.

tants, which led to riots in Quebec. In addition, the Catholic Church strongly influenced all aspects of the Quebec province until the 1960s. The postwar 1940s and '50s were dominated by provincial premier Maurice Duplessis, a very conservative politician who governed with church policy in mind. He remained in power until he died in office in 1959.

By then Quebecers had basically had enough of ultraconservative and Catholic Church rule, which led to the Quiet Revolution of the 1960s. This meant that power moved from the hand of church-backed politicians to a more secular liberal government that introduced changes in the health-care system and education policies.

The 1960s was a time of celebration and turmoil in Quebec. The beginnings of the Quebec separatist movement, which sought a sovereign Quebec nation, was marred by the ultra-left-wing factions of the Front de Liberation du Québec, the Quebec Liberation Front, known as the FLQ. The group was responsible for hundreds of bombings and five deaths. The madness culminated with the October Crisis in 1970, when the FLQ kidnapped and killed a Quebec government minister. At the request of Montreal mayor Jean Drapeau and Quebec premier Robert Bourassa, the Canadian prime minister, Pierre Elliot Trudeau, invoked the War Measures Act, which sent the Canadian Army into the streets of Montreal to restore law and order to the volatile situation.

On the lighter side, the '60s was a time of celebration, when Expo 67 put Montreal on the world map with a party that lasted from April through October 1967. It was a shining moment in Montreal history, an event that is fondly remembered by many Montrealers and Quebecers. The 1976 Montreal Summer Olympics brought the world back to Montreal barely a decade later.

In 1977 the Charter of the French Language, also known as Bill 101, made French the official language of Quebec. In 1980 the Parti Québecois, led by liberal politician René Lévesque, held a referendum on whether Quebec should secede as a sovereign nation. The referendum was defeated by about a 60-to-40 percent margin. But only a decade and a half later, in 1995, another referendum was held, and it was a real squeaker. The *non* votes won, but barely—50.58 percent opposing secession and 49.42 percent voting yes to create a new nation.

Today, Quebec remains a mix of ideologies. For example, conservatives recently posted national and provincial electoral gains, while the province also passed same-sex marriage laws in 2004. But we're talking politics while you're on vacation! Next subject.

Perhaps French president Charles de Gaulle almost said it best when visiting Montreal during Expo 67. From the balcony of city hall in a famous speech, de Gaulle said, "Vive le Québec libre!"—"Long live free Quebec!"

While the "free" part, as in independence, remains a hot topic of discussion at almost every election time, the "Long Live Quebec" part merits no argument. So here's to Quebec—*la belle province*!

Montreal's City Hall is always lit up at night.

Breaking the Ice
bonjour—good day
salut—hello
au revoir—goodbye
Je m'appelle . . .—My name is . . .
Comment ça va?—How are you?
Bien. Et vous?—Fine. And you?
enchanté— delighted (to meet someone)
s'il vous plaît—please
merci—thank you
bienvenue—you're welcome
à bientôt— see you soon
oui—yes
non—no

Traveling to Canada: Practical Information—Federal and Provincial

Immigration / Passport Requirements / NEXUS

When the U.S. Department of Homeland Security sets a new ID rule or deadline for Canadian visitors into the United States, Citizenship and Immigration Canada reacts with similar requirements for U.S. visitors into Canada. These rules are based on the U.S. Western Hemisphere Travel Initiative, which began after 9/11. The strongest opposition for rule changes mostly stems from politicians whose constituencies live near the border and fear that a decline in cross-border traffic will hurt their local economies. The requirements have changed and deadlines have been delayed more than once in the past, so while this information is current, make sure you check before you travel.

Upon arrival into Canada, you need proof of citizenship. This is best accomplished by showing a passport, a NEXUS card, a birth record, baptismal record, a certificate of citizenship, or certificate of naturalization. If these documents do not have a photo ID, bring that as well. A driver's license or a voter registration card is not considered proof of citizenship. A visa is not required for U.S. citizens traveling to Canada.

If traveling by air, you do need a passport. If traveling by land or sea, the passport requirement may go into effect by mid 2008 (but this was already delayed once from a January 2008 deadline, so keep checking).

In the current state of world affairs, you can pretty much resolve any ID problem by getting a passport or NEXUS card. A NEXUS card isn't a passport, as it is good only for travel between the United States and Canada, but a NEXUS card preclears both Canadians and Americans. In addition, there's usually a dedicated car lane at the border for NEXUS holders. That means you can usually bypass long lines. Everyone traveling in the car needs their own NEXUS card, and you still have to declare all items bought on your trip. A NEXUS card currently costs $80 Canadian or $50 U.S. and is valid for five years. A NEXUS card is free for children under 18 years old.

Children under the age of 16 should have their own valid identification, such as a birth certificate or passport. If a child is traveling with only one parent when both parents are alive, or if you are traveling with a child but are not the child's parent or guardian, you should have a letter from the child's parent granting permission to travel to Canada. Having this letter notarized is the best way to go.

For more information visit Citizenship and Immigration Canada at www.cic.gc.ca or call 1-800-622-6232. Also visit U.S. Citizenship and Immigration Services at www.uscis.gov, the Department of Homeland Security at www.dhs.gov, and the U.S. Department of State at www.travel.state.gov or 1-800-333-4636.

Letters to Père Noël

Every year, Canada Post invites kids to send letters to Père Noël, also known as Santa Claus. Instead of a zip code, Canada Post uses a postal code, a six-letter/number address designation. The address for Santa Claus: North Pole, HOH OHO Canada (get it? HO HO HO!). In 2007 some 1 million letters were received in more than two dozen languages from kids around the world, according to Canada Post. Include your return address and you'll get a reply. It costs 93 cents to mail first-class envelopes and postcards from Canada to the United States. Visit www.canadapost.ca.

Canadian Customs

Anything to declare? Your personal clothing and sundries are permitted in Canada. Bringing alcohol and cigarettes is allowed, but amounts are limited. A large bottle of wine or liquor, or a case of beer, and up to a carton of cigarettes is permissible. You must report if you have more than $10,000 in Canadian funds with you.

Some firearms are permissible, like hunting rifles with proper licenses, but you must be at least 18 years old, and you need to declare them. Mace, endangered species, obscene materials, and hate propaganda are prohibited. Packaged foods are usually OK, but fruits and vegetables have their own restrictions and are subject to seizure, as are most plants. There are restrictions for the amounts of dairy products you can bring into the country. Prescription medications should be left in their original container complete with label and doctor information.

You can bring gifts to your Canadian friends duty free if the gifts are valued at $60 or less (alcohol and cigarettes do not apply as gifts). You will have to pay duty on the amount over the limit. For more information visit www.cbsa-asfc.gc.ca. You can also call Border Information Services, BIS, at 204-983-3500 or 506-636-5064.

Crossing the Border: by Car

Montreal is only a 45-minute drive from the U.S. border in New York State. The main highway crossing is Interstate 87 in New York / Autoroute 15 in Quebec. Interstate 89 in Vermont / Route 133 in Quebec is another frequently used crossing.

It's a good bet you will take the I-87 crossing when coming from New York City, Philadelphia, Washington, D.C., or the Mid-Atlantic States. Here's a tip for visitors traveling on New York's I-87: Busy weekend summer traffic and construction upgrades at the U.S. border at Champlain can sometimes mean a crossing with upward of a 45-minute wait—even longer—depending on the time of day you arrive. You can bypass the interstate-highway crossing and potential delays by taking a smaller side crossing. These smaller border inspection stations are a bit out of the way—perhaps 10 miles more on the odometer—but usually the wait time is reduced, and at least you keep moving instead of sitting in traffic.

If you are indeed traveling north on I-87 in New York State (and be careful not to speed between the city of Plattsburgh and the border) take exit 42 and turn right on US 11. Continue for about 2 miles and turn left on NY 276. You'll be at the Lacolle Route 221 Canadian border in less than 2 miles. After crossing, drive 2 miles north and turn left at Montée Guay (the street sign says "Mtee Guay." There is also an indication for Highway 15 Nord). You'll be on the highway heading to Montreal in just 2 more miles.

The Rules of the Road

Canada converted to the metric system in 1970. That means the speed limit on highways is usually 100 km/h (kilometers per hour), or about 60 miles per hour. Many highway signs are bilingual, but some are just in French. Some words that come in handy when driving: *sortie* means exit; *pont* means bridge, *ralentissez* means slow down.

Your own state-issued current driver's license is valid for driving in Quebec for a maximum of six consecutive months. The license class must correspond to the vehicle that you are driving.

You need the proper liability car insurance to be adequately covered in Quebec. A motor vehicle liability insurance card is available at your insurance broker (although in 15 years of crossing the border, I have never once had to show it).

Right turns on red lights are legal throughout the province, except where noted. Right turns on red are prohibited on the island of Montreal.

When waiting to turn left at a Montreal city intersection, a flashing green light indicates it is OK to proceed with your left turn.

Using your cell phone while driving in the province of Quebec is still legal, but a ban on cell phone use while driving comes up for a vote by the legislature in autumn 2007. The use of radar detectors is illegal in Quebec.

Finally, fill up the gas tank before you enter the province, as gas is cheaper in the States. Gas is sold in liters in Canada; 1 gallon of gas equals about 4 liters (3.78 liters). Gas currently ranges from $1 to $1.20 (Canadian) a liter, or about $4 Canadian per gallon.

Cussing in Quebec

Many cusswords in present-day Quebec vernacular have religious origins. For example, say the words *tabarnac*, which translates to the tabernacle of a church altar, *hostie*, the Eucharistic host, or *câlice*, the chalice, and you're swearing like a Quebec sailor.

Crossing the Border: by Plane

Visitors must pass through Canadian Customs and Immigration upon their arrival in Canada. A passport is required for all travel to and from Canada and the United States when traveling by air.

Montreal is serviced by Pierre Elliot Trudeau Airport, formerly Dorval Airport. The three-letter airport code is YUL. Visit www.admtl.com.

Quebec City is serviced by Jean Lesage Airport. The airport code is YQB. Call 418-640-2600 or visit www.aeroportdequebec.com.

The key point to make here concerns your return flight, as U.S. Customs and Border Protection is processed in Canada when departing from Montreal. Add a minimum 30 to 45 minutes of travel time when leaving from Montreal. More information on travel to and from the airport is included within the respective chapters about Montreal and Quebec City.

Crossing the Border: by Train

Daily Amtrak service to Montreal from New York City is available on the Adirondack line. The trip takes about 10 hours. The train crosses the border in Rouses Point, New York. The border crossing time is worked into the train schedule. Call 1-800-872-7245 or visit www.amtrak.com.

VIA Rail is the Canadian rail equivalent. The thing to remember here is that your ticket must be purchased before 8:30 AM on the day of your departure when returning to the States, according to VIA Rail. This ensures that your name will appear on the passenger list, which is submitted to U.S. Customs. If your name is not on the list, you won't be able to cross the border. Visit www.viarail.ca or call 1-888-842-7245.

Return Trips to the U.S.

You need to prove that you are a U.S. citizen when returning to the States, so don't forget your ID. And once again, a passport is now required if you are traveling by air.

Items purchased in Canada must be declared at the U.S. border, and some restrictions apply. It's a good idea to pack purchases separately and have them ready to show if asked. Save your receipts and keep them handy as well.

If your stay in Canada was 48 hours or less, you're allowed to bring back merchandise worth up to $200 without paying duty. This includes purchases of cigarettes and alcohol, but amounts are restricted. Once every 30 days residents can return with merchandise for personal use valued up to $800. Family members traveling together can each claim this amount and combine purchases. Here, the limit for cigarettes is one carton, and the limit for alcohol is 1 liter.

There are many restrictions on food, specifically fruits and vegetables. Other prohibited items include counterfeit materials, and non FDA-approved prescriptions made outside the U.S. And while those Cuban cigars are legal to buy and smoke in Canada, you are prohibited from bringing them back into the States.

For more information visit Know Before You Go on the U.S. Customs and Border Protection Website at www.cbp.gov.

Tax Refunds

The Quebec provincial government formerly offered a refund to nonresidents on taxes spent on goods and services, as long as certain minimums were met. As of April 2007 the province eliminated this tax-refund program. A new version, the Foreign Convention and Tour Incentive Program, introduced in 2007, is now geared to nonresidents who hold conventions in Canada and for the short-term accommodations portion of tour packages. To see if you meet the requirements, visit www.cra-arc.gc.ca/tax/nonresidents/visitors.

Traveling with Pets

Dogs and cats are permitted into Canada if accompanied by a valid health certificate and proof of rabies vaccination (for dogs) from your vet. These documents are important for your return to the United States as well. Pet birds, wildlife, and fish all have their own requirements.

Medical Insurance

In case of a medical emergency, visitors have to pay up front for all medical costs and then submit paperwork for reimbursement through their own insurance company. Local hospital and medical emergency numbers are listed within the Montreal and Quebec City information chapters.

Banking / Currency Exchange

Most places accept major credit cards. For cash on hand, use your checking, savings, or debit card and withdraw money from any Canadian bank ATM. A withdrawal fee is applied, and the money is automatically converted according to the current exchange rate. If the card is a credit card–based debit card, the credit card will also charge a small foreign transaction fee. Avoid airport and private currency exchange counters, as you don't get the best rate. Many Canadian hotels and restaurants accept American dollars, but once again the exchange rate will be to their advantage.

Canadian money is colorful and similar to U.S. paper bill denominations of $100, $50, $20, $10, and $5. Coins are used for lesser amounts, like the bronze-colored "loonie" $1 coin, and the silver-and-gold-colored $2 coin—a "toonie."

Tipping

Tipping is customary in most service industries. Although the hourly wage for service workers is a bit higher in comparison to the States, tipping amounts are similar to U.S. rates. Depending on the service—and your generosity—a 15 to 20 percent tip is adequate for restaurant servers, a loonie or toonie for a drink order, a 10 to 15 percent tip should satisfy any cab driver, and porters get $1 to $2 a bag, depending on how many souvenirs you bought. Housekeeping staff usually deserve an acknowledgment of between $2 and $5 a day. Remember, tipping is not an obligation, but a reward for good service. Use your discretion.

When to Visit / Weather

High season in both Montreal and Quebec City runs from mid-May through mid-October. But don't dismiss a winter visit, either. One of Montreal's most popular winter draws is the High Lights Festival, a foodie's dream come true with some 350 culinary tastings and food workshops; or Quebec City's Winter Carnival, a three-week midwinter nonstop party held since 1955.

In Montreal and Quebec City, spring arrives a few weeks later than in cities like Boston or New York. While the calendar says spring, the after-winter warm-up seems to take forever. But as soon as the weather does warm up, the outdoor terraces are open for business. In comparison, summer weather is usually warm to hot, and sometimes humid, but nothing like New York or Boston. Let's put it this way—I don't have an air conditioner in my Montreal apartment. Fall weather arrives in September and October. At times you can feel a definite chill in the air, and other times you can wear shorts for one last summer fling. Ah, but Old Man Winter—now that's a season. It may start off mild in December, but by January and February the cold temperatures and snow are here to stay at least until the end of March and into April. Snow removal in these parts is an art unto itself. If you drive, snow tires are recommended. So expect cold temperatures, snow, slush, and wait until you meet the wind chill. That said, residents take the cold weather in stride. Try keeping a Montreal senior citizen from her afternoon rounds at the local bingo parlor in the middle of a February snowstorm—*c'est impossible!*

Speaking of temperatures, the country uses the metric system, and that means degrees in Celsius, not Fahrenheit. Spring temperatures average between 32 and 50 degrees Fahrenheit, or 0 to 10 degrees Celsius. Summer weather is ideal—65 to 85 degrees

A winter carriage ride in Montreal's Mount Royal Park.

Fahrenheit, or 18 to 29 degrees Celsius. In fall expect a range from 40 to 55 degrees F, or 5 to 13 degrees C. And in winter, temperatures hover between 8 to 22 degrees Fahrenheit, or -13 to -5 Celsius.

Legal Holidays
New Year's Day / *Jour de l'An*—January 1.
　Good Friday and Easter Monday / *Vendredi Saint* and *Lundi de Pâques*. Many Quebecers get a four-day weekend around Easter.
　Victoria Day / *Fête de la Reine*—the third Monday in May, which is the three-day weekend before the U.S. Memorial Day three-day weekend. It began as a celebration to Queen Victoria and then

encompassed whoever the reigning monarch was. With Quebecers not too keen on celebrating the Queen, the holiday was known for decades as *Fête de Dollard*, which recognizes French settler Dollard des Ormeaux, until that was changed in 2002 to National Patriotes Day in honor of the French rebels who fought against British rule during the Rebellions of 1837–38. Most of all, it's the unofficial start to summer, as many Quebecers take to their gardens for summer planting or hold city-wide garage sales.

St. John the Baptist Day / *St-Jean-Baptiste* or *Fête Nationale*—June 24. This one's a pretty big deal for Quebecers. Think St. Patrick's Day and July 4 all rolled into one. Lots of musical celebrations, barbecues, and Quebec flag-waving pride.

Canada Day / *Fête du Canada*—July 1. Celebrates the Canadian confederation.

Labour Day / *Fête du Travail*—the first Monday in September. Same as the States, except for English spelling.

Canadian Thanksgiving / *Action de Grâce*—the second Monday in October. The day always coincides with Columbus Day in the United States. Yes, turkey is served on Canadian Thanksgiving, but the day is not as popular as its American counterpart and is more popular with English Canadians than French Canadians.

Remembrance Day / *Jour du Souvenir*—November 11. This day commemorates Canada's war dead.

Christmas / *Nöel*—December 25.

Other Holidays and Calendar Oddities

Moving Day: While July 1 is Canada Day, it's also known in Quebec as Moving Day. Moving day has its roots in the days of New France when seigneurs, or landowners, would hire workers to toil the land and then send them on their way just as winter approached—nice guys. It soon became law that these landowners had to provide accommodations that lasted past winter. The modern-day tradition had one-year apartment leases that ran until the end of April. But in 1974, as to not disrupt the school year, Quebec province mandated that apartment leases run from July 1 to June 30. Coincidentally, July 1 happens to be Canada Day, a national legal holiday that's not particularly beloved of French-speaking Quebecers (they prefer St-Jean-Baptiste Day on June 24), except for the fact that it's an extra day to move. And move they do. Some 100,000 Quebecers change their address every year on or around the end of June / early July. The result: tons of garbage—we're talking big-ticket items like appliances and sofas—piled high amidst the middle of tourist season. But the city does a decent job of cleaning up quite quickly. It's also known that Moving Day week is an economic boom for local pizza parlors.

Construction Holiday: The last two weeks in July means many construction workers receive a mandatory two-week summer holiday. This translates to sometimes heavy weekend traffic and long lines at the Quebec / New York and Vermont borders.

Halloween: Instead of "trick or treat," kids in Quebec sing, "L'Halloween!" (the "H" is silent, so it sounds like *"l'alloween!"*).

Boxing Day / *Lendemain de Noël*: December 26. Many Canadians have this day off in addition to Christmas Day. Lots of store sales and crowds. *Non, merci!*

What to Bring

Casual neat attire wears well in Montreal and Quebec City. You can bring something dressy for special occasions. You can also bring shorts and sandals. A light jacket for cool summer nights, a good pair of sneakers, and a portable umbrella all come in handy (you can always buy an umbrella at the local dollar store). In winter, bring long johns, thick socks, long-sleeve T-shirts, gloves, boots, hats, scarves, and the warmest coat you've got—I'm not kidding!

Travel between Montreal and Quebec City: by Car/Train/Air/Boat

By car, Autoroutes 20 and 40 are the two quickest options. Autoroute 20 runs south of the St. Lawrence River. It's most easily accessed by taking the Jacques Cartier Bridge in Montreal, to 132/20 East, to Autoroute 20 East. The road is a bit bumpy in spots and isn't the most scenic of drives. The rest stops could use a makeover as well. Autoroute 40 runs along the north shore of the St. Lawrence River. Travel time on Autoroute 40 is a bit longer than Autoroute 20, but the scenery is nicer in parts, as you can actually see the river for a short clip. Traffic in the Montreal section of Highway 40, also known as the Metropolitan or the Met, can be incredibly busy. Travel time on either highway takes about two hours and 45 minutes.

VIA Rail offers three or four departures between Montreal and Quebec City daily. Both the Montreal and Quebec City train stations are conveniently located. The trip takes about three hours. Round-trip discounted prices go as low as about $100 (Canadian). The trains are clean and a pretty good deal. And you can now use your laptop computer aboard, as the train offers wireless Internet access for a nominal fee. Visit www.viarail.ca or call 1-888-842-7245.

Air Canada's Tango brand offers direct air service between Montreal and Quebec City. The flight takes about 50 minutes, but add typical airport check-in and screening time. Current round-trips cost in the neighborhood of $350. Visit www.aircanada.com or call 1-888-247-2262.

During the summer months, Croisières Évasion Plus offers St. Lawrence River cruise service between Montreal and Quebec City that costs about $120 one-way. The cruise takes six hours. Call 514-364-5333 or visit www.evasionplus.com.

Time Zones

Montreal and Quebec City are in the Eastern Standard Time Zone. To avoid a time-change conflict, Canada followed the U.S. extension of daylight saving time in 2007. That means daylight saving time begins the second Sunday in March and ends the first Sunday in November.

Liquor Laws

The legal drinking age in the province of Quebec is 18 years old. Incidentally, all restaurants and bars in Quebec are nonsmoking.

Electricity

Electrical outlets in Canada provide 110 volts of power, the same as in the States. European travelers will need an adapter for their small appliances.

Language

French is the official language of Quebec. Many residents are bilingual, especially those who work in the travel industry. Brush up on your high school French, as a little French on your part goes a long way.

Useful Web Sites

Government of Canada: www.canada.gc.ca

National Historic Sites of Canada: www.pc.gc.ca

Tourisme Montréal: www.tourisme-montreal.org

Montreal Plus: www.montrealplus.ca

More Montreal: www.moremontreal.com

The City of Montreal: www.ville.montreal.qc.ca

Montreal Webcam Network: www.montrealcam.com

Tourisme Québec: www.bonjourquebec.com

About.com Montreal & Quebec City: www.about.com

2

Montreal Transportation and Practical Information

Geography and General Orientation

Montreal is a triangular-shaped island surrounded by the St. Lawrence River. The city is about 40 miles north of the U.S. / New York State border.

The main tourist areas of Montreal are centrally located in the southern heart and tip of the island, which encompass downtown or *centre-ville*, Old Montreal and the Old Port, the Latin Quarter, and residential city neighborhoods like the Plateau and the Gay Village.

Suburban sprawl surrounds the main city core to the mostly English-speaking west, which is only 20 minutes from the Ontario border, as well as to the mostly French-speaking north in the suburbs of Laval, Mascouche, and Terrebonne. Also to the north, you'll find the Mont Tremblant ski resort, 90 minutes from Montreal. The northeastern tip of the island is a two-and-a-half to three-hour drive to Quebec City. Montreal's South Shore includes bridge and highway access to the city of Longueuil, the Montérégie and Eastern Townships regions, and the United States farther south.

Montreal's namesake is indeed Mount Royal. Explorer Jacques Cartier was the first European to climb the mountain, led by the island's Hochelaga inhabitants in 1535. To prevent the mountain's real estate from being bought by only those who had the money to do so, Mount Royal Park was inaugurated in 1876 as a public space for use by all the city's residents. The park was designed by landscape architect Frederick Law Olmsted, who also designed New York's Central Park and Boston's Emerald Necklace.

Boulevard St-Laurent is the official east-west divider of the city. This means if a street address is listed as west (*ouest*), then it's west of Boulevard St-Laurent. If the address is east (*est*), then it's east of Boulevard St-Laurent. In addition, the lower the number of an address on a street that runs east-west, the closer you'll be to Boulevard St-Laurent. The street is also the symbolic language divider of the city: mostly Francophone to the east, and mostly Anglophone to the west. Montrealers affectionately call their beloved Boulevard St-Laurent "The Main."

To be thoroughly confusing, Boulevard St-Laurent, and the streets parallel to it, actually run closer to east-west than north-south—even though, for convenience sake, Montrealers call it north to south, more or less envisioning the St. Lawrence River as running west to east. So to make directions easier, make believe the island points due east, rather than sharply northeast. So Boulevard St-Laurent and its parallel streets are considered to run north-south, and the crossing streets are considered to run east-west.

That said, major east-west downtown thoroughfares include Rue Sherbrooke, the one-way Rue Ste-Catherine, and Boulevard René-Lévesque (pronounced "lay-VECK"). Many smaller north-south side streets run one-way. And if you find yourself lost, just say a little prayer, as every other street in Montreal as well as neighboring Quebec towns are named after saints.

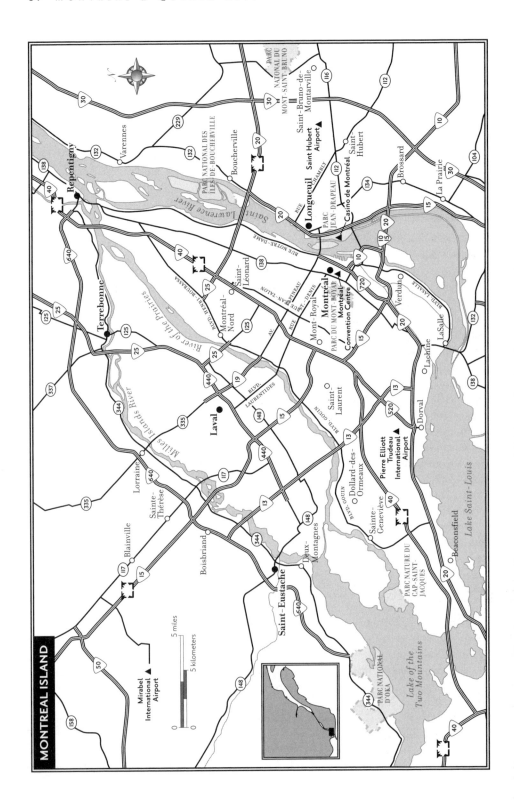

MONTREAL ISLAND

The Montreal Flag

The flag of the city of Montreal is based on the city's coat of arms and was first used in 1939. The flag contains four equal quarters separated by a bright red cross. Each quarter highlights an indigenous flower or plant from the country of origin of the four largest groups of European immigrants to the city. A blue fleur-de-lis in the top left quadrant represents the French. A Lancastrian rose in the top right quarter stands for the English. In the lower right section a shamrock symbolizes the Irish. And in the lower left, a thistle represents the Scottish.

Population

The population of the Montreal metropolitan area is 3,606,700 as of 2006, according to Tourism Montreal. It is the second-largest metropolitan area in Canada after Toronto. The city merged into a "one island, one city" concept in 2002, thinking that combined public services like snow removal would save money. It lasted only a few years, when individual urban boroughs like Westmount and many of the island's western suburbs voted to de-merge. In essence, the population of Montreal island proper stands at 1,813,000 residents.

Neighborhoods

DOWNTOWN

Bustling nightlife, fine restaurants, eclectic museums, endless shopping, and luxury and budget hotels, Montreal's downtown core has it all. There's a lot of ground to cover when downtown, but there's plenty of public transportation to help you get around. Downtown is bordered by the Latin Quarter to the east; Rue Sherbrooke, the Plateau, and Mount Royal

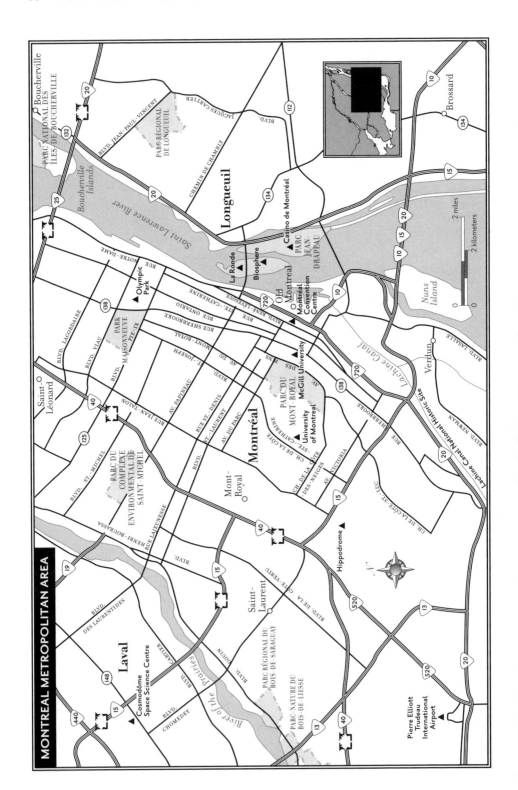

MONTREAL METROPOLITAN AREA

Brossard

Longueuil

PARC RÉGIONAL DE LONGUEUIL

PARC NATIONAL DES ÎLES DE BOUCHERVILLE

Boucherville

Boucherville Islands

Saint Lawrence River

BLVD. JEAN-PAUL-VINCENT

CHEMIN DE CHAMBLY

JACQUES CARTIER

Casino de Montréal

PARC JEAN-DRAPEAU

La Ronde

Biosphere

Old Montréal

Montréal Convention Centre

Olympic Park

PARC MAISONNEUVE PIE-IX

RUE NOTRE-DAME

RUE SHERBROOKE

RUE ONTARIO

RUE STE-CATHERINE

BLVD. RENÉ-LÉVESQUE

RUE ST-JEAN-TALON

AV. DU PARC

BLVD. ST-LAURENT

RUE ST-DENIS

AV. PAPINEAU

BLVD. ST-JOSEPH

AV. DU MONT-ROYAL

McGill University

University of Montreal

PARC DU MONT-ROYAL

RUE STE-CATHERINE

CH. DE LA CÔTE-DES-NEIGES

AV. VICTORIA

Montréal

Mont-Royal

Saint Léonard

BLVD. LACORDAIRE

BLVD. VIAU

BLVD. ST-MICHEL

PARC DU COMPLEXE ENVIRONMENTAL DE SAINT-MICHEL

RUE JEAN-TALON

RUE HENRI-BOURASSA

RUE LAJEUNESSE

BLVD.

Saint-Laurent

Laval

Cosmodôme Space Science Centre

BLVD. DES LAURENTIDES

BLVD. CARTIER

BLVD. POIRIER

BLVD. CHOMEDEY

River of the Prairies

PARC RÉGIONAL DU BOIS-DE-SARAGUAY

PARC-NATURE DU BOIS-DE-LIESSE

BLVD. DE LA CÔTE-VERTE

Hippodrome

Lachine Canal

Lachine Canal National Historic Site

BLVD. NEWMAN

BLVD. LASALLE

Verdun

Nuns Island

Pierre Elliott Trudeau International Airport

CH. DE LA CÔTE-ST-LUC

RUE SHERBROOKE

2 miles

2 kilometers

19

148

440

15

125

40

138

20

132

25

20

112

134

15

10

134

10

15

20

10

720

720

138

15

40

15

520

13

520

20

13

40

13

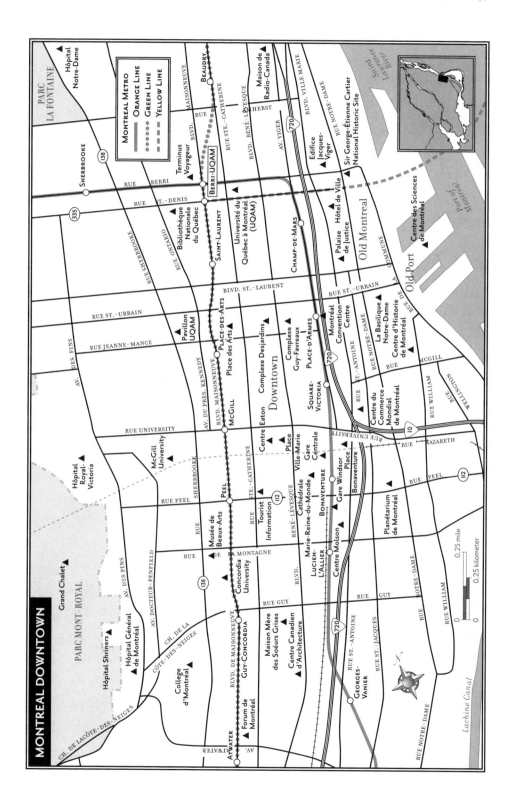

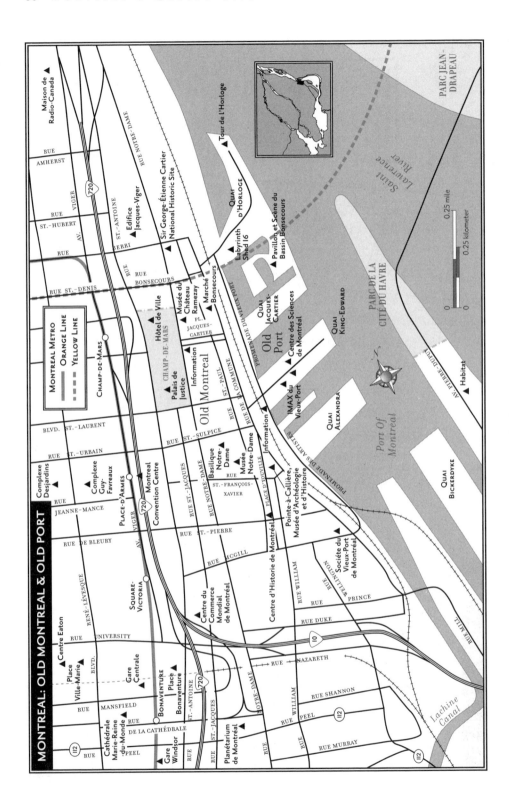

MONTREAL: OLD MONTREAL & OLD PORT

MONTREAL MÉTRO
— Orange Line
- - - Yellow Line

Maison de Radio-Canada

RUE AMHERST

RUE ST.-HUBERT

RUE NOTRE-DAME

Sir George-Étienne Cartier National Historic Site

Edifice Jacques-Viger

Tour de l'Horloge

QUAI D'HORLOGE

Labyrinth Shed 16

Pavillon et Scène du Bassin Bonsecours

RUE BONSECOURS

Musée du Château Ramezay

Marché Bonsecours

Hôtel de Ville

PL. JACQUES-CARTIER

QUAI JACQUES-CARTIER

Palais de Justice

CHAMP-DE-MARS

Information

Centre des Sciences de Montréal

QUAI KING-EDWARD

PARC DE LA CITÉ-DU-HAVRE

Saint Lawrence River

PARC JEAN-DRAPEAU

0.25 mile
0.25 kilometer

Old Montreal

RUE ST.-PAUL

PROMENADE DU VIEUX-PORT

Old Port

Basilique Notre-Dame

Musée Notre-Dame

IMAX du Vieux-Port

Information

QUAI ALEXANDRA

Port Of Montreal

Habitat

AV. PIERRE-DUPUY

BLVD. ST.-LAURENT

BLVD. ST.-URBAIN

Pointe-à-Callière, Musée d'Archéologie et d'Histoire

PLACE D'YOUVILLE

PROMENADE DES ARTISTES

Complexe Desjardins

Complexe Guy-Favreaux

RUE ST.-JACQUES

RUE NOTRE-DAME

ST.-FRANÇOIS-XAVIER

Montreal Convention Centre

AV. VIGER

RUE JEANNE-MANCE

RUE DE BLEURY

RUE ST.-PIERRE

Centre d'Histoire de Montréal

QUAI BICKERDYKE

RUE MCGILL

Centre du Commerce Mondial de Montréal

Société du Vieux-Port de Montréal

RUE WILLIAM

RUE WELLINGTON

RUE PRINCE

RENÉ-LÉVESQUE

SQUARE-VICTORIA

RUE DUKE

Centre Eaton

Place Ville-Marie

UNIVERSITY

Gare Centrale

BONAVENTURE

Place Bonaventure

ST.-ANTOINE

RUE NAZARETH

RUE SHANNON

MANSFIELD

Cathédrale Marie-Reine-du-Monde

PEEL

RUE DE LA CATHÉDRALE

Gare Windsor

Planétarium de Montréal

RUE ST.-JACQUES

RUE WILLIAM

RUE PEEL

RUE MURRAY

Lachine Canal

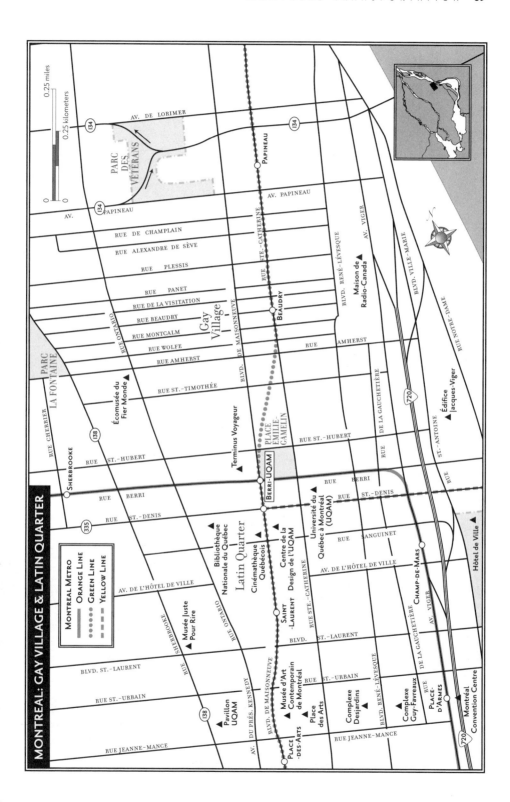

MONTRÉAL: GAY VILLAGE & LATIN QUARTER

MONTREAL METRO
ORANGE LINE
GREEN LINE
YELLOW LINE

Gay Village

Latin Quarter

PARC LA FONTAINE

PARC DES VÉTÉRANS

0.25 miles
0.25 kilometers

AV. DE LORIMER

AV. PAPINEAU

AV. PAPINEAU

RUE DE CHAMPLAIN
RUE ALEXANDRE DE SÈVE
RUE PLESSIS
RUE PANET
RUE DE LA VISITATION
RUE BEAUDRY
RUE MONTCALM
RUE WOLFE
RUE AMHERST
RUE ST.-TIMOTHÉE

RUE CHERRIER
SHERBROOKE
RUE ST.-HUBERT
RUE BERRI
RUE ST.-DENIS
AV. DE L'HÔTEL DE VILLE
SHERBROOKE
RUE ONTARIO

RUE STE.-CATHERINE
RUE DE MAISONNEUVE

BLVD. RENÉ-LÉVESQUE
AV. VIGER
BLVD. VILLE-MARIE
RUE NOTRE-DAME

RUE AMHERST
RUE ST.-HUBERT
RUE DE LA GAUCHETIÈRE
RUE ST.-ANTOINE

▲ Maison de Radio-Canada

▲ Édifice Jacques-Viger

PAPINEAU
BEAUDRY
BERRI-UQAM
PLACE ÉMILIE-GAMELIN
Terminus Voyageur

▲ Écomusée du Fier Monde

▲ Bibliothèque Nationale du Québec

▲ Cinémathèque Québécois
▲ Centre de la Design de l'UQAM
▲ Université du Québec à Montréal (UQAM)

RUE BERRI
RUE ST.-DENIS
RUE SANGUINET
AV. DE L'HÔTEL DE VILLE

SAINT-LAURENT

▲ Musée Juste Pour Rire

RUE ONTARIO
RUE SHERBROOKE
AV. DU PRÉS.-KENNEDY
BLVD. DE MAISONNEUVE
RUE STE.-CATHERINE
BLVD. ST.-LAURENT
RUE ST.-URBAIN

▲ Musée d'Art Contemporain de Montréal
▲ Place des Arts

▲ Pavillon UQAM

PLACE-DES-ARTS

RUE JEANNE-MANCE

BLVD. ST.-LAURENT
RUE ST.-URBAIN

▲ Complexe Desjardins

BLVD. RENÉ-LÉVESQUE

▲ Complexe Guy-Favreaux

DE LA GAUCHETIÈRE
AV. VIGER
RUE
CHAMP-DE-MARS
PLACE-D'ARMES
Hôtel de Ville

▲ Montréal Convention Centre

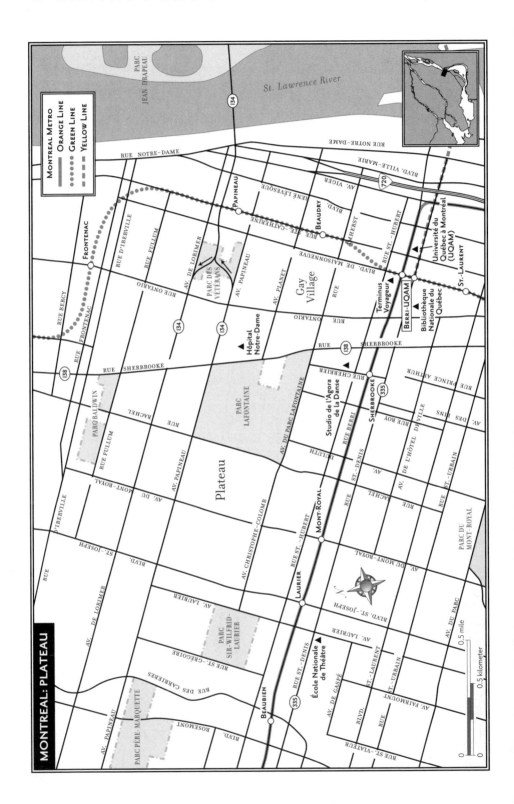

MONTREAL: PLATEAU

Montreal Metro
Orange Line
Green Line
Yellow Line

St. Lawrence River

PARC JEAN DRAPEAU

RUE NOTRE-DAME
RUE NOTRE-DAME

BLVD. VILLE-MARIE
720

Frontenac
Papineau
Beaudry
Berri-UQAM
St-Laurent

Terminus Voyageur
Bibliothèque Nationale du Québec
Université du Québec à Montréal (UQAM)

RUE BERCY
RUE D'IBERVILLE
RUE FULLUM
RUE ONTARIO
AV. DE LORIMER
PARC DES VÉTÉRANS
AV. PAPINEAU
AV. PLANET
BLVD. DE MAISONNEUVE
RUE STE.-CATHERINE
RENÉ LÉVESQUE
AV. VIGER
AMHERST
RUE ST.-HUBERT

Gay Village

RUE ONTARIO

Hôpital Notre-Dame
134
134

RUE SHERBROOKE
138

Studio de l'Agora de la Danse
SHERBROOKE
335
RUE CHERRIER
RUE PRINCE ARTHUR

PARC LAFONTAINE
PARC BALDWIN
RACHEL
RUE FULLUM
RUE

AV. DU PARC LAFONTAINE
RUE BERRI
RUE ST.-DENIS
RUE ROY
RUE DE L'HÔTEL DE VILLE
RUE ST.-URBAIN
AV. DES PINS

Plateau
DULUTH
RACHEL
AV. DU MONT-ROYAL

Mont-Royal

AV. DU MONT-ROYAL
AV. PAPINEAU
AV. CHRISTOPHE-COLOMB
RUE ST.-HUBERT
PARC DU MONT-ROYAL

AV. D'IBERVILLE
BLVD. ST.-JOSEPH
AV. DU MONT-ROYAL

Laurier
AV. LAURIER
AV. LAURIER
BLVD. ST.-JOSEPH
AV. DU PARC

AV. DE LORIMER
PARC SIR-WILFRID-LAURIER
RUE ST.-GRÉGOIRE
RUE DES CARRIÈRES
AV. LAURIER

École Nationale de Théâtre
Beaubien
335
RUE ST.-DENIS
AV. DE GASPÉ
ST.-LAURENT
BLVD.
RUE ST.-URBAIN
AV. FAIRMOUNT

AV. PAPINEAU
PARC PÈRE-MARQUETTE
ROSEMONT
BLVD.
RUE ST.-VIATEUR

0.5 mile
0.5 kilometer

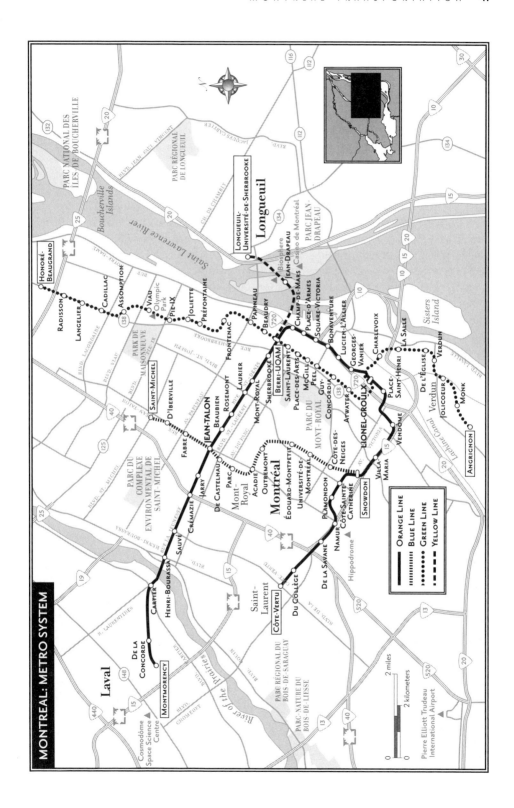

MONTRÉAL: METRO SYSTEM

ORANGE LINE
BLUE LINE
GREEN LINE
YELLOW LINE

Park to the north; Atwater Avenue and Westmount to the west; and Chinatown, the Old Port, and Little Burgundy to the south. The main campuses of Montreal's two English universities—McGill and Concordia—call downtown home. And what do city officials do with Rue Ste-Catherine, one of the busiest thoroughfares in the city, come summertime? Close it down to traffic. Twice. Two of summer's biggest draws, the Montreal Jazz Festival and the Francofolies Festival, with its flair for French music, are held in the center of downtown. With plenty of hotels, bars, and restaurants, Crescent Street has a decidedly Anglo/touristy feel, and is home to nonstop nightlife come Canada Grand Prix time in June. But the locals are never far away and add their own French flavor to the mix.

GAY VILLAGE

Montreal's Gay Village began about 25 years ago during the 1980s when local business merchants sought to open bars and clubs in an area where many gay residents lived. By the 1990s many gay bars, which had been scattered about downtown, closed because they could not compete with the bustling nightlife of Rue Ste-Catherine's concentrated selection of clubs, bars, saunas, and fetish shops. Many quality restaurants and cozy bed-and-breakfast establishments added to the destination, and remain today. In addition, a dozen-plus retro antiques shops along Rue Amherst remain a popular draw for all—the '70s are definitely in! While centered along Rue Ste-Catherine, the Gay Village, also referred to as the *Centre Sud* part of town, is bordered by Boulevard René-Lévesque to the south; Avenue Papineau to the east; Rue Sherbrooke and Lafontaine Park to the north; and the Latin Quarter at Rue Berri to the west. When you get to the Beaudry metro station, complete with its rainbow-colored façade, you know you've arrived. A good Web resource for the area is www.unmondeunvillage.com.

Man by Alexander Calder at Jean Drapeau Park.

HOCHELAGA/MAISONNEUVE

Hochelaga/Maisonneuve is a working-class residential neighborhood home to a number of major Montreal cultural institutions like the Montreal Botanical Garden, the Biodome, Olympic Stadium, Château Dufresne, and the Maisonneuve Market, a centerpiece for the locals who aim to make the area Montreal's next up-and-coming neighborhood. Local officials are pushing the trendy moniker "HoMa" (à la New York's SoHo), but the nickname is still trying to catch on. For tourists, restaurants and hotels are limited, so day trips are highly recommended. The neighborhood is conveniently accessed by the Pie-IX (say "pee-noof") and Viau metro stations.

JEAN DRAPEAU PARK

In the middle of the St. Lawrence River you'll find Jean Drapeau Park, a big-city respite for locals and tourists alike. The park is made up of two islands: Île Notre-Dame and Île Ste-Hélène. In the 1960s when the Montreal metro was under construction, officials wondered what to do with all that dirt. The answer: Take 28 million tons of earth from underneath the streets of Montreal, move it to the middle of the St. Lawrence River, create Île Notre-Dame, and enlarge Île Ste-Hélène. The park hosted the 1967 World's Fair, aka Expo 67, and some events for the 1976 Summer Olympics. Today the park plays home to Fêtes des Neiges, Montreal's winter carnival, as well as outdoor summer concerts that attract tens of thousands of fans. Formerly named Parc des Îles, in 2000 the park was renamed to honor Jean Drapeau, the mayor so instrumental in bringing the metro, Expo 67, and the Olympics to Montreal. The Montreal Casino, the Biosphere, La Ronde Amusement Park, and the Stewart Museum call Jean Drapeau Park home.

Old Montreal skyline.

Old Montreal architecture.

LATIN QUARTER

If downtown's Crescent Street has a decidedly English feel, then the Latin Quarter's main artery, Rue St-Denis, can be called the French equivalent. The main reason: the presence of the University of Quebec at Montreal—UQAM—centered in the middle of the Latin Quarter and home to about 40,000 students. And where there are students, there are dozens of cafés, bars, and a great big public library—in 2005 the massive Grande Bibliothèque opened its doors in the neighborhood. There are a few chain hotels in the area—perfect for budget travelers and groups. The Latin Quarter offers easy access by foot power to the Gay Village to the east, Old Montreal and the Old Port to the south, the downtown core to the west, and the Plateau to the north. The Berri/UQAM metro station is a main transfer point and offers easy public transportation options to all points of the city. Come spring, the outdoor café terraces are among the first to open. And in summer, the Just for Laughs Festival aims to tickle your funny bone with hundreds of free events along Rue St-Denis.

OLD PORT AND OLD MONTREAL

The birthplace of the city, Old Montreal and the Old Port feature centuries-old structures, designer boutique hotels, iconic cobblestone streets, and a grand view of the majestic St. Lawrence River. It's truly a special place beloved by locals and tourists alike. The area comprises a mix of old and new, from dozens of historic buildings and museums to the modern realms of science portrayed at the Montreal Science Center. The area is bordered by Rue Berri to the east; the Latin Quarter, Chinatown, and downtown to the north; Autoroute Bonaventure or Autoroute 10 to the west; and of course the St. Lawrence River to the south. A few years back, the Old Port became the Quays of the Old Port as local officials sought to distinguish the area from neighboring Old Montreal. Everyone still calls it the Old Port.

THE PLATEAU

Decidedly Francophone and carefree, the Plateau residential neighborhood has bustled to the tune of a French accent since the beginning of the 20th century. The district evolved into a Bohemian artist community in the 1970s and has grown to one of the most desirable places to live in Montreal. In addition, the area has been chronicled in the literary lore of playwright Michel Tremblay and novelist Mordecai Richler. The Plateau features rows of urban apartment houses, usually containing three to five units in each, complete with architectural niceties like stained-glass windows and winding staircases. The area boasts numerous art galleries, hundreds of restaurants, and "Main Street" shopping. Take a stroll along Rue St-Denis, Boulevard St-Laurent, or Avenue du Mont-Royal for the people-watching alone and you won't be disappointed. It's city living—any city—at its very best. The Plateau is located to the north of downtown, the Latin Quarter, and the Gay Village, and to the east of Mount Royal Park.

SURROUNDING RESIDENTIAL NEIGHBORHOODS

Mile End, Outremont, and Little Italy, located mostly north of the Plateau district, are residential neighborhoods full of ethnic flavor—from a prominent Portuguese population along Boulevard St-Laurent in the Plateau, a large Hasidic Jewish population in Outremont, to more than just Italians in the Little Italy mix. These listings will mostly include restaurant and food options like the Jean Talon Market.

West of Decarie Highway or Autoroute 15, the residential neighborhood Notre-Dame-de-Grâce—NDG—is home to Concordia University's Loyola campus and busy Monkland

Architectural details in the Plateau.

Avenue. Just east of the Decarie in the Côtes des Neiges / Snowdon residential neighborhoods you'll find St. Joseph's Oratory and the Segal Centre for Performing Arts. Victoria
Avenue in Côtes des Neiges also boasts many Caribbean immigrants and restaurants.

The St-Henri and Little Burgundy neighborhoods southwest of the downtown core hug
the Lachine Canal to the south and the tony Westmount neighborhood to the west of Rue
Atwater. The Atwater Market, Lachine Canal, and "Antiques Alley" along Rue Notre Dame
highlight any visit to the neighborhood.

Safety
Montreal has to be one of the safest cities on the planet. But there are a few places where
you should proceed with caution.

While illegal, pockets of prostitution do exist. Montreal's most notable red-light district
of peep shows and strip joints mostly runs along Boulevard St-Laurent between Rue Ste-
Catherine and René-Lévesque Boulevard. There are hints of seediness along Rue Ste-
Catherine in this area as well, just a few blocks from Place des Arts, when the street
connects the downtown core to the Latin Quarter and Gay Village to the east. As a tourist,
you'll probably walk the eight or so blocks, turn around, and say: What the hell was that?

The Village has a few spots that require mentioning. Male hustlers frequent Rue Ste-
Catherine near Rue Champlain, and at night Rue Ontario from Rue Amherst to Avenue
Papineau is visited by girls in patent-leather high-heeled boots and boys who look like
girls in patent-leather high-heeled boots.

Homeless panhandlers and street squeegee kids assemble all along Rue Ste-Catherine
from downtown to the Village. Many congregate at Émilie Gamelin Park near the Berri/UQAM
metro station entrance in the Latin Quarter. Despite the prominent police presence, visitors
may be approached by those selling drugs in this area and nearby Rue St-Denis.

The neighborhoods of St-Henri and Hochelaga/Maisonneuve have had their share of
headlines. The bottom line: Proceed with caution and remember these areas are very safe—
especially during the day and even at night. So don't dismiss a visit, as you'd miss out on
some great attractions and restaurants.

If you're driving, don't leave any visible items of value inside your car. In addition, those
great big expensive SUVs with American license plates are sometimes the targets of local car
theft rings. There are cars stolen at the airport parking lot, hotel parking garages, and off
the street. I had one stolen in Montreal myself—but c'mon guys, it was a '93 Oldsmobile! Oh
well, it didn't stop me from coming back. As a visitor, you're most likely to have your bicycle
stolen—even if it's locked up. And when riding the metro, no wallets in your back pocket.

Airport and Shuttles
Montreal is serviced by Pierre Elliot Trudeau International Airport—YUL (formerly Dorval
Airport).

L'Aérobus shuttle service is a convenient and inexpensive way in and out of the airport to
points downtown. The shuttle departs every 20 minutes and stops at the Sheraton, Queen
Elizabeth, and Château Champlain hotels, as well as the Central Bus Station in the Latin
Quarter. From the bus station you can transfer to their minibus at no additional charge for
connections to another 40 downtown hotels. The fare costs about $14 for adults. Discounted
fares are available for seniors, children, and round-trips. For reservations call 514-843-4938.

A taxicab ride from the airport is a flat rate of $35 to any point downtown.

There is no direct metro access to the airport, just a nearby commuter rail line with

Typical Plateau staircase looks easy enough to climb—but wait until you need to bring a refrigerator up to the second or third floor!

limited service at Dorval station. While this is the most inexpensive option from the airport to downtown—the price of a bus and commuter rail ticket—you have to time this endeavor just right (I prefer the shuttle). Take the 204 bus from the airport to the Dorval station and then wait for the commuter train, which stops at the Vendôme and Lucien-L'Allier metro stations.

Orléans Express bus line offers bus transportation from the airport to the Eastern Townships and Quebec City. Call 514-999-3977 or visit www.orleansexpress.com.

The Mont Tremblant ski resort offers an express shuttle service called Skyport. Call 514-631-1155 or 1-800-471-1155. Also visit www.skyportinternational.com.

Don't forget to check with your hotel to see if it provides airport shuttle service.

Also remember that when you depart by air from Montreal back to the United States, U.S. Customs and Border Protection is handled in Montreal. Add a minimum 30 to 45 minutes to your usual check-in time for customs clearance. Visit Aéroports de Montréal at www.admtl.com.

Bus Station

The Central Bus Station, Station Centrale, is located at 505 Boulevard de Maisonneuve, across from the Berri/UQAM metro station. The terminal handles buses to and from the United States on Greyhound, 1-800-231-2222 in the U.S. or 1-800-661-8747 in Canada, www.greyhound.com; also on Adirondack Trailways, 1-800-776-7548, www.trailswaysny.com; and Vermont Transit, 1-800-552-8737, www.vermonttransit.com. Canadian destinations to Quebec City and throughout the province are offered on Orléans Express at 514-999-3977, www.orleansexpress.com. And Montreal to Toronto is serviced on Coach Canada, www.coachcanada.com.

Train Station

Montreal's main train station is Central Station, or Gare Centrale (don't confuse it with the main bus station, Station Centrale). The station is centrally located downtown at 895 Rue de la Gauchetière Ouest. The station connects with the Bonaventure metro station and Montreal area commuter rail.

Service to Quebec City and Toronto is handled by VIA Rail, 1-888-842-7245, www.viarail.ca. Service to the U.S. is operated by Amtrak, 1-800-872-7245, www.amtrak.com.

Car Rentals

Tip number one: Don't rent a car in Montreal—this town's made for walking and traveling by convenient public transportation.

Just in case, all major car rental agencies have counters in Montreal at the airport and some downtown locations.

At Trudeau Airport: National Alamo, 1-800-462-5266; Avis, 1-800-879-2847; Budget, 1-800-472-3325; Dollar-Thrifty, 1-800-800-4000; Enterprise, 1-800-261-7331; Hertz, 1-800-263-0600.

> **Jaywalking**
>
> I grew up in the New York City television viewing area, where a popular public service announcement exclaimed: "Cross at the green, not in between" (does anyone remember that?). I don't know if there's a French equivalent, but as of spring 2007 Montreal police began a crackdown on jaywalkers to reduce car accidents involving pedestrians, especially along Rue Ste-Catherine in the downtown core, the Latin Quarter, and the Village. Careful, those cops on bikes sneak up fast. The offense will set you back $37 in fines. So if you see a cluster of folks waiting to cross against a red light when there's no traffic around, you'll know why.

Taxis

Taxicabs are driven by registered drivers who use their own cars. That means the cab can be any make, model, or color. Cabs are recognizable by the sign on the car roof. An illuminated sign means the cab is available. Hailing a cab in Montreal is very safe. A cab ride currently costs $3.15 for the initial meter activation, $1.45 for each kilometer, and 55 cents for each minute of waiting. Popular cab companies in the city include Diamond Taxi, 514-273-6331 or 1-800-716-6727; or Taxi Coop Montreal, 514-725-2667, www.taxi-coop.com.

Public Transportation—STM Metro and Bus

When you're not walking, public transportation is the way to go in Montreal. The city's public transit system is operated by the Société de Transport de Montréal, or STM.

Go green! The Mont-Royal metro station offers a place to park your bike.

Options include an efficient and easy-to-use subway system called the metro. Montreal's metro system was born under the administration of Jean Drapeau, the popular mayor who also welcomed the world to Montreal at Expo 67. Coincidentally, the metro opened the same year.

The metro boasts four color-coded lines: green, blue, orange, and yellow. Hours of operation are from about 5:30 AM to about 1 AM. It's a fairly quiet ride, too, as the tires are made of rubber. Transfers for the bus are available at the silver boxes near the turnstiles once you've accessed the metro—you need to take the transfer from your departing station, not the station where you arrive.

The system shares access to the city's extensive bus system, which is equally recommended. Popular routes include the 97 bus, which runs east-west along Avenue du Mont-Royal in the Plateau, and the 24 bus, another convenient east-west route that runs along Rue Sherbrooke into the downtown core from the Village, the Plateau, and the Latin Quarter. The driver will offer a transfer for a connecting bus or the metro as soon as you board.

A one-way fare currently costs $2.75. A discount strip of six tickets costs $11.75. Tourist cards, which are good for unlimited use, are available for a one-day pass at $9, and a three-day option for $17. Purchase a weekly pass for longer stays for $19. Call 514-786-4636 or visit STM at www.stm.info.

Highways / Bridges and Tunnels / Rush Hour

The major east-west highway in Montreal is Autoroute 40, also known as the Metropolitan, the Met, or the TransCanada Highway. Take Autoroute 40 west to Ottawa and Toronto, and east to Quebec City. Bisecting the city north-south is Autoroute 15, which will transport you from the Champlain Bridge to the Laurentians, Mont-Tremblant, and points north.

The easiest access into Montreal from the South Shore is by the Jacques Cartier Bridge for destinations in the Plateau, Hochelaga/Maisonneuve, the Gay Village, and the Latin Quarter. The Champlain Bridge offers convenient access to the airport, and directly downtown by taking Autoroute Bonaventure, the second exit after crossing the bridge—careful, the exit comes up fast. And while the Mercier Bridge exit precedes the other bridge exits along Autoroute 15 North, the longer drive isn't worth the trip.

Like any other major city, Montreal indeed lays claim to a rush hour. Avoid driving during typical morning and evening work drive times. In addition, there's also a summer festival rush hour. What's that? Let's put it this way—don't attempt driving in the city during Jazz Festival when Rue Ste-Catherine and more are closed to traffic, especially on the same nights when the Fireworks Festival closes the Jacques Cartier Bridge and the FIMA Arts Fest closes parts of the Gay Village. Now that's a traffic jam. These red flag days include the last Saturday every June and the first Wednesday and Saturday of every July.

Parking/Signage

Like in any major city, parking is an art. Montreal is no exception. Parking signs are written in French. You'll need to know the days of the week abbreviated in French—here you go: Lun./Mon., Mar./Tue., Mer./Wed., Jeu./Thu., Ven./Fri., Sam./Sat., Dim./Sun. In addition, signs are posted in military time. For example, 17h means 5 PM (just subtract 12). There are seasonal restrictions for snow removal during winter and street cleanings spring through autumn. There are daily parking restrictions all year long for rush hour and residential parking. Look for the signs with the numbered red boxes and don't park there during restricted times unless your car has a city-issued sticker that corresponds to the number in the red box. If you can't decipher the sign, just ask a local to help with the translation. Parking tickets will set you back a minimum of $42. And, oh, they LOVE to give tickets in Montreal, so you'd better be quick!

Emergency Contacts

For emergencies dial 911.

The City of Montreal Police Service, Service de Police de la Ville de Montréal or SPVM, handles local police matters in the city. There are 49 neighborhood police stations—NPS—on the island of Montreal. Downtown, NPS 21 is at 1180 Rue Ste-Elisabeth near Boulevard René-Lévesque, 514-280-0121. NPS Centre Sud in the Gay Village is at 1200 Ave. Papineau, 514-280-0122. NPS 38 West in the Plateau is at 380 Rue Prince Arthur Ouest at the corner of Rue Hutchison, 514-280-0119. Also visit www.spcum.qc.ca.

Sûreté du Québec is equivalent to highway or state police. For emergencies dial 310-4141 or *4141 on your cell phone. Also visit www.suretequebec.gouv.qc.ca.

The RCMP, Royal Canadian Mounted Police, those guys and gals in those crisp red suits, handles federal matters. The Montreal headquarters is at 4225 Dorchester Blvd. in Westmount, 514-939-8300 or 1-800-771-5401. Also visit www.rcmp-grc.gc.ca.

Hospitals and Dental Emergencies

Local hospitals include Montreal General Hospital, 1650 Cedar Ave., 514-934-1934; St. Luc Hospital near the Old Port and Latin Quarter, 1058 Rue St-Denis, 514-890-8000; Notre Dame Hospital, 1560 Rue Sherbrooke Est across from Lafontaine Park, 514-890-8000; Hôtel-Dieu (hospital) near the mountain downtown, 3840 Rue St-Urbain, 514-890-8000; Royal Victoria Hospital, 687 Ave. des Pins Ouest, 514-934-1934.

For dental emergencies contact Carrefour dentaire at 1101 Rue Bélanger Est. Call 514-721-6006 or visit www.carrefourdentaire.com.

Persons with Limited Physical Abilities

Kéroul is an organization that ranks local establishments on their ability to accommodate people with limited physical ability. Call 514-252-3104 or visit www.keroul.qc.ca.

Consulates

The United States Consulate General is at 1155 Rue St-Alexandre downtown, 514-398-9695.

Old Montreal Weddings

It's a peak summer weekend in Old Montreal. So what will you find? Plenty of tourists, of course. But wait until you meet the newlyweds. Montreal holds justice of the peace wedding ceremonies at a building on Rue St-Antoine. The wedding parties then make their way by limo or by foot to nearby Rue Notre Dame, where the main City Hall building or Château Ramezay make the perfect backdrop for wedding photos. And don't be surprised to see same-sex couples tying the knot and posing for pictures, too. They have been able to marry legally in Quebec since 2004.

Tourism Offices

All the tourist information you'll need, including brochures, maps, and pamphlets, can be found year-round at the Infotourist Centre at 1255 Rue Peel, 514-873-2015 or 1-877-266-

Montreal City Hall is a favorite backdrop for wedding photos.

5687. This phone number is the tourism information phone line for the entire province. Also visit www.bonjourquebec.com.

There's also the Tourist Welcome Office in Old Montreal at 174 Rue Notre Dame Est. The Museums Pass and metro cards may be purchased here. Open daily from April until the beginning of November; Wednesday through Sunday during winter.

Post Offices

Full-service Canada Post counters are most readily available at local Jean Coutu and Pharmaprix drugstore/health and beauty chains. Visit Jean Coutu in the Plateau at 1990 Ave. du Mont-Royal Est, 514-527-3485. Visit Pharmaprix downtown at 1 Place Ville-Marie (near Rue University), 514-866-9881, and in the Village at 901 Rue Ste-Catherine Est, 514-842-4915.

Pharmacies and Health and Beauty Aids

Here are some other pharmacy locations. Jean Coutu in the Plateau at 3745 Blvd. St-Laurent, 514-843-6697. Pharmaprix downtown at 390 Rue Ste-Catherine Ouest, 514-875-7070. Also downtown at 1500 Rue Ste-Catherine Ouest, 514-933-4744. In the Plateau at 3861 Blvd. St-Laurent, 514-844-3550. And Uniprix Pharmacy in Complexe Desjardins (across from Place des Arts), 150 Rue Ste-Catherine Ouest, 514-281-8229.

Grocery Stores and Supermarkets

There are a number of supermarkets large and small throughout the city. Provigo downtown at 1953 Rue Ste-Catherine Ouest, 514-932-3756. Provigo in the Plateau at 50 Ave. du Mont-Royal Ouest, 514-849-8028. And Metro (it's not the subway, it's the name of the supermarket) in the Gay Village at 1955 Rue Ste-Catherine Est, 514-525-5090.

Area Codes

The Montreal island area code is 514. A new area code, 438, was introduced in 2006, but I don't know anyone who has it yet. The off-island area code is 450. You need to dial the full 10-digit phone number with area code when making a local call in Montreal.

Cell Phone Rentals

Cell phone rentals in Montreal are available at Cellulaire Plus. Call 1-877-244-6621 or visit www.cellulaireplus.net.

Media

The French-language entertainment industry is a thriving business in Quebec, complete with its own television stations and original programming, as well as its own crop of celebrities and fan magazines. The Canadian Broadcasting Company—CBC, Global Network, and CTV offer national programming in English—much the same fare that's available in the States, although some shows are revamped into a French version, like *Deal or No Deal*, called *Le Banquier* (The Banker) on the French network TVA. In Montreal, the American ABC, CBS, and NBC affiliates usually originate from Plattsburgh, New York, or Burlington, Vermont. Similarly, regional radio offers a mix of French and English music and talk stations. Fans of National Public Radio should give a listen to CBC Radio One at 88.5 FM and CBC Radio Two at 93.5 FM.

The *Montreal Gazette* is Montreal's English-language daily newspaper. The newspaper dates to 1778 and currently boasts a weekday circulation of about 140,000. The Thursday Arts and Life section offers plenty of concert listings, while the Friday Preview section offers a calendar of things to do. Also locally available are the *National Post* and the *Globe and Mail*, which offer a national Canadian perspective. The larger weekend edition of Canadian newspapers is published on Saturday in Canada, not Sunday like in the States. *Le Devoir*, *La Presse*, and *Le Journal de Montréal* are the largest daily French-language newspapers in the city.

The *Montreal Mirror* and the *Montreal Hour* are two free local alternative weeklies that offer tons of entertainment listings. They're published every Thursday and are available everywhere.

Another free publication is the monthly *Fugues*, a colorful compact guide to the Gay Village. It's mostly in French, but it includes lots of bilingual special-event advertisements and happenings in and around the Gay Village. *Fugues* is available throughout the Gay Village.

Also published monthly is *Scope*, a free guide that includes restaurant and hotel ads, and more than a few strip club listings. The *POM* guide is produced annually and bears the brand name of a local commercial bakery. It offers discount coupons to many area attractions. Both *Scope* and the *POM* guide are available at the tourist information centers, the airport, and participating vendors like hotels and restaurants throughout the city.

Worthy Causes: Dans La Rue / *L'Itinéraire* Magazine

Dans la Rue is the brainchild of Father Emmett Johns, also known as Pops, a much-loved man to many of Montreal's homeless street kids. While you're in town you may see his trademark RV delivering these youths a meal and a short break from the streets. Dans La Rue's day center offers high school and employment skills courses. For more information call 514-526-5222 or visit www.danslarue.com.

L'Itinéraire magazine is a monthly publication sold by street vendors who are trying to earn an honest wage. You'll usually see these friendly sellers in front of grocery stores, metro stations, or any busy city street corner. The cost is only $2, and the profits are split between the publisher and vendor. They are not written in English, so think of them as a chance to practice your French reading skills. Visit www.itineraire.ca.

Montreal summer skyline at dusk.

Alexandre Logan B&B offers comfortable
accommodations in Montreal's Gay Village.

1631

Alexandre
(1870)

3

MONTREAL LODGING— *S'HÉBERGER* (MEANS "TO STAY/LODGE")

There are plenty of places to stay in Montreal—it all depends on what you're looking for. Old Montreal features fancy—and pricey—boutique hotels. They're perfect for a romantic getaway. The downtown area offers lots of big-name hotels. Many of these feature rooms with a view. In addition, some of these chains have more than one location in Montreal, but are individually operated. A number of small guesthouses have made their mark on the Plateau for decades. And bed-and-breakfasts are best experienced in the Gay Village—remember, you may have to share a bath. While those popular village B&Bs are mostly gay owned and operated, they are straight-friendly as well.

Here is a general price guide (in Canadian dollars) for a one-night stay, based on double occupany, in Montreal. I say general price guide because there is often a huge swing in what the property publishes as its regular rate to what's really offered when the competition kicks, especially during low season. On the other hand, you'll have to book well in advance and pay top dollar during peak travel season like Canada Grand Prix time. There are bargains to be found, so check online, make some calls, and shop around.

$	up to $75
$$$	76 to $150
$$$$	151 to $250
$$$$$	251+

Downtown

Best Western Europa
514-866-6492
www.europahotelmtl.com
1240 Rue Drummond, Montréal, QC H3G 1V7
or

Best Western Ville Marie Hotels and Suites
514-288-4141
www.hotelvillemarie.com
3407 Rue Peel, Montréal, QC H3A 1W7
Price: $$–$$$

There are two downtown locations from which to choose if you're loyal to the Best Western name. Each property features about 170 rooms. The Ville Marie is more stylish inside—some rooms offer a four-poster bed—and out, and a bit more expensive. The Europa offers more discounted

1000 de la Gauchetière and the Marriott Chateau Champlain soar past Windsor Station.

prices—special rates in fall can start as low as about $125 a night—and the rooms reflect the price. The hotels are within just two blocks of each other and are close to the Redpath Museum, the McCord Museum, and the Museum of Fine Arts, as well as the metro and shopping along Rue Ste-Catherine.

Cantlie Suites Hotel

514-842-2000
www.hotelcantlie.com
110 Rue Sherbrooke Ouest, Montréal, QC
    H3A1G9
Price $$–$$$

This 250-unit property is situated along a stretch of Sherbrooke Street that boasts almost a dozen hotels in a row. Le Cantlie emerges as one of the nicer of the bunch, complete with sleek bar, nicely appointed lobby, elegant rooms with frilly fabrics, gym, and rooftop swimming pool. It's close to the metro, the mountain, and the Museum of Fine Arts. The trendy restaurant Garçon! is just downstairs.

Château Versailles

514-933-8401
www.versailleshotels.com
1659 Rue Sherbrooke Ouest, Montréal, QC
    H3H 1E3
Price: $$$–$$$$

or

Meridian Versailles Montréal

514-933-8111, 1-888-933-8111
www.versailleshotels.com
1808 Rue Sherbrooke Ouest, Montréal, QC
    H3H 1E5
Price: $$$

Château Versailles and Meridian Versailles have a few things in common: same owner-ship, almost the same location—they're just next door to each other—same Web site, and both boast upscale accommodations.

Château Versailles features 65 rooms in a beautiful setting—a stately, opulent chateau-style house along Rue Sherbrooke. Complimentary amenities feature gym, continental buffet breakfast, in-room safe, and evening turndown. Their classic and deluxe rooms are colorful, clean, and start at about $185; their elegant Versailles Suite features a king-size bed, ornate fireplace, crown moldings, and Jacuzzi. Special rates for that room start at about $359 a night. The Meridian Versailles offers a more tra-ditional hotel exterior with standard rooms that start at about $185. The immensely popular high-end restaurant Brontë is at street level.

Dauphin Hotel

514-861-0808
www.hoteldauphin.ca
1025 Rue de Bleury, Montréal, QC H2Z 1M7
Price: $$

The Dauphin is a small chain of local hotels. This is one of their newest. It's in a very convenient location bordering downtown and Old Montreal in the business area known as Quarter International. The Dauphin is just across the street from Palais des Congrès (the convention center), Toqué! restaurant—perhaps the best in town—and the beautiful outdoor sculpture La Joute by Jean-Paul Riopelle. It's within walking distance to Old Montreal and cen-tral downtown and two metro stations: Place d'Armes and Square Victoria. It opened in 2007, so the six dozen rooms feature a clean and contemporary décor, like vessel-style sinks, in an affordable setting.

Delta Hotel

514-286-1986
www.deltamontreal.com
475 Ave. du President Kennedy, Montréal,
    QC H3A 1J7
Price: $$$

The address of the Delta is on President Kennedy, while access is available on Rue Sherbrooke as well—they must be trying to distinguish themselves from the other dozen or so hotels that run along Sherbrooke, which is a bit of a concrete canyon. This is one of the better big-name properties in the immediate vicinity. There are about 456 rooms, many with a view. Some offer traditional décor, while the premier rooms offer a more inviting updated look (crisp clean linens can do wonders for a room). The Delta is very close to everything downtown has to offer: shopping, the metro, and museums. Rooms cost about $200 a night.

Hilton Bonaventure

514-878-2332
www.hilton.com
900 Rue de la Gauchetière Ouest, Montréal, QC, H5A 1E4
Price: $$$–$$$$

This Hilton property features almost 400 rooms decorated in a classic urban style. Amenities include a gym, a bar, and an inviting outdoor swimming pool—the pool is heated so you can take a swim during winter (do all Hiltons do that?). It's very conveniently located to local public transportation and just across the street from Central Station—Gare Centrale—the main train station for VIA rail service to Quebec City and Amtrak service to the States. The location is also perfect if you're in town for a convention at Place Bonaventure just next door. Advance bookings and room selection at time of check-in are the most inexpensive way to go—about $175 a night in high season.

Hyatt Regency

514-982-1234, 1-800-361-8234
www.montreal.hyatt.com
1255 Rue Jeanne-Mance, Montréal, QC H5B 1E5
Price: $$$–$$$$

One of the best locations in town. The Hyatt is located just across the street from Place des Arts and Musée d'Art Contemporain. If your room faces Rue Ste-Catherine, and it's late June or early July, you'll be able to see the throngs of revelers in town for the Montreal Jazz Festival. Downtown shopping runs all along Rue Ste-Catherine to the west. And the Latin Quarter, the Gay Village, and Old Montreal are about 10 minutes away by foot. In addition, the Place des Arts metro station is just across the street. Amenities include an indoor pool, gym, well-appointed business club, inviting contemporary working lobby, and bar as well. The 600-plus rooms are clean, with up-to-date furnishings and marble baths.

Le Germain Hotel

514-849-2050, 1-877-333-2050
www.hotelboutique.com
2050 Rue Mansfield, Montréal, QC H3A 1Y9
Price: $$$$

Boutique elegance like this is usually reserved for Old Montreal. Le Germain offers 100 ultra-chic, contemporarily designed rooms with full amenities and always the best linens around. You can buy the linens, as well. You're close to the Peel metro station, Museum of Fine Arts, and lots of downtown shopping.

Loews Hotel Vogue

514-285-5555, 1-800-465-6654
www.loewshotels.com
1425 Rue de la Montagne, Montréal, QC H3G 1Z3
Price: $$$$

It may not look it from the outside, but inside the Loews Vogue features a more elegant and stately approach, with some rooms featuring canopy beds. There are 125 rooms in all and full amenities in this property. You're three blocks from the Peel metro station and close to some of downtown's best restaurants, like Brontë,

Garçon!, and Ferreira Café. The Museum of Fine Arts is just around the corner. Expect to pay about $250 per night for a standard room.

Marriott Courtyard

514-844-8855
www.courtyardmontreal.com
410 Rue Sherbrooke Ouest, Montréal, QC
   H3A 1B3
Price: $$–$$$

or

Marriott Château Champlain

514-878-9000, 1-800-228-9290
www.mariotthotels.com/yulcc
1050 Rue de la Gauchetière Ouest,
   Montréal, QC H3B 4C9
Price: $$$–$$$$

or

Marriott SpringHill Suites (in Old Montreal)

514-875-4333, 1-866 875 4333
www.springhillmontreal.com
445 Rue St-Jean-Baptiste, Montréal, QC
   H2Y 2Z7
Price: $$$–$$$$

The Marriott name offers a number of Montreal options. There are two downtown locations and the SpringHill brand in Old Montreal. The Marriott Courtyard downtown is near five or six similar big-box-style city hotels along Rue Sherbrooke. The location is great, but they all look like they could use an exterior steam cleaning. The Courtyard offers 157 rooms and two dozen suites. It's nearby the McCord Museum, McGill University, and downtown shopping. With early booking, rates can start as low as $139. The Château Champlain is the nicer of these Marriott properties. The 600 rooms are traditional in décor but offer great views. The location is near the Bonaventure metro station, the Bell Centre,

Queue de Cheval Steakhouse and Decca 77 restaurants, and a short walk to Old Montreal. The Marriott Springhill Suites in Old Montreal offers 124 suite-style rooms with kitchenette, mini-refrigerator, microwave, and living area with sofa bed. Other amenities include a swimming pool and buffet breakfast. Check online for free parking promotions. The style isn't typical Old Montreal elegance, but the price is reasonable for the neighborhood, from $175 to $245 a night. It's close to the Square-Victoria metro station.

Novotel Montréal Centre

514-861-6000, 1-866-861-6112
www.novotelmontreal.com
1180 Rue de la Montagne, Montréal, QC
   H3G 1Z1
Price: $$–$$$

Novotel offers a contemporary loft-style feel with open bath concept. This downtown property offers about 225 rooms at fair prices. The location is near Crescent Street bars and nightlife and Rue Ste-Catherine shopping. The best deals start as low as $139 a night with breakfast.

Opus Hotel

514-843-6000
www.opushotel.com
10 Rue Sherbrooke Ouest, Montréal, QC
   H2X 4C9
Price: $$$–$$$$

The emphasis is on ultra-chic retro style. Accents like fuchsia club chairs, olive banquettes, and dark wood adorn the lobby, while clean lines and comfy living highlight the rooms. The property has undergone many changes recently—most specifically the name; the space was formerly the Godin Hotel, which was renamed Opus Montréal in 2007, the newest member of the Opus Canadian boutique hotel chain. There are 136 very stylish rooms, the Opus Bar, a gym, and it's centrally located—perfect if you need to work downtown during the day and want to play in the nearby Plateau at night.

Queen Elizabeth Hotel

514-861-3511
www.fairmont.com
900 Blvd. René-Lévesque Ouest, Montréal,
  QC H3B 4A5
Price: $$$–$$$$

Ladies and gentlemen, the Queen. The Queen Elizabeth Hotel is a Fairmont property—think upscale iconic accommodations like the Château Frontenac in Quebec City or the Plaza in New York. That means the well-appointed stately rooms often come with a view and the price tag to match. But with more than 1,000 rooms, there are less expensive rates during low season, like a $179-a-night price found for the October Columbus Day weekend. The place has every amenity available and is close to the train station, the metro, and Place Bonaventure.

Ritz Carleton

514-842-4212, 1-800-363-0366
www.ritzmontreal.com
1228 Rue Sherbrooke, Montréal,
  QC H3G 1H6
Price: $$$–$$$$

The Ritz Carleton luxury hotel has offered opulent classy rooms since it opened in 1912. While rates often range in the $200 to $300 range, last-minute deals can go as low as about $170. It's located downtown near the Montreal Museum of Fine Arts and fine shopping at Holt Renfrew. Afternoon tea is a popular pastime at the Ritz Carleton. Impeccably-dressed doormen mean you have arrived.

Sofitel Montreal

514-285-9000, 1-877-285-9001
www.sofitel.com
1155 Rue Sherbrooke Ouest, Montréal, QC
  H3A 2N3
Price: $$$–$$$$

Simple stylish Sofitel added a touch of contemporary class to Rue Sherbrooke when it opened in 2001. The hotel features 250 fashionable rooms with modern baths, ample windows, and full amenities. The on-site Renoir restaurant is a hit as well. It's just down the block from the Montreal Museum of Fine Arts and McGill University.

Square Phillips

514-393-1193, 1-866-393-1193
1193 Place Phillips, Montréal, QC H3B 3C9
www.squarephillips.com
Price: $$–$$$

The Square Phillips features apartment-style suites, some with kitchenette, along with more traditional rooms. Amenities include complimentary breakfast, indoor swimming pool, gym, and laundry room. It's close to the Bay department store, downtown shopping, the casual Grand Comptoir French bistro, and a 10-minute walk to Old Montreal. Daily, weekly, and monthly rates available.

W Montréal

514-395-3100, 1-888-625-5144
www.whotels.com
901 Rue Square Victoria, Montréal,
  QC H2Z 1R1
Price: $$$–$$$$

These digs ooze über cool with a capital . . .W. It's an ultra-mod designed indulgent space for the young and hip and those who want to be. The rooms are decorated in taupes and tans, with cool blue mood lighting, curtains, and accents. Amenities include Bliss Spa skin care products, a gym, on-site spa, and the oh-so-fabulous Wunderbar for cocktails. The location hovers between Old Montreal and downtown. It's just across from the Square-Victoria metro station. It's hard to find a deal here for less than $275 a night.

CITQ

450-679-3737, 1-866-499-0550

www.citq.qc.ca

1010 Rue De Sérigny, Suite 810, Longueuil, QC
J4K 5G7

CITQ stands for the Corporation de l'Industrie Touristique du Québec. It's a nonprofit provincial organization that ranks and classifies tourist hotels and accommodations. The CITQ is a reliable reference to help you select your accommodations in Quebec. The CITQ evaluates eight different types of properties: hotels, B&Bs, tourist homes, resorts, hospitality villages, youth hostels, educational institutions like college dorms open to the public when school is not in session, and marinas. Participation on the part of all accommodation businesses is mandatory.

The criteria for each property category varies, which means a hotel and a youth hostel are not evaluated the same way. Lodgings are evaluated on qualities like availability of amenities, appearance, and cleanliness—there are dozens of characteristics that the CITQ team evaluates. After the evaluation, the hotel or B&B receives a ranking as well as a sign that must be clearly posted near the entrance of the establishment. Classification levels range from zero to five stars for hotels and zero to five suns for B&Bs. Marinas are ranked from zero to five anchors. The ranking for any accommodation is valid for two years. All of that said, I've stayed at smaller three-star accommodations that I've liked better than larger four-star hotels. The CITQ Web site provides rankings in all of Quebec's 21 tourist regions. Their guide is published annually and is available free at area tourist bureaus.

Gay Village

Alexandre Logan (1870)

514-598-0555, 1-866-895-0555

www.alexandrelogan.com

1631 Rue Alexandre DeSève, Montréal, QC
H2L 2V8

Price: $$–$$$

This residential Village B&B is no stranger to awards, having won Quebec Tourism accolades three years in a row. The B&B is just far enough away from the action for a quiet night's sleep and close enough to the hustle and bustle of Rue Ste-Catherine that you can walk there in two minutes. It's also close to the Beaudry metro station. The house dates to 1870 and features a spacious common room with ornate woodwork, a sunny terrace, and five well-appointed rooms—some with small balcony and private bath. The parking is free—yes, free! On-street parking is available if you properly follow the rules. Minimum night stays sometimes apply.

Aubergell

514-597-0878
www.aubergell.com
1641 Rue Amherst, Montréal, QC H2L 3L4
Price: $$

Aubergell B&B host Yvon Jussaume has been a genuinely friendly fixture in these parts for almost two decades—he owned one of the first gay bars in the village and has owned a B&B since the 1990s (Aubergell was formerly the L'Un et L'Autre B&B). Aubergell features six cozy and clean rooms in a sincerely lighthearted atmosphere. The prices are very reasonable—some rooms start at $95 a night. Most share a bath. The hearty breakfast includes quiche, croissants, and coffee. The intimate Gotha Lounge is at street level and the perfect way to start off your evening. Aubergell is close to all Gay Village bars, nightclubs, restaurants, and retro antiques shopping. The Berri/UQAM metro station is less than a five-minute walk.

Gouverneur Hotel Place Dupuis

514-842-4881, 1-888-910-1111
www.gouverneur.com
1415 Rue St. Hubert, Montréal, QC H2L 3Y9
Price: $$-$$$

The Gouverneur offers 350-plus classy nononsense rooms with full amenities and great views—especially when facing downtown and the mountain. The hotel's central location in the Latin Quarter makes for easy access to the Village, downtown, and Old Montreal. Features include an indoor swimming pool, gym, and on-site parking. Purchase a tasty patisserie treat or fresh fruit at Poivre et Sel (Pepper and Salt) inside the Place Dupuis shopping center / food court at street level. The Berri/UQAM metro station is just downstairs, and La Grande Bibliothèque, the library, is just across the street.

La Loggia

514-524-2493
www.laloggia.ca
1637 Rue Amherst, Montréal, QC H2L 3L4
Price: $-$$

It's not called a bed-and-breakfast, although that's what it is. It's dubbed "art and breakfast." The newest B&B in the Gay Village offers comfortable accommodations and an artistic workshop. After three decades in Vancouver, artist and owner Joël Prévost and his partner Rob Ross returned to Quebec to establish a combination guesthouse and art studio. The space offers workshops, apprenticeships in sculpting, artists-in-residence, gallery space, exhibitions, as well as a place to sleep and breakfast. The building was once the studio of Quebec Automatist artist Marcel Barbeau. The four rooms range in price from $90 to $125. La Loggia is close to Berri/ UQAM metro, retro antiques shopping along Rue Amherst, and some great Village restaurants.

Sir Montcalm Bed and Breakfast

514-522-7747
www.sirmontcalm.com
1455 Rue Montcalm, Montréal, QC H2L 3G9
Price: $$-$$$

Sir Montcalm Bed and Breakfast offers a contemporary urban feel with all the comforts of home—and then some—like communal space with fireplace, an intimate well-manicured courtyard bordered by puffy white hydrangeas, inviting outdoor shower, flat-screen TVs, and a hearty breakfast. The true comforts of home wouldn't be complete without mentioning the ever-affable owner André Bergeron, who will go out of his way to make sure your stay is perfect. The three rooms and two suites offer private baths, and the place is meticulously clean. The location is great— on a quiet residential street near bustling Rue Ste-Catherine in the Village close to bars, restaurants, and the Beaudry metro station. The B&B also features a residence apartment for longer stays.

The Sir Montcalm B&B courtyard is an inviting place to relax.

Turquoise B&B

514-523-9943, 1-877-707-1576
www.turquoisebb.com
1576 Rue Alexandre DeSève, Montréal,
    QC H2L 2V7
Price: $$

Residential-style lodgings, but this one's
been around since 1993—owner Gilles was
one of the first to operate a Village B&B,
and it's still going strong. The accent here is
on high ceilings, five colorful rooms with
shared bath, and lovely backyard garden
with small pond.

Latin Quarter

There are about two dozen guesthouses as
well as mid- and moderate-size hotels in
the Latin Quarter. Many offer basic accom-
modations at affordable prices—properties
geared toward groups or budget travelers.
There are many low-budget less-than-
mediocre accommodations in the area as
well—so choose wisely. Here are a few of the
better choices. The area is convenient to
Old Montreal, the Gay Village, Rue St-Denis
bars, the city public library, and
Berri/UQAM metro station.

All Suite VIP Loft Montreal

514-448-4848
www.viplofthotel.com
329 Rue Ontario Est, Montréal, QC H2X 1X7
Price: $$

Twelve loft-style rooms located in the thick
of things near busy Rue St-Denis. Discount
online rates from about $119 to $139 a night.

Candlewood Suites Montréal

514-667-5002, 1-888-561-7666
191 Blvd. René-Lévesque Est, Montréal,
    QC H2X 3Z9
Price: $$–$$$

and

All Suite VIP-Loft accommodations in the Latin Quarter.

Holiday Inn Express
514-448-7100, 1-888-465-4329
155 Blvd. René-Lévesque Est, Montréal, QC
H2X 3Z8
Price: $$–$$$

Two of the newer properties along the downtown / Latin Quarter boundary. The Holiday Inn Express opened in 2003. Half a block away, the Candlewood Suites opened in 2007. Although they have different names, they have an uncanny resemblance to each other. That's because they have the same owner. Kitchenettes are available in both. A short walk to Old Montreal. Rates start at $140 in either hotel. A good value for the price.

Château de l'Argoat
514-842-2046
www.hotel-chateau-argoat.qc.ca
524 Rue Sherbrooke Ouest, Montréal, QC
H2L 1K1
Price: $–$$

Colorful Euro-style accommodations centrally located on the border of the Plateau, downtown, and the Latin Quarter. No two rooms are alike. The Sherbrooke metro station is a few blocks away, and the Sherbrooke bus 24 offers easy access to the downtown core. It's a 10-minute bus ride, depending on traffic, to the McCord Museum, the Redpath Museum, and the Museum of Fine Arts. Rooms start at $85 to $150.

La Conciergerie Guest House
514-289-9297
www.laconciergerie.ca
1019 Rue St-Hubert, Montréal QC, H2L 3Y3
Price: $$

Before there was a Gay Village B&B, there was La Conciergerie, owned by hosts Michael and Luc since 1985. The space now encompasses two side-by-side Victorian homes for a total of 17 rooms, 9 of which feature private bath. The rooms are clean and comfortable, and the price is affordable, from about $100 to $150 a night. While not technically in the Gay Village, it's as close as you can get. Amenities include on-site gym and sunny rooftop terrace. Steps from the Old Port.

Le Relais Lyonnais
514-448-2999
www.lerelaislyonnais.com
1595 Rue St-Denis, Montréal, QC H2X 3K3
Price: $$–$$$

One of the nicer accommodations in the Latin Quarter, with a contemporary look and feel. Room accents include exposed brick, wood shutters, and crisp linens. On busy Rue St-Denis just across from Cinémathèque Québécoise. Rates from $145 and up from mid-April through September.

Le Roberval
514-286-5215, 1-877-552-2992
www.leroberval.com
505 Blvd. René-Lévesque Est, Montréal, QC
H2L 5B6
Price: $$

Very easy access to the Old Port. Rooms start at $99.

Lord Berri
514-845-9236, 1-888-363-0363
www.lordberri.com
1199 Rue Berri, Montréal, QC H2L 4C6

One of the larger properties in the Latin Quarter, with 50-plus rooms. More amenities than their guesthouse-style neighbors as well, like indoor parking. Rates start at about $135 a night.

The Art of Snow Removal

The average snowfall in Montreal is about 89 inches or 7.4 feet annually. The city removes it with timely efficiency. When orange no-parking signs are posted on the street, you'll have to move your car or it will be towed. After a heavy snowfall, a number of vehicles are deployed—a sidewalk-sized mini-plow to get the snow in the street, a street plow to push the snow from the road toward the sidewalk, and a scary-looking super-sized snowblower that removes the snow into a dump truck riding tandem. Don't get in the way. It's quite a production, and an efficient one at that.

Old Montreal

Auberge Bonaparte

514-844-1448

www.bonaparte.ca

447 Rue St-François-Xavier, Montréal, QC H2Y 2T1

Price: $$$–$$$$

Thirty elegantly styled rooms in an Old Montreal five-story building that was built in 1886. Wrought-iron furnishings add substance throughout. Full breakfast included and a great on-site restaurant of the same name—Restaurant Bonaparte. Steps to the Centaur Theatre. Room rates from $170 to $350.

Hostellerie Pierre du Calvet

514-282-1725

www.pierreducalvet.com

405 Rue Bonsecours, Montréal, QC H2Y 3C3

Price: $$$$

The place for opulent New France elegance—you'll truly feel as if you've been transported back in time. Nestled along the cobblestone streets of Old Montreal, Maison Pierre du Calvet dates to 1725 and is considered Montreal's oldest inn. Now a bed-and-breakfast with 10 rooms, the space boasts appropriate period furnishings like four-poster beds and decadent décor like rich flowing drapery. Previous guests have included Benjamin Franklin and the occasional Hollywood celebrity. Makes for a most romantic getaway. The auberge also features two restaurants—Le Pierre du Calvet for fine French fare—highly recommended for weekend brunch—and Les Filles du Roy for traditional Quebecois dining. It's close to Champ-de-Mars metro station and Bonsecours Market.

Hotel Gault

514-904-1616, 1-866-904-1616

www.hotelgault.com

449 Rue Ste-Hélène, Montréal, QC H2Y 2K9

Price: $$$–$$$$

Take a good look at the façade of Hotel Gault, because from the looks of the inside, you'd never know you were staying in a building that dates to the 1800s. OK, they did leave the exposed brick walls, but the interior design is über chic and modern. Nice touches like heated floors, oak cabinetry, and original artworks. Rates start at about $190, but larger lofts begin in the $500-a-night range.

Hôtel Le St-James

514-841-3111, 1-866-841-3111

www.hotellestjames.com

355 Rue St-Jacques, Montréal, QC H2Y 1N9

Price: $$$$

Mingle with Madonna? She's stayed here. Relax with the Rolling Stones? They've lodged here as well. These opulent luxury digs in Old Montreal are not for the faint of wallet. You're surrounded by lavish furnishings, fine art and antiques, and their private car fleet, which includes a Rolls-Royce Phantom, is available upon your whimsy. Classic rooms start at $280, while the terrace apartment suite will set you back $5,000 a night. Equally exclusive is the hotel's XO Restaurant.

Hotel Nelligan

514-788-2040, 1-877-788-2040
www.hotelnelligan.com
106 Rue St-Paul
    Ouest, Montréal, QC H2Y 1Z3
Price: $$$–$$$$

Poetry in refined motion defines the Hotel Nelligan, named after 19th-century Montreal poet Émile Nelligan. The 100 rooms and suites are housed in three historic Old Montreal buildings that date to the 1830s. The rooms feature a clean look, contemporary furnishings, and exquisite linens. Many include a romantic fireplace as well. Room rates begin at $190 a night. In keeping with the poetic theme, the space is also home to Montreal's highly acclaimed Verses Restaurant.

Hotel Place d'Armes

514-842-1887, 1-888-450-1887
www.hotelplacedarmes.com
55 Rue St-Jacques, Montréal, QC H2Y 3X2
Price: $$$$

The Place d'Armes defines the neighborhood's boutique chic. Three 19th-century buildings compose the space and offer iconic architectural features, like thick ornate stone exterior. Once inside, two centuries collide as exposed brick walls meet contemporary furnishings. You could live in some of the bathrooms, they're so nice. There are 135 rooms, 55 of them suites. The best views overlook Place d'Armes square and the Notre Dame Basilica. You're steps to the Place-d'Armes metro station and Palais des Congrès convention center, and a 15-minute walk to Place des Arts. Stated prices range from $225 a night for a standard room to $1,200 for the penthouse suite, but I did find a late-booking special for as low as $195 a night for the standard room and $230 for the deluxe. Superior service as well. The hotel offers a busy summer rooftop terrace for lunch, the trendy Suite 701 lounge for drinks, and fine dining at Aix Cuisine du Terroir.

Hôtel XIXe Siècle

514-985-0019, 1-877-553-0019
www.hotelxixsiecle.com
262 Rue St-Jacques Ouest, Montréal, QC H2Y 1N1
Price: $$$–$$$$

The name translates to the Hotel 19th Century —the Victorian-era building dates to 1870 and was first the headquarters of the Montreal City and District Savings Bank— Rue St- Jacques was Canada's version of Wall Street back then. The hotel opened in 2001 and features comfortable elegant rooms in one of Old Montreal's better boutique properties. Classic rooms start at $145 and suites start at $185. If you can get that classic room at that price in this neighborhood, grab it. But expect to pay a bit more than what the Web site states. Close to the Centaur Theatre, Pointe-à-Callière, the Montreal Museum of Archaeology and History, and the Square-Victoria metro station.

InterContinental Hotel

514-987-9900, 1-800-361-3600
www.montreal.intercontinental.com
360 Rue St-André Ouest, Montréal, QC H2Y 3X4
Price: $$$–$$$$

For upscale elegant accommodations in Old Montreal. The edifice shares the space with the grand Nordheimer Building, which dates to 1888. The lobby sets the mood: fancy mosaic floor tiles, ornate ceiling details, and columns made of cast iron. Even if you're not staying there, it's worth a walk through. There are 350 tastefully decorated rooms with full amenities. Some suites are housed in the building's impressive turret. The hotel offers a fitness center, a 45-foot rooftop lap pool, two restaurants, a lobby bar, and 18 meeting rooms. Rooms with a view along Rue St-André will be able to see the magnificent *La Joute* sculpture in Place Riopelle just across the street. The Palais des Congrès convention center and the highly acclaimed restaurant Toque! are just across the street as well. Standard rooms start at about $180 to $220 a night.

Le Saint-Sulpice Hotel

514-288-1000, 1-877-785-7423
www.lesaintsulpice.com
414 Rue St-Sulpice, Montréal, QC H2Y 2V5
Price: $$$–$$$$

The boutique Saint-Sulpice offers 108 luxury loft-style contemporary suites in Old Montreal. There's a minimum of 500 square feet of space in each room, with ample room amenities that include inviting linens, dark-wood furnishings, sofa bed, in-room safe, and bar-type kitchenette. Off-season and early booking rates come in at a bargain for this place if you do a little work—from $210 to $250 a night. You're located in the heart of Old Montreal, steps to the Notre Dame Basilica and the Old Port, and not far from Place-d'Armes metro station. The space features a lovely terrace garden, and you won't have to go far for a good meal. The site also features the acclaimed Restaurant S.

Extra, Extra!
Don't forget that these taxes will be added to the price of your hotel room:
3 percent Hospitality Tax
6 percent Goods and Services Tax (GST)
7.5 percent Provincial Sales Tax (PST)

The Plateau

Anne ma soeur Anne Hôtel-Studio

514-281-3187, 1-877-281-3187
www.annemasoeuranne.com
4119 Rue St-Denis, Montréal, QC H2W 2M7
Price: $–$$

Anne my sister Anne is not my sister, but the translation of the hotel name. The hotel offers 17 colorful, basic but comfortable rooms on busy Rue St-Denis in the heart of the Plateau neighborhood. The guesthouse is nearby restaurants like Au Pied du Cochon, bars, and trendy city shopping. Room rates from $70 to $265.

Auberge de la Fontaine

514-597-0166, 1-800-597-0597
www.aubergedelafontaine.com
1301 Rue Rachel Est, Montréal, QC H2J 2K1
Price: $$–$$$

You can't get any closer to Lafontaine Park than this. Guesthouse style lodgings with 21 very colorful rooms in a residential Plateau location. You're across the street from the park, which offers tennis courts, sunbathing, and plenty of benches—bring a book. Shopping, cafés, and bars are nearby along Avenue du Mont-Royal. Sherbrooke or Mont-Royal are the closest metro stations, perhaps 10 blocks away or about a 10-minute walk. Breakfast is included. Bike rentals nearby as well. High season rates start between $153 and $219.

Doubletree Hilton

514-842-8581
www.cpmontreal.com
505 Rue Sherbrooke Est, Montréal, QC
    H2L 4N3
Price: $$$

Hotel names can sometimes be confusing. This one definitely wins a prize. It's the Doubletree. No wait, it's the Hilton. Hold on, wasn't this the Crowne Plaza Metro Centre? Officially it's the Doubletree by Hilton Montréal Centre-Ville (whew!), and yes it is the former Crowne Plaza. Basically it's a Hilton-style hotel, almost moderately priced, with typically decorated rooms, some—not all—updated in the past year or two when Hilton took over in 2006. It is in one of the best locations in town. It's technically the Plateau because it's on the north side of Rue Sherbrooke, but you're very centrally located. The Sherbrooke metro station is just around the corner, and you're

The Château de l'Argoat.

The Doubletree Hilton.

Hôtel de l'Institut de Tourisme et d'Hôtellerie du Québec is a hotel, a restaurant, and a school.

within walking distance to the rest of the Plateau, downtown, the Latin Quarter, the Gay Village, and Lafontaine Park. There are about 300 rooms in all, and about half—if you're facing Sherbrooke or Rue Berri—come with a nice view. Amenities include heated indoor swimming pool. Room rates range from about $160 to $300 a night.

Hôtel de l'Institut de Tourisme et d'Hôtellerie du Québec
514-282-5120, 1-800 361-5111
www.ithq.qc.ca
3535 Rue St-Denis, Montréal, QC H2X 3P1
Price: $$–$$$

A working hotel and restaurant school that offers 42 contemporary rooms, an inviting modern lobby, and a surprising dining experience of refined French fare in an elegant setting. Tasting menu costs $45 and includes cold and hot appetizer, main course, dessert, and coffee. Reserve separately at 514-282-5161. Both the hotel and restaurant are staffed by an enthusiastic class of young professionals. Room rates range between $125 and $295. It's in the Plateau near restaurants, the Sherbrooke metro station, and Sherbrooke bus 24 for easy access into the downtown core.

Rue St-Denis Shopping Tour

Rue St-Denis offers fun bars, great restaurants, and some unique boutiques. Here's a quick shopping tour from south to north, starting in the Plateau near Rue Roy just north of Rue Sherbrooke.

Structube

514-282-1666
3782 Rue St-Denis, Montréal, QC H2W 2M1
For contemporary urban furnishings and accessories.

Les Verriers St-Denis

514-849-1552
www.glassland.com
4326 Rue St-Denis, Montréal, QC H2J 2K8
Glassland's motto—glass and light: eternal dance partners. Original glass panels that are custom made to order and decorative objects like suncatchers, night-lights, picture frames, lamps, and more.

Montreal Images

514-284-0192
www.montreal-images.com
3854 Rue St-Denis, Montreal, QC H2W 2M2
Posters, greeting cards, and Tin Tin products.

John Fluevog Shoes

514-509-1627
www.fluevog.com
3857 Rue St-Denis, Montréal, QC H2W 2M4
Footwear that's fun to wear.

Couleurs

514-282-4141
www.couleurs.qc.ca
3901 Rue St-Denis, Montréal, QC H2W 2M4
How to get to retro. One-of-a-kind finds from the '50s to the '70s.

Bleu Nuit

514-843-5702
www.arthurquentin.com
3913 Rue St-Denis, Montréal, QC H2W 2M4

Arthur Quentin for the kitchen on Rue St-Denis.

Blue Nuit has the same owner as nearby Arthur Quentin. What AQ exquisitely does for the kitchen, Bleu Nuit elegantly does for bed and bath.

Chapofolie
514-982-0036
3944 Rue St-Denis, Montréal, QC H2W 2M2
Hats for every occasion and gloves to match. A St-Denis staple for a dozen years.

Suite 88 Chocolatier
514-844-3488
www.suite88.com
3957 Rue St-Denis, Montréal, QC H2W 2M4
A chic boutique for gourmet chocolates. Warning: you may never leave.

Arthur Quentin
514-843-7513
www.arthurquentin.com
3960 Rue St-Denis, Montréal, QC H2W 2M2
Bring back a souvenir from here, and the cook will kiss you! One of Montreal's premier shops for the kitchen and gourmet chef.

Lush
514-849-5333
www.lush.com
4067 Rue St-Denis, Montréal, QC H2W 2M7
A colorful shop that offers all-natural hand-made bath products in fun shapes like wheels of cheese or deli spreads sold by the pound.

Senteurs de Provence
514-845-6867
4077 Rue St-Denis, Montréal, QC H2W 2M7
For a splash of southern France. Tablecloths, runners, fabrics, home scents, and bath accessories.

Kanuk
514-284-4494, 1-877-284-4494
www.kanuk.com
485 Rue Rachel Est, Montréal, QC H2J 2H1
Proudly made in Quebec. Take a quick detour onto Rue Rachel two blocks east of St-Denis if you're in the market for the warmest winter coat you will ever buy. Kanuk manufactures all their clothes right here at their factory and retail store. For men's, women's, and children's coats, jackets, outerwear, and gear.

Chandells & Cie
514-286-6109
4116 Rue St-Denis, Montréal, QC H2W 2M5
For colorful candles that are all made in Quebec.

Dix Mille Villages
514-848-0538
4128 Rue St-Denis, Montréal, QC H2W 2M5
Where the world is a much smaller place and where you'll find a variety of fair-trade products. The name translates to ten thousand villages.

Essence du Papier
514-288-9691
www.essencedupapier.com
4160 Rue St-Denis, Montréal, QC H2W 2M5
Pens, paper products, and stationery in every color of the rainbow.

Zone
514-845-3530
www.zonemaison.com
4246 Rue St-Denis, Montréal, QC H2J 2K8
Get in the Zone for two floors of unique housewares.

Bohemia Global Market
514-288-0850
4282 Rue St-Denis, Montréal, QC H2J 2K8
Imports from around the world, including a wide selection of colorful tangine ceramic covered pottery.

Depart en Mer
514-288-62 73
www.departenmer.com
4306 Rue St-Denis, Montréal, QC H2J 2K8
Ships ashore. This colorful shop boasts nautical flair. For furniture, accessories, navigational instruments, clothing, and exquisite ship models.

Céramic Café Studio
514-848-1119
www.leccs.com
4338 Rue St-Denis, Montréal, QC H2J 2K9
Don't buy your own souvenir, *make* your own souvenir. Add your own artistic flair to an unpainted piece of pottery. A fun rainy day activity to do with the kids. Light meals and coffee.

Galerie Flowerbox
514-843-4400
www.flowerbox.ca
4400 Rue St-Denis, Montréal, QC H2| 2LI
The live potted plant sculptures from Galerie Flowerbox defy gravity because they're hung vertically on the wall. You may not be able to bring these plants across the border, but still fun to browse.

Le Valet d'Coeur
514-499-9970
www.levalet.com
4408 Rue St-Denis, Montréal, QC H2| 2LI
The name translates to the jack of hearts. You'll find fun in the form of games, puzzles, classic toys, collectibles, and juggling apparatus.

Nüspace
514-845-6868
www.nuspace.ca
4689 Rue St-Denis, Montréal, QC H2| 2L5
For futuristic and fun furniture like Eero Aarnio–style globe chairs.

Montreal Best Bets: *Gratuit!*—Free!
The best things en vie are free. Here are some great Montreal freebies.

Montreal Museum of Fine Arts
Admission to the permanent collection is free; temporary exhibitions are half-price for adults Thursday night.

Canadian Centre for Architecture
CCA offers free admission Thursday evening from 5:30 to 9.

Musée d'Art Contemporain
The place for avant-garde contemporary art. Free admission every Wednesday evening from 6 to 9.

Montreal International Fireworks Competition
There are 10 fireworks shows (it's actually a competition) every summer. The place to be is the Jacques Cartier Bridge.

Montreal Jazz Festival
With 300 free shows every summer, you're bound to find something you like.

Place Jean-Paul-Riopelle
Adjacent to Palais de Congrès, Place Jean-Paul-Riopelle offers *La Joute*, an outdoor sculpture in a public park that's a must-see Montreal moment. The seasonal visit (summer evenings) will only take about 20 minutes, but the memory will last a lifetime.

Mount Royal Park
Take a hike—literally. A stroll in Mount Royal Park is a great idea any time of year—especially during autumn foliage season when there's a light rain shower under an umbrella and the rest of town stays away—magic!

Théâtre de Verdure
Lafontaine Park hosts dozens of free shows under the stars every summer. Even Les Grands Ballets Canadiens takes to the stage for five free performances every year.

Surrounding Area: Airport Options

Most major hotel chains have a location near the airport. Here are four options if you get delayed during Montreal winter weather or need a quick departure out of town. There are no attractions in this area, just the airport. The hotels are best accessed by airport shuttle or cab.

Best Western Montreal Airport
514-631-4811
www.bwdorval.ca
13000 Côte-de-Liesse, Dorval, QC H9P 1B8

Hampton Inn & Suites
514-633-8243, 1-866-633-8243
www.hamptoninnmontreal.com
1900 TransCanada Highway, Dorval, QC
    H9P 2N4

Hilton Montreal Airport
514-631-2411
www.montreal-airport.hilton.com
12505 Côte-de-Liesse, Dorval, QC H9P 1B7

Ramada Hotel Montreal Airport
514-733-8818
www.ramada.com
7300 Côte-de-Liesse, St-Laurent, QC
    H4T 1E7

4

Montreal Dining—*MANGER* (means "to eat")

Dining in Montreal can be a euphoric culinary experience, a substantial quick sandwich, or a relaxing afternoon of appetizers and drinks in the company of good friends. Here are some wonderful recommendations for a variety of tastes and budgets. With about 5,000 restaurants in the city, this is definitely not an all-inclusive list, just a little something for everyone.

Price Guide
(for a dinner entrée)

$$ 1 to $15
$$$ 16 to $30
$$$$ 31 to $40
$$$$$ 41+

The restaurants are broken down into the following neighborhoods:
Downtown
Gay Village / Latin Quarter
Jean Drapeau Park
Little Burgundy
Old Montreal
Mile End
Outremont and Mile End / Avenue Laurier Ouest
The Plateau

A word of note: The Plateau and neighboring Outremont and Mile End may be undistinguishable to a tourist in terms of geography, but probably not to a local. These three districts are grouped last because of their proximity to one another. And even though Avenue Laurier Ouest runs through Outremont and Mile End, it got its own geographic selection of restaurants as well.

Boulangerie les Co'pains d'Abord is the perfect Plateau café for croissants and pastries.

Downtown

Altitude 737

514-397-0737
www.altitude737.com
1 Place Ville-Marie (near Rue University),
Suite 4340, Montréal, QC H3B 5E4
What's nearby: McGill metro station, Rue
Ste-Catherine shopping
Price: $$$$

Every city has a restaurant that boasts the
best view in town, right? Well, Altitude 737
wins that Montreal title hands down, as it's
located near the top floor of the Place Ville-
Marie Building in the heart of downtown.
The menu is traditional French fare, but it's
best for pre-dinner drinks and the view.
The restaurant turns into a nightclub by the
10 o'clock hour. Those nightclub patrons
look quite young.

Arahova

514-935-3339
www.arahova-souvlaki.ca
1825 Rue Ste-Catherine Ouest, Montréal
H3H 1M2
What's nearby: Canadian Centre for
Architecture, AMC Forum 22
Price: $

The popular Arahova franchise chain of
Greek eateries now numbers about 12 in the
Montreal area. This Rue Ste-Catherine
location is one of the newest. Arahova
offers affordable, consistently good Greek
basics like spinach pie, gyros, souvlaki,
Greek salads, and tasty fried calamari. I like
to lunch here after a visit to the CCA
because it's nearby and the price is right.
Lunch specialties like the calamari start at
about $5, spinach pie about $4. Also in Old
Montreal at 480 Blvd. St-Laurent, 514-282-
9717. Open daily.

Brontë

514-934-1802
www.bronterestaurant.com
1800 Rue Sherbrooke Ouest, Montréal, QC
H3H 1E4
What's nearby: Château Versailles Hotel,
Montreal Museum of Fine Arts, Guy-
Concordia metro station
Price: $$$–$$$$

Sleek, stylish, and seriously epicurean,
Brontë pays fine attention to detail. Chef
Joe Mercuri's market-cuisine menu experi-
ence consistently ranks as one of
Montreal's more pleasant upscale dining
experiences. The hip décor seduces with
clean lines and soft, colorful lighting. Open
for dinner. Closed Sunday and Monday.

Café Rococo

514-938-2121
1650 Ave. Lincoln, Montréal, QC H3H 1H1
What's nearby: Guy-Concordia metro sta-
tion, Concordia University
Price: $–$$

Pass the paprika—this is the place for
affordable and hearty Hungarian fare. Try
the beef goulash, of course. There's also a
vegetarian goulash version and a tasty
selection of authentic homemade
Hungarian pastries. Closed Sunday.

Decca 77

514-934-1077
www.decca77.com
1077 Rue Drummond, Montréal, QC
H3B 4X4
What's nearby: Bonaventure metro station,
Bell Centre
Price: $$–$$$$

Swanky digs, trendy menus, and a surpris-
ingly affordable table d'hôte: about $35 for
dinner or $25 for lunch (the reason for the
moderate price rating). The inventive menu
does not disappoint. The evening table
d'hôte starters include grilled shrimps with
tapenade and confit tomatoes. Continue the
sensuous seafood theme with tempura soft-
shell crab accompanied by jasmine rice

with banana and spicy mayonnaise. Everything looks beautiful, too. Comfortable atmosphere with a decidedly business crowd for lunch. Open Monday through Friday for lunch and dinner; Saturday for dinner. Closed Sunday.

Ferreira Café

514-848-0988

www.ferreiracafe.com

1446 Rue Peel, Montréal, QC H3A 1S8

What's nearby: Peel metro station

Price: $$$$

Montreal has a number of excellent Portuguese restaurants in town. Ferreira is the high-end version with the price tag to match. Best for expertly prepared fish dishes. The grilled seafood mix will set you back $45. The setting offers a rich wood bar and sunny yellow walls complete with broken bits of blue and white pottery.

Garçon!

514-843-4000

www.restaurantgarcon.com

1112 Rue Sherbrooke Ouest, Montréal, QC H3A 1G6

What's nearby: Museum of Fine Arts, Redpath Museum, Sofitel Hotel, McGill metro station

Price: $$$–$$$$

One could walk past Garçon! along this busy stretch of Rue Sherbrooke and not realize it—the main visual clue is the orange metal silhouette sculpture of Garçon!'s iconic waiter (that and the low-profile sidewalk terrace, busiest during the lunch hour and for afternoon drinks and appetizers between 5 and 7). That's what we had: afternoon drinks and appetizers. Once inside, the pleasant ambience of Garçon! includes stone walls, wood bar, pink fluorescent accent lighting—and a tale of two waitresses: one seriously dressed in typical black server attire, the other in va-va-vavoom skin-tight cocktail dress cut up to

here—her wine pour proved a bit skimpy (or the glasses were just way too big). The duck confit appetizer proved moist and meaty and surprisingly came with a luscious *amuse-bouche* of chilled asparagus cream. Based on that, I'd come back for drinks and starters anytime, and even dinner, as well.

Grand Comptoir

514-393-3295

1225 Square Phillips, Montréal, QC H3B 3E9

What's nearby: Square Phillips Hotel, McGill metro station

Price: $$

One of the better, affordable, and modest French bistros in town. For tasty soups, hearty cassoulets, and a variety of European-style sausage plates. The outdoor terrace seems to be the center of the downtown universe during summer. It's nice for a late lunch after a morning of serious shopping along Rue Ste-Catherine, just after the business lunch crowd has gone back to work. Steps from the Bay department store. Always polite service. Open for lunch and dinner. Closed Sunday.

Il Cortile

514-843-8230

1442 Rue Sherbrooke Ouest, Montréal, QC H3G 1K4

What's nearby: Museum of Fine Arts, Guy-Concordia metro station

Price: $$–$$$

For genuine Italian fare in a beautiful setting—one of the nicer outdoor courtyards in town.

La Capannina

514-845-1852

2022 Rue Stanley, Montréal, QC H3A 1R6

What's nearby: Peel metro station

Price: $$–$$$

For affordable traditional Italian fare in a cozy central downtown setting. Lunch and dinner Monday through Friday. Dinner Saturday. Closed Sunday.

L'Entrecôte St-Jean

514-281-6492
www.lentrecotestjean.com
2022 Rue Peel, Montréal, QC H3A 2W5
What's nearby: Peel metro station
Price: $$

L'Entrecôte St-Jean's specialty is their simple French bistro formula of potage, greens with walnuts and vinaigrette, sirloin steak, heaping fries, and profiterole for dessert. It's consistently good. There's one in Quebec as well, but different owners. Weekdays for lunch and dinner. Weekends for dinner.

MBCo

514-284-0404
www.mbco.ca
1447 Rue Stanley, Montréal QC H3A 1P4
and
514-845-8887
Complexe Desjardins, 150 Rue Ste-
    Catherine Ouest
Price: $–$$

First, say "em-bee-co." It stands for the Montreal Bread Company. The egg specialties include oven-baked omelets with roasted French baguette, or chopped egg salad with herbs on hearty pumpernickel. Salads for lunch and Danish for snacks. Two downtown locations: across from the YMCA and inside Complexe Desjardins food court. Also at the Trudeau Airport.

Newtown

514-284-6555
www.newtown.ca
1476 Rue Crescent, Montréal, QC H3G 2B6
What's nearby: Peel metro station, Loews
    Hotel Vogue
Price: $$$$

Newtown, owned by Formula One race car driver Jacques Villeneuve (Villeneuve translates to new town) has remained popular since opening in 2001. Located on the busy Crescent Street strip, the complex hosts a restaurant, lounge, terrace, and nightclub. The atmosphere boasts a colorful urban vibe. Lunch specials are reasonably priced and recommended for pastas and salads. Happy hour is fun, but martinis will set you back about $12 (hey, gasoline for those racing cars is expensive!). Nice summer terrace. Open daily. Nightclub open Friday and Saturday.

Queue de Cheval

514-390-0090
www.queuedecheval.com
1221 Blvd. René-Lévesque Ouest, Montréal,
    QC H3G 1T1
What's nearby: Sheraton Hotel,
    Bonaventure metro station
Price: $$$$

One of Montreal's premier steakhouses—with the price tag to match. The quality is superb and the $27 lunch table d'hôte is the most affordable way to go. There are a dozen lunch choices—recommended is the filet mignon with scallop and garlic mashed potatoes that will linger all afternoon long. Dinner entrées à la carte will cost in the $40 range, and sides, like a baked potato or a quarter head of iceberg lettuce with dressing, will set you back about $9 each. Very friendly but spotty service at lunch—it appeared that some of the young wait staff was learning the ropes. That said, the lunchtime price for the quality of food will leave serious steakhouse aficionados pleased.

Renoir

514-285-9000
www.restaurant-renoir.com
1155 Rue Sherbrooke Ouest, Montréal, QC
    H3A 2N3
What's nearby: Redpath Museum, McGill
    metro station
Price: $$$–$$$$

Located inside the Sofitel Hotel, which modernized a concrete stretch of Sherbrooke Street hotels a few years back, Renoir offers a pricey but superbly fine market cuisine menu. The lunch gourmet market dish includes appetizer, main, and dessert for $26. The dinner table d'hôte costs about $49. At that price go for the truffled corn gnocchi with Parmesan starter and the lobster and herb with apricot salad, almonds, and green onions. Classy contemporary atmosphere.

Thursdays

514-288-5656
www.thursdaysbar.com
1449 Rue Crescent, Montréal, QC H3G 2B2
What's nearby: Guy-Concordia metro station, Montreal Museum of Fine Arts
Price: $$

Thursdays is a popular Crescent Street mainstay that's fun for drinks and weekend brunch, which is a bit pricey—about $19 for adults and $9 for children—but comes with live entertainment in the form of a roving magician. There are a number of similar eateries that cater to the Crescent Street tourist and young local student crowd like Hard Rock Café, Wienstein and Gavinos, and Sir Winston Churchill's Pub. (You may see some of these re-listed under the downtown nightlife section.) Crescent Street is the hub of downtown activity during Canada Grand Prix weekend. Visit www.crescentmontreal.com.

Trinity

514-787-4648
www.trinity-restaurant.com
1445 Rue Drummond, Montréal, QC H3A 0A1
What's nearby: Peel metro station, Ritz Carleton Hotel
Price: $$$–$$$$

Trinity is the latest culinary endeavor by restaurateur Peter Morentzos (he also owns the upscale Queue de Cheval steakhouse a few blocks away). This time high-end Greek fare and seafood highlight the menu. Trinity boasts a spacious Las Vegas-esque lushness and wow factor about it complete with white birch décor, sleek ample bar, and miniature Mediterranean pool. The seating includes banquettes with colorful pillows, round bronze Middle Eastern–style serving tray tables, as well as convivial picnic tables. The lunch table d'hôte at $28 is the most affordable way to go. The open kitchen concept is clean and inviting—you can touch the clams on ice if you wish, they're so close. Hands down the most fun is the kitchen help. These women—dressed in black from head to toe just like they do in the Old Country—look as if they just got off the boat. Open daily.

Troika

514-849-9333
2171 Rue Crescent, Montréal, QC H3G 2C1
What's nearby: Guy-Concordia metro station, Montreal Museum of Fine Arts, Le Cantlie Hotel
Price: $$$–$$$$

A Montreal institution that serves high-end Russian fare in a lavish setting. For classics like caviar, beef Stroganoff, chicken Kiev, and any one of the designer Russian vodkas. Open Tuesday through Saturday for dinner.

Zen Ya

514-904-1363
486 Rue Ste-Catherine Ouest, Montréal, QC H3B 1A6
What's nearby: McGill metro station, Rue Ste-Catherine shopping
Price: $$

For Japanese delights in a modern and meditative space tucked away on the second floor of a downtown building. The bento box of miso soup, tasty tempura (eat them first before they get cold), grilled beef and vegetables, sushi sampler, and dessert for about $16 is a lunchtime favorite. Open weekdays for lunch and dinner; weekends for dinner.

Gay Village / Latin Quarter

Au Petit Extra
514-527-5552
www.aupetitextra.com
1690 Rue Ontario Est, Montréal, QC
    H2L 1S7
What's nearby: Lion d'Or nightclub, retro
    antiques shops nine blocks away
Price: $$–$$$

OK, do you want the food or the location first? I like to end on a high note, so we'll start with the location. The restaurant is situated along the Papineau Avenue access to the Jacques Cartier Bridge in the northeast outskirts of the Gay Village, which has been in gentrification mode since the 1990s. Just across the street is a stretch of tattoo parlors. It's not like you're in danger of your life or anything—you can walk these streets in safety—but a cab is the most convenient way to get here. That said, kudos to chef Nathalie Major for standing her ground as Au Petit Extra is a culinary oasis in this slowly evolving part of town. It is basic and hearty French fare that's expertly prepared. Weekdays for lunch; daily for dinner.

Bistro le Porto
514-527-7067
www.bistroleporto.com
1365 Rue Ontario Est, Montréal, QC
    H2L 1S2
What's nearby: Beaudry metro station, St-
    Jacques Market, theater Usine C
Price: $$

Le Porto stands for casual Portuguese cuisine. Try the house soup with hearty chorizo sausage and the smoky grilled calamari for an appetizer. Other house specialties

include tasty grilled sardines—de-bone on your own—and *cataplana*, a luscious seafood casserole. Steaks and salads as well. Also the perfect spot for a cheese platter with a glass of Porto, of course—there are 60 varieties of Porto wines from which to choose.

Carte Blanche
514-313-8019
www.restaurant-carteblanche.com
1159 Rue Ontario, Montréal, QC H2L 1R8
What's nearby: St-Jacques Market,
    Ecomusée du Fier Monde
Price: $$–$$$

One of the newer entries in the Village neighborhood. Carte Blanche offers fine French fare and seasonal menu themes in a cozy and stylish atmosphere. Dinner tables d'hôte range between $18 and $30. Sample luscious linguine with cream of asparagus and prosciutto, and the chef's own marinated beef bavette.

Chez Cora
514-285-2672
www.chezcora.com
1017 Rue Ste-Catherine Est, Montréal, QC
    H2L 2G4
What's nearby: Berri/UQAM metro station,
    Colisée bookstore
Price: $

The Chez Cora story in a nutshell: Yes, there really is a Cora, founder Cora Mussely Tsouflidou. She opened her first restaurant 20 years ago, and now the Chez Cora franchise numbers more than 80 restaurants throughout Canada. Chez Cora quiches and products are sold in local supermarkets, and her CORA Foundation helps underprivileged children. The menu offers substantial and affordable breakfast and lunch fare. Most open daily for breakfast and lunch only. Also in the Plateau at 1396 Ave. du Mont-Royal Est, 514-525-9495.

La Paryse is the place for burgers.

Cuba Saveur Tropicale

514-389-7222
1799 Rue Amherst, Montréal, QC H2L 3L7
What's nearby: Berri/UQAM metro station
Price: $–$$

Next stop: Cuba—and no visa needed. Authentic Cuban/Caribbean dishes in a very casual atmosphere. Open for dinner Tuesday through Saturday; and from 2 PM to 10 PM on Sunday.

Élla Grill

514-523-5553
1237 Rue Amherst, Montréal, QC H3L 3K9
What's nearby: Berri/UQAM metro station
Price: $$

Greek has come to the Village. I haven't had the chance to sample the menu of this fairly new restaurant offering typical Greek and Mediterranean fare, but from the looks of things on a recent summer Saturday night, Élla Grill is quite festive and promising.

Euro Polonia

514-223-4240
1565 Rue Amherst, Montréal, QC H2L 3L4
What's nearby: Berri/UQAM metro station, retro antiques shops, Ecomusée du Fier Monde
Price: $

While walking along Rue Amherst one day, I actually did a double take when I first saw Euro Polonia. It seemed out of place for the Gay Village, which is usually reserved for retro antiques shops, gay bars, and small French bistros. But there it was—comfort-style homemade Polish delicacies like pierogies and Polish sausage. The small store boasts a deli counter for takeout specialties and a few tables where you can stay and enjoy a hearty delicious Polish lunch for less than $10.

La Loïe

514-527-1016
1351 Blvd. René-Lévesque Est, Montréal, QC H2L 2M1
What's nearby: Beaudry Metro station
Price: $$–$$$

When the weather is just right, and the front door is open, you may notice the aromatic scents of the duck *magret* grilling a half block away at La Loïe (pronounced lew-wee, I think). The food is so good at La Loïe bistro, and the portions seem a bit larger than typical plates of French cuisine. The place is small but airy, busier for lunch, quieter for dinner—a good or bad thing, depending on the atmosphere you're looking for. The lunchtime creamy seafood linguini at about $14—with generous chunks of seafood combined with hints of fresh herbs and lemon zest—is so filling, it's enough to share. The service is sincere, casual, and friendly.

La Paryse

514-842-2040
302 Rue Ontario Est, Montréal, QC H2X 1H6
What's nearby: Berri/UQAM metro station, Jello Bar
Price: $

The most popular burger joint in town, with a very dedicated and loyal clientele.

Ô Chalet

514-527-7070
www.restaurantochalet.com
1393 Blvd. René-Lévesque Est, Montréal, QC H2L 2M1
What's nearby: Beaudry metro station
Price: $$$–$$$$

Inventive fun for foodies. The menu combines French fare with Quebecois flair like the smoked Îles de la Madeleine mackerel starter and Quebec cheese plate for two. The décor offers a rustic feel, right down to the blue-and-brown upholstered booths and the cowhide-covered counter stools. It's open for lunch—which is quite busy from the Radio Canada business clientele who work across the street—happy hour on the summer terrace, and dinner Tuesday through Saturday.

O Thym

514-525-3443
1112 Blvd. de Maisonneuve Est, Montréal, QC H2L 1Z5
What's nearby: Berri/UQAM metro station, retro antiques shops, Gotha Lounge
Price: $$$

A lovely little quality French bistro where the menu is written on a chalkboard and you can bring your own wine. Open Tuesday through Friday for lunch, weekends for brunch, daily for dinner.

Piccolo Diavolo

514-526-1336
www.piccolodiavolo.com

1336 Rue Ste-Catherine Est, Montréal, QC H2T 2H5
What's nearby: Beaudry metro station
Price: $$

A village mainstay for Italian fare for more than a decade. The food is hearty and affordable, with à la carte plates priced at less than $20. For pizza, pasta, salads, and grilled specialties. There's also an all-you-can-eat antipasti lunch at about $10. Weekdays for lunch and dinner, weekends for dinner.

Saloon

514-522-1333
1333 Rue Ste-Catherine Est, Montréal, QC H2L 2H4
What's nearby: Beaudry metro station
Price: $

A Village staple since 1992, Saloon is always busy and consistently good for burgers, sandwiches, nachos, and the like. The décor has evolved over the years but always

Ô Chalet restaurant combines modern cuisine and a rustic atmosphere.

remains hip and trendy. Open daily for lunch and dinner.

St-Hubert

514-286-9661
www.st-hubert.com
1019 Rue Ste-Catherine Est, Montréal, QC
  H2L 2G4
What's nearby: Berri/UQAM metro station
Price: $

The St-Hubert chain of rotisserie chicken restaurants has been on the Montreal food map since the 1950s. Some locations are takeout/delivery operations, but many, like the Village location, is a popular restaurant setting for chicken, fries, cole slaw, and their trademark brown gravy.

Jean Drapeau Park

Nuances

514-392-2708
www.casino-de-montreal.com
1 Ave. du Casino, Montréal, QC H3C 4W7
What's nearby: It's inside the Montreal
  Casino
Price: $$$$

New décor highlights Nuances, one of Montreal's most upscale restaurants. A spring 2007 makeover saw the restaurant transform from stately country club to modern urban oasis with cream upholstered seats, flowing white curtains, and a sumptuous crystal chandelier. The serene view of Montreal remains, as does the inventive menu. In these digs, if you can afford it, go for the $165 tasting menu with wine. The starter Chilean sea bass proved succulent and moist, while the caribou tenderloin with gnocchi provided a wise meat segue but came with way too much information (the wild caribou is killed by bow and arrow in the Canadian north by indigenous Inuit peoples). The cheese selection was the most surprising element and was served slightly warm atop crusty bread with apricot and beet. It was simple, smooth, and satisfying. Dessert of Genoa spice cake with almond, mascarpone, fig, and pearls of caviar completed this journey to culinary indulgent land. The wine pairings for each course were superb—particularly the Francis Coppola zinfandel. Incidentally, each server is trained as a sommelier. The staff offers impeccable professional efficiency, and you don't just get one server, you get them all. It's a dressy affair, upscale casual works fine, but a suit jacket doesn't hurt either. Save this one for a special occasion. The atmosphere may be a bit too polite for one to completely relax—unless you just hit it big on the slots, that is.

Little Burgundy

Joe Beef

514-935-6504
2491 Rue Notre Dame Ouest, Montréal, QC
  H3J 1N6
What's nearby: Lionel-Groulx metro station, Rue Notre Dame antiques shops
Price: $$$–$$$$

One of Montreal's current hot dining spots since it opened in 2005. For seafood and steaks with a twist. It's named after a tavern owner from the 1800s, whose real name was Charles McKiernan, who always offered a meal to those in need. Open Tuesday through Saturday for dinner. There are only 25 seats, so reservations are a must.

Le Limón

514-509-1237
2472 Rue Notre Dame Ouest, Montréal, QC
  H3J 1N5
What's nearby: Lionel-Groulx metro station, Atwater Market, Rue Notre Dame
  antiques shops
Price: $$

Vibrant lime green is the color of choice. My favorite part of a Mexican meal (sometimes my favorite part of any meal) is the appetizer. Early evening frozen margaritas and appetizers like shrimp ceviche are suggested after strolling Rue Notre Dame for antiques or a nearby boat ride on the Lachine Canal. Open lunch weekdays, dinner daily.

Quoi de N'Oeuf

514-931-3999
2745 Rue Notre-Dame Ouest, Montréal, QC H3J 1N9
What's nearby: Lionel-Groulx metro station, Atwater Market
Price: $

A French lesson with your breakfast—and a play on words: oeuf means egg; quoi de neuf means what's new? For hearty crepes, breakfast skillets and brunch.

Little Italy

In Little Italy, traditional and satisfying old-world Italian fare can best be enjoyed at **Casa Napoli**, 6728 Blvd. St-Laurent, 514-274-4351, and **Via Roma**, 7064 Blvd. St-Laurent, 514-277-3301.

Tipping and Taxes

Fifteen percent is a decent and expected tip for good service at any Montreal or Quebec City restaurant. The easiest way to calculate this is to add the federal tax, the GST (Goods and Services Tax), which is abbreviated in French as TPS on your bill, and the provincial tax—on your bill as TVQ. Together the TPS and TVQ total 13.5 percent on whatever you buy—including meals at restaurants. You will have to add just a bit more to tip the full 15 percent. Incidentally, I always suggest making reservations for dining in Montreal. Bon appétit!

Old Montreal

Aix Cuisine du Terroir

514-904-1201
www.aixcuisine.com
711 Côte de la Place d'Armes, Montréal, QC H2Y 2X6

What's nearby: It's inside the Place d'Armes Hotel; Place-d'Armes metro station
Price: $$$–$$$$

Market fresh and fine, Aix delivers fanciful and traditional French cuisine with local flair. Sample seared duck breast with mascarpone and squash purée, sided with blood orange and ginger confiture, or if it's a really special occasion, just go for it—the Aix Platter satisfies with oysters, house smoked salmon, shrimp, king crab legs, and half a lobster. Sumptuous Old Montreal digs. Spectacular summer terrace for lunch and drinks. Open weekdays for lunch and dinner; weekends for breakfast, brunch, and dinner.

Aszú

514-845-5436
www.aszu.ca
212 Rue Notre Dame Ouest, Montréal, QC H2Y 1T3
What's nearby: Place d'Armes metro station
Price: $$$–$$$$

Wine and combine. This upscale Old Montreal wine bar offers eclectic nouvelle cuisine that's impeccably presented. A suggested wine pairing is offered for each menu item. Open weekdays for lunch, daily for dinner.

Bonaparte

514-844-4368
www.bonaparte.ca
447 Rue St-François-Xavier, Montréal QC H2Y 2T1
What's nearby: It's inside the Auberge Bonaparte; Place-d'Armes metro station
Price: $$$$

Bonaparte boasts classic simple French fare with a modern twist. It's elegant and romantic but not uptight. The Old Montreal setting comes complete with iconic stone walls and cozy atmosphere with an impeccable menu to match. The evening tables d'hôte range from about $28 to $42, quite reasonable considering the place and locale. But if you're truly celebrating, stick around for the seven-course tasting menu/epicurean pampering. Weekdays for lunch and daily for dinner.

Cluny ArtBar

514-866-1213
www.cluny.info
257 Rue Prince, Montréal, QC H3C 2N4
What's nearby: Square-Victoria metro station, Old Port of Montreal, Centaur Theatre
Price: $$

Industrial light fare that's magic. Take an Old Montreal warehouse and convert it into a condo, an art gallery, or a restaurant. Cluny combines the latter two as it shares a space with the Quartier Ephémère Creative Arts Centre, locally known as the Darling Foundry. Most popular for lunch, Cluny attracts many locals who work in the nearby multimedia industry. The food is always incredibly fresh and served cafeteria-style on bright yellow trays with communal-style seating. Try the smoked salmon on soft focaccia bread with cream cheese and roasted eggplant, a daily hot al dente pasta, and chocolate pudding that surpasses mom's. Open Monday through Friday until 5 PM, and Thursday evenings. Incidentally, Cluny happens to be the name of co-owner Rob Hack's pet black pug—the dog's mug adorns the fun business card.

Gandhi

514-845-5866
230 Rue St-Paul Ouest, Montréal, QC
    H2Y 1Z9
What's nearby: Square-Victoria metro station
Price: $$–$$$

Always ranked as one of the best Indian restaurants in town. And the price is affordable for Old Montreal. Weekdays for lunch and dinner, weekends for dinner.

Garde Manger

514-678-5044
408 Rue St-François-Xavier, Montréal, QC
    H2Y 2S9
What's nearby: Centaur Theatre, Place-d'Armes metro station
Price: $$$–$$$$

Boisterous fun and food. Fantastic Mediterranean and seafood specialties presented in an energetic atmosphere. Open for dinner. Closed Monday.

Gibbys

514-282-1837
www.gibbys.com
298 Place d'Youville, Montréal, QC H2Y 2B6
What's nearby: Square-Victoria metro station, Centre d'Histoire de Montréal
Price: $$$–$$$$

A charming old-fashioned Old Montreal staple for steaks and seafood. The menu features classic seafood starters like crab cakes, curried shrimp, and shrimp cocktail, as well as 16 cuts of steaks and meats for the grilling. Housed in the Youville Stables, which date from 1765 to 1850, the building features rustic ceiling beams and a cozy cocktail lounge. Expect to pay $25 and up for entrées. Appetizers and desserts extra.

Jardin Nelson

514-861-5731
www.jardinnelson.com
407 Place Jacques-Cartier, Montréal, QC
    H2Y 3B1
What's nearby: Château Ramezay, Montreal Science Centre
Price: $$

It is perhaps the liveliest outdoor terrace in all of Old Montreal. Make that terraces—there's one in front, but the bustling garden terrace in back is where it's at. Lunch proves most popular, with the majority of meals in the $15 price range—the 10 varieties of stuffed crepes are the big draw. Live jazz music accompanies your lunch every weekday. Popular weekend brunch, too.

Le Nantua

514-288-4288
275 Rue Notre Dame Ouest, Montréal, QC
    H2Y 1T8
What's nearby: Notre Dame Basilica,
    Centaur Theatre
Price: $$$–$$$$

For classic high-end seafood in a refined Old Montreal setting.

Olive et Gourmando

514-350-1083
www.oliveetgourmando.com
351 Rue St-Paul Ouest, Montréal, QC H2Y 2A7
What's nearby: Square-Victoria metro sta-
    tion, Old Port of Montreal
Price: $–$$

A popular fancy sandwich shop in Old Montreal that's always crazy busy for lunch. If you can't get a seat, you can order your sandwich to go and enjoy it at the nearby Old Port. Suggested is the hot panini called the Cubain, with ham, pork, Gruyère cheese, and chipotle, lime, and coriander mayo. The staff moves with efficiency, and to my sur-prise I got a wink when my sandwich was ready. I did manage to wait to eat my creation until I got to the Old Port, but could smell the aromas through the wrapper and was tempted to rip open the brown paper bag, sit down on the curb, and eat the thing right there. I must admit, it was sinfully tasty, with an ever slight slow burn. Was it worth $9 for a sandwich? You make up your own mind. But the wink was worth every penny.

Ora

514-848-0202
www.restaurantora.com
394 Rue St-Jacques, Montréal, QC H2Y 1S1
What's nearby: Square-Victoria metro sta-
    tion, Centaur Theatre
Price: $$$–$$$$

Jardin Nelson in Old Montreal has a busy summer terrace in front, and an even busier terrace in back.

Ora is a new contemporary Old Montreal restaurant that caters to a business crowd for lunch. The menu features a succulent crab cake appetizer and a reasonably priced selection of lunch tables d'hôte, like the seafood pizza, which cost about $15 and was good. But not so reasonably priced was the $38 exotic mushroom and truffle oil risotto. It's not something you do often—order $38 risotto—especially for lunch. But it was worth every orgasmic mouthful and was accompanied by audible "Mmmmms." Share it with a friend and talk about it for years to come. Phenomenal desserts, too.

Pierre du Calvet / Les Filles du Roy

514-282-1725
www.pierreducalvet.ca
405 Rue Bonsecours, Montréal, QC
    H2Y 3C3
What's nearby: Champ-de-Mars metro station , Bonsecours Market
Price: $$$–$$$$

You can't beat the 18th-century Old Montreal atmosphere at Pierre du Calvet. The setting includes thick stone walls, grand fireplace, hedonistic furnishings, bright gold and yellow accent molding, and the occasional cobweb between the antlers on the mounted deer. The Pierre du Calvet weekend brunch is a favorite and a delicious bargain at about $16. The apple-stuffed crepes and the eggs Benedict are perfect to share—there are two on each plate. Brunch also comes with fresh salad to start and endless cups of coffee. Open for dinner as well, for fine French fare. The adjacent Les Filles du Roy offers weekday fare like gourmet burgers and traditional Quebecois Lac St-Jean *tourtière* meat pie. The staff is young, friendly, and professional.

Stash Café

514-845-6611
www.stashcafe.com
200 Rue St-Paul Ouest, Montréal, QC
    H2Y 1Z9

An antique tapestry adorns a stone wall in the Filles du Roy Restaurant at Hotel Pierre du Calvet in Old Montreal.

What's nearby: Place-d'Armes metro station, Notre Dame Basilica
Price: $$–$$$

Delectable Polish recipes at a very fair price for Old Montreal. Lunch costs between $10 and $15. For dinner, try the Polish Primer for about $26, which includes borsch, salad, a main plate of *bigos* (a sausage and cabbage stew), *placki* (a fried potato pancake), and meat and potato pierogis. Then try the Polish poppyseed cake for dessert. Open daily.

Toqué!

514-499-2084
www.restaurant-toque.com
900 Place Jean-Paul-Riopelle, Montréal, QC H2Z 2B2
What's nearby: Intercontinental Hotel, *La Joute* outdoor sculpture, Palais des Congrès
Price: $$$$

The name rhymes with "OK," but Toqué! is much better than that. Normand Laprise has been a celebrated fixture in Montreal since the mid-1990s, and his Toqué! restaurant consistently wows serious foodies, local critics, and the vacationing diner enjoying a special night out. The local market cuisine tasting menu costs about $147 with five wine pairings. It's the indulgent way to go in a place like this. A real Montreal treat. Open Tuesday through Saturday for dinner.

Version Laurent Godbout

514-871-913
www.version-restaurant.com
295 Rue St-Paul Est, Montréal, QC H2Y 1H3
What's nearby: Rasco Hotel, Place Jacques-Cartier, Marché Bonsecours
Price: $$$–$$$$

In Montreal's abundant land of fancy French-style fare comes locally renowned chef Laurent Godbout's culinary take on things. His Version is all about Mediter-
ranean surprises from Italy, southern France, Spain, and Portugal. Start with nacho-style gravlax salmon. Then sample main dishes like scallop, shrimp, and grilled chorizo with smoked paprika, asparagus purée, and snow peas; or the veal chop with chili-pineapple glazed bok choy and coriander sweet potatoes. Very relaxed atmosphere, inviting terrace, and on-site boutique. Lunch is a bargain, starting at about $14. Tuesday through Friday for lunch, Tuesday through Saturday for dinner.

Mile End

Berlin

514-270-3000
www.geocities.com/berlinmtl
101 Ave. Fairmount Ouest, Montréal, QC H2T 2M4
What's nearby: Corner of Rue St-Urbain; Blvd. St-Laurent bus 55
Price: $–$$

The place is nothing to look at from the outside, but once inside you'll discover casual hearty German fare in a friendly atmosphere. Start with fried Camembert with cranberries, or Berliner meat dumplings. For the mains, sample schnitzel, sausage, or sauerbraten with spaetzle and sauerkraut sides. The décor features authentic pieces of the Berlin Wall. The German and European beers in bottle or on tap, as well as the apple schnapps, readily flow. Sometimes there's live music. Lederhosen optional. Open for dinner. Closed Monday.

Bu

514-276-0249
www.bu-mtl.com
5245 Blvd. St-Laurent, Montréal, QC H2T 1S4
What's nearby: Corner of Ave. Fairmount; Blvd. St-Laurent bus 55
Price: $$ for food, $$$ for wine

This trendy Mile End wine bar offers mod-ern Italian fare and 500 wines from which to choose. Happy hour features an appetiz-ing *amuse-bouche* trio for $15—try the cheese pie with balsamic cream. Cold main plates include prosciutto and papaya roulades or piping-hot eggplant lasagna. Late menu after 10 PM; open daily for din-ner until 1 AM.

Cuisine et Dépendance

514-842-1500
www.cuisineetdependance.ca
4902 Blvd. St-Laurent, Montréal, QC
    H2T 1R5
What's nearby: Just south of Blvd. St-
    Joseph; Blvd. St-Laurent bus 55
Price: $$–$$$

There is no specialty at Cuisine et Dépendance because there's a specialty every day. For that fact, there's no menu either, because there's a new menu every day: five appetizers and five main courses for dinner (three and three for lunch), which is tem-porarily written on a roll of butcher paper and torn off for the next seating. There is one thing you will find: the ever-affable co-owner Danielle Matte who works the dining area with genuine panache, and the expert cuisine of co-owner chef Jean Paul Giroux, the *dépendance* or addiction part of this very casual and friendly French restaurant. Main courses about $22.

L'Atelier

514-273-7442
www.restaurantlatelier.com
5308 Blvd. St-Laurent, Montréal, QC
    H2T 1S1
What's nearby: North of Ave. Fairmount;
    Blvd. St-Laurent bus 55
Price: $$–$$$

An atelier is a workshop. L'Atelier is the inventive culinary kind. The fun fusion tast-

At Wilensky's, the specialty of the house is a fried baloney sandwich.

ing menu features 20 items that range from $9 to $15. Three choices make a full meal. It's a whimsical feast that may take you a while to make a decision. Selections include poutine with thick-cut fries, rabbit, barbecue sauce, and Allegretto cheese; cod with red lentils and wild mushrooms; or medallions of deer with Espelette pepper *pipérade*. Open Tuesday through Friday for lunch, Tuesday through Sunday for dinner. Closed Monday.

Milos

514-272-3522
www.milos.ca
5357 Ave. du Parc, Montréal, QC
    H2V 4G9
What's nearby: Between Rue St-Viateur and
    Ave. Fairmount
Price: $$$–$$$$

Immensely popular Mile End high-end Greek restaurant renowned for its seafood specialties. The $20 business lunch is the most affordable way to go. Open weekdays for lunch and dinner, weekends for dinner.

Soy

514-499-9399
www.restaurantsoy.com
5258 Blvd. St-Laurent, Montréal, QC
    H2T 1S1
What's nearby: North of Ave. Fairmount;
    Blvd. St-Laurent bus 55
Price: $–$$

Don't think fusion at Soy, says manager Manny Cheng, who runs Soy with his wife, chef Suzanne Liu. He prefers to call it a modern take on Asian cuisine, which means using less oil and lighter batter. The result of this delectable philosophy includes baked scallops with spicy tobiko and nori seaweed; Szechuan duck sided with cucumber, spring onions, hoisin sauce, and pancakes; and Korean barbecue Kalbi beef with romaine and marinated

cucumber. All of these dishes are available à la carte or as affordable table d'hôte that cost about $25. Soups start at $3, appetizers cost about $6, and lunch tables d'hôte average about $10. Inventive Asian-inspired martinis with ginger, coriander, and lemongrass flavors are the perfect start to your meal.

Wilensky Light Lunch

514-271-0247
34 Ave. Fairmount Ouest, Montréal, QC
    H2T 2M1
What's nearby: Rue Clark
Price: $

This isn't your grandfather's corner luncheonette. Wait a second—uh, yes it is. Wilensky's has been a Montreal institution for the past seven decades. It's a corner luncheonette that's full of baloney—literally—the "Wilensky Special" is fried baloney, salami, with mustard on a kaiser roll. You don't even get a plate—it's tucked inside a pocket of wax paper. Wash it down with an egg cream. Open weekdays for breakfast and lunch.

Best Quick Bites: Montreal Bagels

The Montreal bagel has been touted as the best in the world. They're more compact than their New York counterparts—not so thick, but still chewy. They're first boiled in honey water, then baked, and always best when served fresh from the oven. The topping of choice: a generous coating of sesame seeds. So are Montreal bagels really the best in the world? You decide. Try **St-Viateur Bagel** at 263 Rue St-Viateur Ouest (514-276-8044) or 1127 Ave. du Mont-Royal Est (514-528-6361), www.stviateurbagel.com; and **Fairmount Bagel** at 74 Ave. Fairmount Ouest (514-272-0667, www.fairmountbagel.com). Open 24 hours.

Petits Gâteaux on Avenue du Mont-Royal has cupcakes in every color.

Outremont and Mile End / Avenue Laurier West

Avenue Laurier West (Ouest), which runs through parts of Outremont and Mile End, is about 10 blocks east of the Laurier metro station. St-Laurent Boulevard and Avenue du Parc (the official boundary between Outremont and Mile End) are your two main cross streets. These are not listed alphabetically, but from St-Laurent Boulevard walking west.

Chao Phraya

514-272-5339
www.chao-phraya.com
50 Ave. Laurier Ouest, Montréal, QC
    H2T 2N4
Price: $$

A Montreal staple now for two decades, Chao Phraya offers authentic Thai flavors and dishes in an elegant setting. The menu is quite ambitious and includes hearty—and spicy—soups, starters like grilled shrimp with chili paste and mint leaves, and entrées of chicken, duck, beef, and vegetarian specialties as well. Many dishes are spicy, but you get to choose the level of heat. Open daily for dinner.

Bazaar Anise

514-276-6999
www.anise.ca
104 Ave. Laurier Ouest, Montréal, QC
    H2T 2N7
Price: $$–$$$

In 2007 this popular restaurant changed names from Anise to Bazaar Anise, and changed menus from fancy French fare to more casual Mediterranean and French-infused grilled specialties. It's cozy—maybe four dozen seats in all, with a separate lounge. Enjoy drinks and appetizers like grilled Lebanese sausage with pomegranate molasses. Open for dinner Tuesday through Saturday.

Raza

514-227-8712
www.restaurantraza.com
114 Ave. Laurier Ouest, Montréal, QC
    H2T 2N7
Price: $$$–$$$$

The cuisine is dubbed Nuevo Latino. Raza artfully bridges South American flavors with a French-style approach The culinary combinations include foie gras empanada with purple corn, duck with barbecue guava and quinoa grains, and shrimp with pumpkin, cheese, and amarillo chilies.

Jun-i

514-276-5864
158 Ave. Laurier Ouest, Montréal, QC
    H2T 2N7
www.juni.ca
Price: $$$–$$$$

The upscale spot for sushi and sake on Laurier West. The menu offers inventive Japanese and French entrée concoctions like organic chicken stuffed with risotto, mushroom, and Parmesan cheese topped with a creamy lemongrass sauce; or filet mignon with mushroom, carrots, and celery with hints of maple syrup, beef stock, and miso. Open for lunch Tuesday through Friday, dinner Monday through Sunday.

La Petite Ardoise

514-495-4961
222 Ave. Laurier Ouest, Montréal, QC
    H2T 2N8
Price: $$

Bistro-style breakfast, brunch, lunch, and dinner. For lunch try the quiche or hearty sandwich selections, including the open-faced ham and béchamel *croque-madame*, or their quick-formula dinners like the onion soup gratinée, duck confit main plate, and coffee, all for about $20. A half dozen varieties of crepes as well. Relaxing summer terrace. Open daily.

de Gascogne

514-490-0235
237 Ave. Laurier Ouest, Montréal, QC
    H2T 2N9
Price: $

A wonderful gourmet grocery that offers delectable sandwiches to stay or go, as well as prepared meals. Also stick around for pastries, desserts, and coffee. Just look for the rolling-pin door handles.

Juliette & Chocolat

514-510-5651
www.julietteetchocolat.com
377 Ave. Laurier Ouest, Montréal, QC
    H2V 2K3
or
514-287-3555
1615 Rue St-Denis, Montréal, QC H2X 3K3
    (in the Latin Quarter)
Price: $

A menu that revolves around chocolate—and the world is a better place for it. Crepes, chocolate fondue, hot chocolate, pastries, and candy.

Rôtisserie Laurier

514-273-3671
381 Ave. Laurier Ouest, Montréal, QC
    H2V 2K3
Price: $

Another decades-old Montreal institution—it's been around since 1936. This family-style restaurant specializes in rotisserie chicken, barbecue chicken sandwiches, and chicken pot pie. Start with homemade pea soup and finish with homemade chocolate cream pie. You also get crayons with your black and white paper placemat/menu. A value for lunch and dinner.

Chez Lévêque

514-279-7355
1030 Ave. Laurier Ouest, Montréal, QC
 H2V 2K8
Price: $$

One of the better French bistros in Montreal—it's been around for three decades—with a very loyal following to prove it. For breakfast or weekend brunch, lunch or afternoon pastry with coffee, and dinner fare like grilled steaks, chops, and seafood. There's no rush at Chez Lévêque. Open daily.

Gourmet Laurier

514-274-5601
www.gourmetlaurier.com
1042 Ave. Laurier Ouest, Montréal, QC
 H2V 2K8

For fine spices, oils, vinegars, cheeses, chocolates, pastries, jams, teas, and coffees—it's where Van Houtte coffee was born. Open daily.

Leméac

514-270-0999
www.restaurantlemeac.com
1045 Ave. Laurier Ouest, Montréal, QC
 H2V 2L1
Price: $$$–$$$$

This Outremont bistro offers serious French fare. The menu includes everything from a daily fish dish and risotto selections, to the likes of calf liver, veal kidneys, and blood pudding. Lunch table d'hôte starts at about $18 for appetizer and main plate; desserts extra. The delectable appetizer of white asparagus with mushroom topped with a poached egg would have satisfied for brunch. The doré lake fish and rice pilaf was good but ordinary and made me wish I had ordered something else from

this generous menu. Dessert specialties like the indulgent pain perdue with ice cream and maple syrup is fancy French toast in disguise. A late-night menu features appetizer and mains for $22 beginning at 10 PM or later. Upscale crowd, polite atmosphere.

The Plateau

Au Pied du Cochon

514-281-1114
www.restaurantaupieddecochon.ca
536 Ave. Duluth Est, Montréal, QC H2L 1A9
What's nearby: Corner of Rue St. Hubert;
 Lafontaine Park, Sherbrooke metro station
Price: $$$–$$$$

Pied du cochon translates to the foot of the pig—and yes, it's on the menu. There are seven pork entrées in all, including the generously sized happy pork chop, as well as bison ribs, duck in a can, and inventive Quebecois twists like poutine with fois gras. The desserts are homespun and delicious, like the sugar pie for two. It's rustic, lively, and fun—and always considered one of Montreal's bests. Open for dinner. Closed Monday.

Boulangerie les Co'pains d'Abord

514-522-1994
965 Ave. du Mont-Royal Est, Montréal, QC
 H2J 1X4
What's nearby: Shopping on Ave. du
 Mont–Royal, Lafontaine Park
Price: $

The epitome of the perfect Plateau café. This busy cozy café and pastry shop is quite popular with the locals. Go there for fresh-baked baguette, mini homemade chicken pot or vegetarian millet pies (they'll warm them up for you), or a slice of tangy goat cheese pizza to go. But really go there for the incredible pastries and desserts. The brownies with walnuts are perfectly sweet, and the chocolate almond croissants can tastefully be shared with a friend. The small foyer is fun, too, boasting a wall of fliers that offer everything from local garage sale listings to language lessons to bicycles for sale.

Byblos Le Petit Café
514-523-9396
www.geocities.com/cafebyblos
1499 Ave. Laurier Est, Montréal QC H2J 1H8
What's nearby: Laurier metro station, Blvd.
    St-Joseph bus 27 or Ave. Papineau bus 45
Price: $

Byblos is a friendly Plateau neighborhood restaurant that has specialized in Iranian and Middle Eastern fare for two decades. If co-owner Hamid Pourafzal senses it's your first visit, he may suggest that he choose the menu items. My friend and I said yes. He also said that if we didn't like something, we could send it back. We said OK. We didn't send anything back. We sampled the likes of *boranis*, yogurt dips flavored with eggplant, spinach, and beets served with pita, and rouleaux of spinach and cheese, similar to spinach pie with a variation on the crust. The rolls are also available stuffed with ground beef or fish. Top it off with piping-hot Iranian tea, where the hard-candy-like sugar cube slowly melts in your mouth with each sip. The bill came to $40 for two, with a glass of wine. Vegetarian friendly. Very relaxed atmosphere, with large windows that open to the sidewalk. There's also a very popular weekend brunch, but don't expect typical bacon and eggs. Open Tuesday through Sunday for breakfast, lunch, and dinner. As for Hamid, you can't get any nicer than that.

Café Santropol
514-842-3110
www.santropol.com
3990 Rue St-Urbain, Montréal, QC H2W 1T7
What's nearby: Corner of Ave. Duluth; Blvd.
    St-Laurent bus 55
Price: $

Fair is fair trade at Café Santropol, a Montreal staple for sandwiches and coffee for three decades. All coffees are fair-trade certified. For soups, salads, and inventive sandwich combinations—more than two dozen in all—like the Minted Ham of smoked ham, apple and cucumber slices, and mint jelly. Very vegetarian-friendly. Friendly vibe. Open for lunch until midnight. Cash only.

Chez le Portugais
514-849-0550
www.chezleportugais.com
4134 Blvd. St-Laurent, Montréal, QC
    H2W 1Y8
What's nearby: Corner of Rue Rachel; Blvd.
    St-Laurent bus 55
Price: $$

Run by the very affable Henrique Laranjo, Chez le Portugais offers traditional and tasty Portuguese fare. Sample *petiscos*—the Portuguese version of tapas—like *bacalhau a bras* (a fish-cake round made of cod and matchstick potatoes), simple but luscious chicken with mushroom sauce, and braised beef. A fine selection of Porto as well, including a smooth 20-year-old white reserve Porto under the Quinta do Estanho label.

Chu Chai
514-843-4194
4088 Rue St-Denis, Montréal, QC
    H2W 2M5
What's nearby: Corner of Ave. Duluth;
    Mont-Royal metro station
Price: $$

Oh boy, soy! Vegetarians step to the front of the line and carnivores prepare to be delightfully surprised. The menu says words like chicken, duck, and shrimp, but the recipes are all vegetarian. The surprisingly tasty Thai-inspired menu includes dishes with lemongrass, coconut, and yellow curry flavors. Open for lunch takeout only; daily for dinner.

Best of Montreal: Mont-Royal Avenue Food Tour

Don't miss a leisurely stroll along Mont-Royal Avenue. You find restaurants, bars, men's and women's clothing boutiques, gift stores, used CD and book stores, and a tasty selection of food purveyors including fruiteries (fruit stores), boulangeries (bakeries), and patisseries (pastry shops). You will love this street as I do. Start at the Mont-Royal metro station and head east. When you get to the end, just hop on the 97 bus to get back to the metro.

Petits Gâteaux offers gourmet cupcakes in flavors like chocolate ganache with 68 percent cocoa from Cuba (it must be illegal to bring them back into the States; I won't tell if you won't). The shop is designed in brown, to signify the chocolate batter; light yellow walls, representing butter; and pink curtains and trays, for the candy. At 783 Ave. du Mont-Royal Est, 514-510-5488.

Caffè Art Java adds temporary liquid art to your café au lait that disappears after your first sip. Bring your laptop. At 837 Ave. du Mont-Royal Est, 514-527-9990.

L'Aromate features a fun selection of tableware and unique culinary gifts. At 1106 Ave. du Mont-Royal Est, 514-521-6333.

Diabolissimo offers homemade prepared fresh pastas and sauces as well as tasty sandwiches to go. At 1256 Ave. du Mont-Royal Est, 514-528-6133.

La Soupière offers kitchen gadgets and utensils. At 1272 Ave. du Mont-Royal Est, 514-527-4626.

Folie en Vrac offers an abundant selection of Mediterranean olive oils, vinegars, spices, and a satisfying healthy falafel pita sandwich for about $4. At 1307 Ave. de Mont-Royal Est, 514-523-4622.

La Maison du Rôti is a *boucherie* or butcher shop that also offers a fine selection of spices, packaged goods, coffees, and teas. At 1669 Ave. du Mont-Royal Est, 514-521-2448, www.lmdr.net.

Pâtes à Tout means homemade pasta for all. Italian specialties to stay or go like eggplant Parmesan or stuffed cannelloni. At 1846 Ave. du Mont-Royal Est, 514-525-0897.

La Coquille offers fun kitchen gadgets, Asian-inspired tableware, and the occasional Hello Kitty kitchen appliance. At 1915 Ave. du Mont-Royal Est, 514-313-9880.

William J. Walter offers 50 varieties of sausage. It's not the kind of souvenir you can bring back, but you can grab lunch there like gourmet hot dogs with sauerkraut on fresh baguette. At 1957 Ave. du Mont-Royal Est, 514-528-1901.

Harnois offers delectable gourmet chocolates. At 1957A Ave. du Mont-Royal Est, 514-51-3434.

I dare you to walk past **Le Péché Glacé** without stopping—the smell of waffles topped with artisanal ice cream is intoxicating. At 2001 Ave. du Mont-Royal Est, 514-525-5768.

Of the half-dozen fruit stores all along the street, **Passion des Fruits** has the best music: reggae, world beat, and contemporary sounds. At 2018 Ave. du Mont-Royal Est, 514-521-1151.

La Fromagerie Hamel offers 250 varieties of cheese. Try the local Oka cheese made by monks. At 2117 Ave. du Mont-Royal Est, 514-521-3333.

Finally, at **Café Le Placard** you can buy breakfast, a warm croissant, a cup of fair-trade coffee, and a secondhand dress or necklace. How's that for a combination? At 2129 Ave. du Mont-Royal Est, 514-590-0733.

Dans La Bouches

514-526-1404

2000 Ave. du Mont-Royal Est, Montréal,
QC H2H1S6

What's nearby: Four blocks east of Ave.
Papineau; Ave. du Mont-Royal bus 97

Price: $$

Very popular local eatery with a little some-
thing for everyone: tapas, salads, fajitas,
burgers, and grilled steaks and chicken.
Busy weekend brunch. The décor is mod-
ern, comfy, and inviting—especially when
the large glass garage-door-style windows
are open along Mont-Royal Avenue. The
best feature: there is absolutely no rush.
Open daily for lunch and dinner.

La Banquise

514-525-2415

976 Rue Rachel Est, Montréal, QC H2J 2J3

What's nearby: Sherbrooke metro station,
Lafontaine Park

Price: $

OK, here is your poutine primer. A poutine
is an indigenous Quebec snack made of
french fries topped with grain or farmer's
cheese, all smothered in tangy brown gravy.
Haute cuisine? No way. Just pure Quebec
comfort food, best enjoyed after a few beers.
La Banquise has been serving poutine for
about four decades and offers some 20 dif-
ferent varieties. Newcomers should stick to
the basic poutine recipe, but if you're
adventurous, sample the poutine *galvaude*
(with chicken and peas), poutine Mexicaine
(with hot peppers, tomato, and black
olives), or poutine Elvis (with ground beef,
peppers, and sautéed onions). Hot dogs and
hamburgers, too. Cash only. Open 24 hours.

La Iguana

514-844-0893

www.restaurant-laiguana.com

51 Rue Roy Est, Montréal, QC, H2W 2S3

What's nearby: Two blocks east of Blvd. St-
Laurent

Price: $$

Typical Mexican fare at very reasonable
prices. There's also a generous selection of
tequilas. Nice outdoor summer terrace.
Live music Thursday through Saturday.
Open Tuesday through Saturday for dinner.

Laloux

514-287-9127

www.laloux.com

250 Ave. des Pins Est, Montréal, QC H2W 1P3

What's nearby: Musée des Hospitalières de
l'Hôtel-Dieu de Montréal

Price: $$–$$$

A small but serious French bistro that's
inventive and young in attitude and menu—
and very popular with the locals. Suggested
are the cod filet wrapped in prosciutto with
lentils, diced tomatoes, and garlic confit, or
the roasted guinea-fowl with chanterelle
mushrooms and white asparagus. Both
about $23. Classic Euro look.

La Raclette

514-524-8118

1059 Rue Gilford, Montréal, QC H2J 1P7

What's nearby: In the middle of a Plateau
residential neighborhood; corner of
Ave. Christophe Colomb; Mont-Royal
metro station

Price: $$

First came the cow. Then came the cheese—
Swiss-style raclette. It melts smoothly and
evenly, and melts in your mouth. It's not fon-
due, but fondue is available. The grande table
d'hôte starts at $32 and first features a hearty
potage and salmon gravlax appetizer. For the
main course choose the melted raclette
cheese with thin strips of ham and beef or a
delicious chicken breast stuffed with sun-
dried tomato accompanied by hash-brown
potatoes—a tasty surprise. The dessert

choices include *poire Belle-Hélène*—pear with ice cream, whipped cream, and chocolate sauce, or luscious chocolate torte. The Tuesday evening summer crowd included young lovers, co-workers, girlfriends, and birthday celebrations—a lively authentic Plateau mix—quite endearing. Forgot to order the *Trou Normand* sorbet with lemon, basil, and vodka, but left with a full belly anyway. There's an outdoor sidewalk terrace in front, and this is a bring-your-own-wine restaurant; there is no liquor license (which makes me wonder how they do the *Trou Normand*). Back to the cow—fun black and white cow-themed photographs adorn the walls. Open daily for dinner.

L'Express
514-845-5333
3927 Rue St-Denis, Montréal, QC
    H2W 2M4
What's nearby: North of Rue Roy
Price: $$

L'Express epitomizes Montreal's iconic hardworking French bistros with a busy inviting atmosphere and always great food. It's been open for 25 years, and it's open daily for breakfast until late in the evening, closing at 1 AM.

Mazurka
514-844-3539
64 Rue Prince-Arthur Est,
    Montréal, QC H2X 1B3
What's nearby: A dozen restaurants along
    Prince Arthur in the Plateau just east of
    Blvd. St-Laurent
Price: $$

Mazurka is situated along pedestrian-only Rue Prince-Arthur where you'll find a row of casual neighborhood restaurants, many that offer a bring-your-own-wine policy. Mazurka stands out among the Prince Arthur crowd for quality homemade Polish specialties. Open daily for lunch a nd dinner until midnight.

L'Express restaurant, one of Montreal's best, is open for breakfast, lunch, dinner, and late-night snacks.

Med Bar & Grill
514-844-2534
www.medgrill.com
3500 Blvd. St-Laurent,
    Montréal, QC H2X 2V1
What's nearby: Sherbrooke metro station,
    Doubletree Hotel, Cabaret Juste Pour Rire
Price: $$$

There's a trendy clique of similar restaurants just north of Sherbrooke geared toward Montreal's young, beautiful, and carefree—Quebec City's Grande Allée also comes to mind. Expect menu fare like pastas, fancy salads, seafood specialties, and dancing-on-the-table-kind-of-energy come Canada Grand Prix time. (To be fair, the friendly competition just across the street is at **Globe**, 3455 Blvd. St-Laurent, 514-284-3823; and just down the block at **Buonanotte**, 3518 Blvd. St-Laurent, 514-848 0644, www.buonanotte.com.)

Moishes
514-845-3509
www.moishes.ca
3961 Blvd. St-Laurent, Montréal, QC
    H2W 1Y4
What's nearby: Between Ave. des Pins and
    Ave. Duluth; Blvd. St-Laurent bus 55
Price: $$$–$$$$

One of the city's better steak and seafood grills and a Montreal institution since 1938. Typical quality grill fare like rib steaks, sirloins, veal and lamb chops, and seafood. Signature starters and sides like chopped liver and marinated herring or potato latkes and their trademark french-fried onions. Weekdays for lunch; dinner daily.

Nuevo
514-525-7000
www.nuevorestaurant.com
775 Ave. du Mont-Royal Est, Montréal, QC
    H2J 1W8
What's nearby: Mont-Royal metro station
Price: $$–$$$

The later it gets the livelier it gets—the telltale sign is the DJ booth. Nuevo is a small fun tapas bar dressed in blues and browns. There are three dozen varieties of tapas, and a few selections, like the seared red tuna or filet mignon, can be ordered as a meal. Open daily for dinner; kitchen closes at midnight.

Pullman
514-288-7779
www.pullman-mtl.com
3424 Ave. du Parc, Montréal, QC H2X 2H5
What's nearby: Just north of Rue
    Sherbrooke, McCord Museum
Price: $$

Wine by the glass or the bottle plays a central role at Pullman—so do the bar bites. Fun eats like bison burgers, grilled Perron au porto cheddar cheese sandwiches, and oysters Rockefeller. The restaurant is fashioned after a train car, and while the location just barely classifies it as the Plateau just north of Sherbrooke Street, it's got a great downtown vibe. It's open Tuesday through Saturday from 4:30 PM to 1 AM and accommodates everyone from the casual happy-hour visitor to the late-night snack crowd.

Restaurant Mont-Royal
514-523-3670
1001 Ave. du Mont-Royal Est,
    Montréal, QC H2J 1X7
What's nearby: Mont-Royal metro station
Price: $

The official name is actually Restaurant Mont-Royal Hot Dog Inc. This diner-style Plateau restaurant is great for breakfast, brunch, burgers, and good fish-and-chips. Very friendly staff.

Resto Robin de Bois
514-288-1010
www.robindesbois.ca
4403 Blvd. St-Laurent,
    Montréal, QC H2W 1Z8

What's nearby: Blvd. St-Laurent bus 55,
    Mount Royal Park
Price: $$–$$$

Robin de Bois—or Robin Hood—is run
mostly by volunteers who work the kitchen
and serve the meals. All proceeds go to
local charities. The menu highlights French
fare, with rustic regional influences like
local Quebec cheeses in their sandwiches
and quiches.

Schwartz's
514-842-4813
3895 Blvd. St-Laurent, Montréal, QC
    H2W 1X9
What's nearby: Blvd. St-Laurent bus 55
Price: $

The renowned place for smoked meat in
Montreal. Folks wait in line for the stuff. In
the rain. Without umbrellas. Open daily
until midnight, Saturday until 2:30 PM.

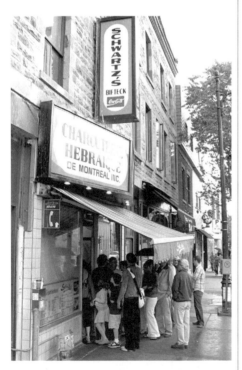

*There's a line-up every day for a Schwartz's smoked
meat sandwich.*

Senzala
514-521-1266
www.senzala.com
1428 Rue de la Roche, Montréal, QC H2J 3H9
What's nearby: Lafontaine Park, Maison des
    Cyclists
Price: $$

Girls and guys from Ipanema to the front of
the line. The specialty is casual Brazilian
fare with dishes that infuse flavors of
coconut, coriander, and chilies. Start with a
traditional *caipirinha* cocktail made with
ice, lime juice, and *cachaça*, a fermented
extract of sugarcane. Very popular weekend
brunch. Open for dinner. Also in Mile End
at 177 Rue Bernard.

SoupeSoupe
514-380-0880
80 Ave. Duluth Est, Montréal, QC H2W 1G8
What's nearby: Corner of Ave. Coloniale
Price: $

Move over, Mom. SoupeSoupe aims to bowl
you over. For soup—a dozen varieties every
day—and sandwiches, too. Cash only. Open
daily.

Truffert Bistro de Christophe
514-590-0897
1481 Ave. Laurier Est, Montréal, QC H2J 1H8
What's nearby: Laurier metro station, Blvd.
    St-Joseph bus 27 or Ave. Papineau bus 45
Price: $$–$$$

Truffert is operated by Garçon! restaurant
alumni Christophe Truffert and chef Trevor
Bird—now that's a winning combination.
The fare is typical French that's expertly
prepared—more restaurant than bistro in
style and portion. The menu changes fre-
quently; the desserts are to die for. It's
located along the very residential stretch of
Laurier East that boasts a number of fun
Montreal restaurants. That means the
crowd includes couples, double-daters, and
even the lone diner who very comfortably

sat at the bar in T-shirt and jeans reading the paper and dinking a glass of wine while waiting for his dinner. The place looks great as well, with generous mirrors, comfortable banquette, open-style kitchen area, ample glass-enclosed wine closet, and a splash of dark red. Open Tuesday through Saturday for dinner and weekend brunch.

Wok du Chef

514-525-2882

1200 Ave. du Mont-Royal Est, Montréal, QC
 H2J 1Y1

What's nearby: Mont-Royal metro station

Price: $–$$

Very popular Plateau eatery for Asian specialties including Szechuan, Cantonese, and Thai fare (this is actually my local Chinese takeout place). I love the hearty meal soups any time of year: noodles, wontons, warm broth, and bok choy. Generous Tonkinese soups, too. The dinner for two is very affordable at about $25 for soup, dumplings with peanut sauce or imperial rolls, and three main choices. Very friendly staff. Open daily for lunch and dinner.

Jean-Talon Market

The iconic Montreal food market and the largest one, at that. Located in Little Italy, Marché Jean-Talon boasts dozens of vendors selling local produce, packaged goods, and fresh flowers. It's busy, colorful, and cheerful. Enjoy fresh fruit, buy flowers for your hotel room, or spy on some serious foodies. At 7075 Ave. Casgrain, 514-277-1379. Accessible by the De Castelnau or Jean-Talon metro stations. Visit www.marchespublics-mtl.com.

La Joute sculpture by Jean Paul Riopelle offers a magical Montreal moment.

5

Montreal Culture, Sightseeing, and Shopping—*S'amuser* (means "to have fun!")

Following the format of the book, sightseeing is grouped according to neighborhood. This is not to say you can't have breakfast in the Plateau, take a stroll up the mountain, visit a downtown museum, and then catch a play in Old Montreal all in the same day—you can. But it's a little more manageable a neighborhood at a time. Here you'll find the best that Montreal has to offer when it comes to major attractions, museums, festivals, parks, outdoor activities, entertainment, and shopping. When you play like a Montrealer, you'll soon discover the meaning of *joie de vivre*!

Price Guide
(for adult admission fees)

$	up to $10
$$$	11 to $20
$$$$	21+

Downtown

CULTURE / MAJOR ATTRACTIONS / ARCHITECTURE

Bell Centre
514-989-2841 (ticket office)
www.bellcentre.ca
1260 Rue de la Gauchetière Ouest, Montréal, QC H3B 5E8
What's nearby: Montreal Planetarium, Central Station (Gare Centrale train station)

The Bell Centre began life as the Molson Centre in 1996 and replaced the Montreal Forum—sacred grounds in these parts—as the home of the Montreal Canadiens. Naming rights were changed to the Bell Centre in 2002. It's not only home to the Canadiens—also known as "the Habs," for *habitants*—the venue offers top-name musical concerts and ice shows. If you need an authentic souvenir from Montreal, the on-site Canadiens team store is the place for you. Check out who's performing when you're in town at Admission Ticket Network at www.admission.com or 514-790-1245.

Canadian Center for Architecture

514-939-7026
www.cca.qc.ca
1920 Rue Baile, Montréal, QC H3H 2S6
What's nearby: Guy-Concordia metro station, AMC 22 Forum Movie Theatre
Price: $

Now that's a beautiful . . . blueprint? The CCA is all about the art of architecture. Montreal native and architect Phyllis Lambert founded the CCA as a research center in 1979 and an architecture museum a decade later (her design credits as planner, along with architect and collaborator Ludwig Mies van der Rohe, include the Toronto Dominion Centre and the Seagram Building in New York—her father was Samuel Bronfman of Seagram distillery fame). It's not your typical museum visit; instead urban planning, landscape design, and environmental concerns highlight the always unique repertoire of exhibitions at the CCA. Past exhibits have explored everything from urban asphalt to vintage architectural books to college dorms. Author Douglas Coupland (Generation X) once displayed a magnificent eclectic installation sculpture called Super City fashioned from his favorite childhood toy building kits. The CCA also features free thematic movie screenings, an outdoor sculpture garden, and a specialized bookstore stacked with hundreds of architecturally themed titles. Free admission on Thursday evenings.

Catch a Habs game at the Bell Centre.

Concordia University Leonard and Bina Ellen Art Gallery
514-848-2424 ext. 4750
www.ellengallery.concordia.ca
1400 Blvd. de Maisonneuve, Montréal, QC H3G 1M8
What's nearby: Guy-Concordia metro station
Price: Free

For an intimate contemporary art experience when Concordia University is in session. It's not specifically a student art gallery, but lifelong students of art are welcome.

McCord Museum
514-398-7100
www.mccord-museum.qc.ca
690 Rue Sherbrooke Ouest, Montréal, QC H3A 1E9
What's nearby: McGill metro station, McGill University, Redpath Museum
Price: $$

Founded in 1921, the McCord Museum is a treasure trove for all things Canadian. The collection numbers 1.3 million objects—everything from period furnishings to authentic folk art to First Nations' artifacts. The archives include an impressive collection of about 1 million photographs—almost half taken by acclaimed photographer William Notman, whose studio captured Montreal history from the 1840s to the 1930s. The collection is displayed through the permanent exhibition Simply Montreal and three temporary exhibition spaces. Past exhibits have highlighted Scotsmen and Scotswomen from Montreal, colorful Inuit tapestries, and iconic west coast Haida art. The on-site McCord Café is a popular lunch eatery with the downtown business crowd.

Montreal Museum of Fine Arts
514-285-2000
www.mmfa.qc.ca
1379-1380 Rue Sherbrooke Ouest, Montréal, QC
What's nearby: Ritz Carleton Hotel, McGill University, Guy-Concordia metro station
Price: Free for the permanent collection, $$ for certain temporary exhibits

The Montreal Museum of Fine Arts boasts a wonderfully inspiring collection that includes classic and modern decorative arts, Canadian and European fine arts, and Mediterranean, Asian, African, and South American antiquities—a little something for everyone. Don't try to tackle the entire collection in a quick visit—but do not miss a visit if you're in town. Best of all, a visit to the permanent collection is free (donations are gladly accepted). There is always a unique temporary exhibition as well, which in the past has paid tribute to Canadian originals like Emily Carr and Jean-Paul Riopelle, American contemporaries like Keith Haring and the art of Walt Disney, and European masters like Matisse, Monet, and Magritte. MFA's buildings are architecturally impressive in their own right—the neoclassic original built in 1912 and the more contemporary edifice that opened in 1991 across the street—the two are linked by an underground exhibition passageway that runs right under Rue Sherbrooke. The nearby Erskine and American United Church, built in 1894, was recently acquired by the MFA and will house its Canadian collection starting in 2010. Half-price adult admission is available on Wednesday evening, and the MFA is open until 9 PM Wednesday through Friday. The museum celebrates its 100th anniversary in 2012.

Montreal Planetarium

514-872-4530
www.planetarium.montreal.qc.ca
1000 Rue St-Jacques Ouest, Montréal QC H3C 1G7
What's nearby: Bonaventure metro station
Price: $

The Montreal Planetarium, the only French one in North America (it's actually bilingual), began life as the Dow Planetarium in 1966. It was named after, and received financial backing from, the Dow Brewery, which once stood nearby (hey, why not—celestial bodies and beer make a perfect match). After an agreed-upon decade-long stint, the city took over all aspects of operation and the name changed. Nowadays the planetarium produces a number of popular multimedia shows annually for stargazers of all ages. The new permanent exhibition, which opened in 2006, celebrates its 40 years in nostalgic style. Tentative plans are in the works for a move to the Olympic Park area in the east end, where the planetarium would probably fare much better in the company of other popular tourist attractions like the Biodome and the Botanical Garden.

Musée d'Art Contemporain

514-847-6226
www.macm.org
185 Rue Ste-Catherine Ouest, Montréal, QC H2X 3X5
What's nearby: Place-des-Arts metro station, outdoor Jazz Festival concerts
Price: $

Musée d'Art Contemporain is the place for contemporary art in Montreal. A visit promises to tantalize, tease, and provoke the senses with eclectic, imaginative, and sometimes provocative paintings, installations, and video productions. I always leave with a smile on my face. Exhibits spotlight an array of international and Canadian artists, including Brian Jungen, who once created a life-size whale skeleton fashioned from white plastic patio chairs. And controversial photographer Spencer Tunick got 3,000 Montrealers in a nude mood when he photographed them naked on the Place des Arts esplanade in 2002. Great guided tours as well, often led by a well-educated staff of young local university art students. Free admission on Wednesday evenings.

Musée des Hospitalières de l'Hôtel-Dieu de Montréal

514-849-2919
www.museedeshospitalieres.qc.ca
201 Ave. des Pins Ouest (Pine Ave. West) Montréal, QC H2W 1R5
What's nearby: Laloux Restaurant, Mount Royal Park
Price: $

Doctors, nurses, hospital workers, and history buffs to the front of the line. Hôtel-Dieu thoroughly chronicles Montreal's first hospital, its co-founder Jeanne Mance, early settlers to New France, and the history of medicine in Montreal. The space packs quite a bit of information on its two floors through a variety of objects including documents, religious artifacts, and vintage medical instruments and devices that look simply barbaric. The Hôtel-Dieu is still a working hospital and religious convent. Guided summer tours of the grounds available by reservation. Closed Monday year-round and Tuesday during winter.

Palais des Congrès

514-871-8122
www.congres.mtl
201 Ave. Viger Ouest, Montréal QC
What's nearby: Chinatown, Old Montreal, Toqué! restaurant, Place-d'Armes metro station

Palais des Congrès, Montreal's main convention center, hosts dozens of public and industry trade shows every year, including the Montreal International Auto Show every January. The building underwent a colorful renovation in 2002 and features public art, including *Lipstick Forest*, a collection of 52 bubblegum-pink tree trunks, and a kaleidoscopic multicolored glass façade on its west end.

Redpath Museum

514-398-4086, ext. 4092
www.mcgill.ca/redpath
859 Rue Sherbrooke Ouest, Montréal, QC H3A 2K6
What's nearby: McCord Museum, McGill metro station
Price: Free

Located on the campus of McGill University downtown, the Redpath Museum was named after donor John Redpath, whose local sugar refinery made him a very rich man. The neoclassic-style building dates to 1882 and is stunning inside and out. The emphasis on natural history includes a formidable collection of fossils, minerals, gems, and even an *Albertosaurus* dinosaur skeleton. In 2007 the museum hosted a fun event that created an anatomically correct life-size flying pteranodon origami, from a single 15-square-foot piece of paper that took one week to fold, under the helm of origami artist Dr. Robert Lang. Fun workshops for the whole family, too. One for the adults is the Stones and Beer Tour, a bike tour that explores local architecture (the stones of buildings) topped off with a light picnic snack. Closed Friday during summer, closed Saturday year-round.

Festivals / Special Events / Guided Tours

Coach Canada / Gray Bus Tours

800-461-1223
www.coachcanada.com
Departure point: 1255 Rue Peel, Montréal
Price: $$$

Coach Canada / Gray Line offers a three-hour sightseeing tram-style bus tour of the city with stops downtown, in Old Montreal, the Old Port, Olympic Park, Mount Royal Park, and St. Joseph's Oratory. About $36 for adults. Double decker–style tours as well.

Montreal International Jazz Festival

514-871-1881, 1-888-515-0515
www.montrealjazzfest.com
Ticketed shows at venues throughout the city; outdoor free shows centered at the Place des
    Arts esplanade
What's nearby: Place-des-Arts metro station, Hyatt Regency Hotel
Price: Free to $$$

The Jazz Festival defines the spirit of Montreal. It's a nonstop summertime party that's accessible to all. The mood is light, the price is right (the outdoor shows are free), and the music is fantastic. The performers range from top-name draws to incredibly talented university students who major in jazz music. Imagine being in your early 20s, having played the Montreal Jazz Fest to an adoring crowd of thousands, and listing the accomplishment on your résumé. Good for them! While jazz takes front and center, the music encompasses blues, funk, world beat, Latin sounds, groove, techno, and dancing in the streets. The atmosphere is equal parts civilized and polite to carefree and festive. Combine the lighthearted mood of that many people with those Amarula alcoholic frozen beverages that are sold on site and you have the potential for one very large conga line. Held for 10 days every summer, from late June to early July. Outdoor performances from noon to midnight.

Stones and Beer Bike Tour
514-398-4086, ext. 4092
www.mcgill.ca/redpath
Price: $$

Hosted by the Redpath Museum every summer and early fall, the Stones and Beer tour explores local history and architecture by bicycle. The stones part features the reflecting pool and building stones of the Grand Seminary on Rue Sherbrooke Ouest, while the beer part tours the McAuslan Brewery. For cyclists only and BYOB—bring your own bike (the beer is provided). Price includes tour booklet, snack of fresh bread and cheese, and tastings of five locally produced ales at the brewery. About $20.

Music fills the air, camaraderie fills the streets at the Montreal Jazz Festival.

PARKS AND PUBLIC GARDENS

Place Jean-Paul-Riopelle
www.qimtl.qc.ca
What's nearby: Palais de Congrès, Square-Victoria and Place-d'Armes metro stations
Price: Free

This outdoor urban space at the colorful west end of the Palais des Congrès is elemental in appeal. The centerpiece is a sculpture titled *La Joute*, which was originally created for the 1976 Summer Olympics by sculptor Jean-Paul Riopelle, one of Quebec's favorite sons. *La Joute* bubbles with water, sprays with steam, and ignites with a ring of fire. It's a mesmerizing mix that's simply a very cool Montreal moment. The seasonal show runs on the hour between 7 and 11 PM.

SHOPPING

Belgo Building / Association des Galeries d'Art Contemporain—AGAC
514-798-5010
www.agac.qc.ca
372 Rue Ste-Catherine Ouest, Montréal, QC H2B 1A2
What's nearby: Place des Arts, Place-des-Arts metro station

If your time is limited and you're in the mood to purchase original Canadian contemporary art, don't go traipsing all about town. Montreal's Belgo Building hosts 30 art galleries on its five floors. Each gallery is privately run, so they're not all open at the same time. In addition, the AGAC Web site includes links to 18 of its gallery members, some located in the Belgo Building, others scattered about the city. It's a good place to start. AGAC offices are located in suite 521.

Canadian Guild of Crafts
514-849-6091
www.canadianguild.com
1460, Rue Sherbrooke Ouest, Suite B, Montréal, QC H3G 1K4
What's nearby: Guy-Concordia metro station, Brontë restaurant

A true Canadian original. Part exhibition space and part art gallery, the Canadian Guild of Crafts was established in 1906 as a nonprofit organization to promote and conserve Inuit and Amerindian-style art and fine crafts. You're not buying just a souvenir here; you're purchasing a high-end work of art. Closed Sunday.

Chapters Books
514-849-8825
www.chapters.indigo.ca
1171 Rue Ste-Catherine Ouest, Montréal, QC H3B 1K4
What's nearby: Trinity Restaurant, Montreal Museum of Fine Arts

Centrally located in the heart of downtown, Chapters, the largest English bookstore in Montreal, boasts three floors of books, bargains, and a café. There is a well-stocked selection of travel books as well. The nearby bookstore partner Indigo at Place Montréal Trust features more French titles. At 1500 Ave. McGill College, 514-281-5549.

ECONOMUSEUMS

Combining museum, atelier, and boutique all in one, "economuseums" highlight traditional arts and crafts trades and their production techniques. Each economuseum features a small exhibit, workshops and classes open to the public, and a place to buy the completed product. Moreover, each one is run by devoted artisans who share the passion of their craft. There are about four dozen economuseums throughout Quebec and the Maritimes; Montreal currently boasts three. In the Plateau, **Les Brodeuses** specializes in embroidery and sewing, 5364 Blvd. St-Laurent, 514-276-4181. Near Place des Arts downtown, violin-making takes center stage at **Luthier Jules Saint-Michel**, 57 Rue Ontario Ouest, 514-288-4343. And at **La Maison de Calico** in the western suburb of Point-Claire, quilting is the specialty of the house, 324 Lakeshore Rd., 514-695-0728. Visit www.economusees.com.

MAJOR URBAN MALLS / UNDERGROUND CITY

The Underground City has to be the most misunderstood thing about Montreal. There, I said it. Why? It's basically one big shopping mall that connects to the metro that connects to another shopping mall that connects to some hotels that connect to another shopping area that connects to the train station or Place des Arts or museums, and along the way: shopping. The concept is admirable—especially during cold Montreal winter days. Yes, you can walk quite a distance without having to set foot outdoors—in all there are an impressive 20 miles (33 kilometers) of connected passageways. But if you're not a shopaholic, you may be disappointed. And if you are a shopaholic and go looking for the Underground City, you're probably already standing in it.

Here are some of the more popular downtown malls. Yes, they are all part of the Underground City. Remember, most downtown retailers close at 5 PM on Saturday. Why? Enough of this shopping, it's Saturday night and time to play or the family is coming for dinner.

Complexe Desjardins. Across from Place des Arts, Complexe Desjardins features smaller boutiques, a food court, a supermarket, a drugstore, and the Hyatt Regency Hotel. Accessible at 150 Rue Ste-Catherine Ouest, or 175 Blvd. René-Lévesque Ouest. Call 514-845-3646 or visit www.complexdesjardins.com.

Complexe Les Ailes / Eaton Centre. The former home to the Canadian retail giant Eaton's, Les Ailes took over the department store space in 1999—it's actually two complexes in one, with some 60 boutiques, including Les Ailes de la Mode, Tommy Hilfiger, Guess, and Swarovski in the Les Ailes side, and another 175 retailers like Levi's, Old Navy, Gap, and Benetton in the Eaton's side (the store may be gone, but the building kept the Eaton Centre name). At 677 and 705 Rue Ste-Catherine Ouest or the McGill metro station. Call 514-288-3759 or visit www.complexelesailes.com; and 514-288-3710 or www.centreeaton.ca.

Gallerie Place Ville-Marie. Place Ville-Marie the building is one of Montreal's tallest at 46 stories. It's the building with the landmark rotating beacon visible at night. The *gallerie* part is the shopping mall located at street level, which features men's and women's fashions, a drugstore, a jeweler, a magazine store, a food court, and easy access to the Bonaventure metro and Gare Centrale train stations. Access at René-Lévesque Blvd., or University, Mansfield, or Cathcart Streets. Call 514-866-8666 or visit www.placeville marie.com.

Les Cours Mont-Royal. Formerly the Mount Royal Hotel, the art deco building dates to 1922. Today the space features residential condos and elegant shopping and boutiques including American Apparel, DKNY, Emporio Armani, and the Spa Diva day spa for facials, massages, and pampering. At 1455 Rue Peel. Call 514-842-7777.

Ogilvy's. An upscale Montreal shopping institution since 1866, and always one of the best window displays during the holidays. The store features the likes of Lacoste, Hugo Boss, Burberry, Louis Vuitton inside, and, to store management's dismay, a spoon-playing street performer who's become somewhat a local celebrity outside. At 1307 Rue Ste-Catherine Ouest. Call 514-842-7711 or visit www.ogilvycanada.com.

Place Montreal Trust. This four-floor mall features some five dozen smaller boutiques like Indigo Books, Omer DeSerres art supplies, Mexx, and Winner's, the Canadian equivalent of T. J. Maxx. Enter at 1500 Rue Ste-Catherine or McGill College Ave. Call 514-843-8000 or visit www.placemontrealtrust.ca.

OTHER DOWNTOWN DEPARTMENT STORES AND SPECIALTY SHOPS

Birks is Canada's premier jeweler. At 1240 Phillips Square, just across from the Bay department store. Call 514-397-2511 or visit www.birks.com. **Holt Renfrew** offers upscale brands like Alexander McQueen, D&G, Gucci, Prada, Ralph Lauren—you know, that gang. At 1300 Rue Sherbrooke Ouest, 514-842-5111, or www.holtrenfrew.com. **Hudson's Bay Company**, better known as the Bay (la Baie), began with the earliest of shoppers, actually settlers who bargained for goods in the fur trade way back in 1670. Today the retail giant operates dozens of department stores throughout Canada. Although now made in England, the Bay's iconic colorful multistriped point blankets make for a great souvenir. The Montreal downtown store is at 585 Rue Ste-Catherine Ouest, 514-281-4422, www.hbc.com. **Simons** is an immensely popular department store for trendy urban men's and women's fashions, and a small but rather nice selection of bed and bath home décor at reasonable prices at sale time. At 977 Rue Ste-Catherine Ouest, 514-282-1840 or www.simons.ca.

SPORTS/BIKING/ACTIVITIES

Atrium Le 1000

514-395-1000
www.le1000.com
1000 Rue de la Gauchetière Ouest, Montréal, QC H3B 4W5
What's nearby: Bonaventure metro station
Price: $

Ice skating in summer? Yes, you can. C'mon, this is Montreal—they're practically born with skates on their feet. Open daily for ice skating all year long, it's a cool way to beat the heat in summer. Skate rentals available. Special thematic skating sessions include student nights on Thursday and DJ music every Saturday night. Housed inside the 51-story office building known as Le 1000—the peaked roof makes it one of the most recognizable structures of the Montreal skyline.

THEATER/NIGHTLIFE/ENTERTAINMENT

AMC Forum 22

514-904-1250
2313 Rue Ste-Catherine Ouest, Montréal, QC H3H 1N2
What's nearby: Atwater metro station, CCA
Price: $$

The AMC Forum 22 building is the former Montreal Forum, the hallowed hockey hall where the Montreal Canadiens won most of their 24 Stanley Cups. Some sections of the original arena seating remain. Today the site features 22 movie screens showing the latest Hollywood releases in both English and French, as well as foreign and art house films.

Cinéma Banque Scotia Montréal

514-866-0111
977 Rue Ste-Catherine Ouest, Montréal, QC H3B 4W3
What's nearby: Peel metro station, Chapters bookstore
Price: $$

Canadian-based Scotiabank has acquired the naming rights to a number of movie houses throughout Canada. This multiplex features screenings mostly in English and an IMAX theater that's used for Hollywood blockbusters. The building was formerly the Famous Players Paramount, which before that was the popular Simpson's Department Store.

DOWNTOWN NIGHTLIFE

With more than two dozen establishments, Crescent Street can be dubbed downtown party central for this touristy part of Montreal, especially during the long Grand Prix weekend in June. A number of restaurants along the strip double as bar, lounge, or nightclub when the sun goes down. For a complete list, visit www.crescentmontreal.com. Among them, **Newtown**, owned by race car driver Jacques Villeneuve, revs things up with a lounge, rooftop terrace, and nightclub open Friday and Saturday night. At 1476 Rue Crescent, 514-284-6555, www.newtown.ca. Grab a pint or two at **Pub Claddagh**, where there are 19 beers on tap, live music, and traditional Irish pub food. At 1433 Rue Crescent, 514-287-9354, www.pubcladdagh.com. **Les 3 Brasseurs** is a popular Quebec microbrewery with three locations in the city. At 1356 Rue Ste-Catherine Ouest, on the corner of Crescent, 514-788-9788, www.les3brasseurs.ca. **Funky Town** revisits '70s-era disco, at 1454 Rue Peel, 514-282-8387, while **Electric Avenue** takes a turn back to the '80s, at 1469 Rue Crescent, 514-285-8885. Both are at www.clubsmontreal.com. A bit off the Crescent Street strip, **Sharx** offers pool and snooker tables and a 10-lane bowling alley, 1606 Rue Ste-Catherine Ouest, 514-934-3105, www.sharx.ca. Farther east, just past Place des Arts, **Club Soda** has featured live musical acts for the past two decades. At 1225 Blvd. St-Laurent, 514-286-1010, www.clubsoda.ca.

Place des Arts

514-842-2112
www.pda.qc.ca
175 Rue Ste-Catherine Ouest, Montréal, QC H2X 2S6

What's nearby: Place-des-Arts metro station, Complexe Desjardins shopping and food court, Hyatt Regency Hotel
Price: $$–$$$, depending on performance

Founded in 1963, Place des Arts is the current home of the Montreal Symphony Orchestra, the Montreal Opera, and the always inventive Les Grands Ballets Canadiens dance company. In addition, it's where local Broadway touring companies, international dance troupes, and a variety of music acts come to perform. The complex boasts five indoor theaters. The largest, Salle Wilfrid-Pelletier, seats just shy of 3,000 guests and was renamed for Pelletier, the former artistic director of the MSO. The outdoor esplanade is the centerpiece of the annual Montreal Jazz Festival and Les FrancoFolies French music fest.

Upstairs Jazz Bar & Grill
514-931-6808
www.upstairsjazz.com
1254 Rue Mackay, Montréal, QC H3G 2H4
What's nearby: Guy-Concordia metro station

You actually go a few steps downstairs to get into Upstairs, an intimate, friendly jazz nightclub and restaurant. There are two dinner services, at 7 and 10 PM, and young affable owner Joel has the delicate task of informing the early patrons when it's time to scoot—but he does so with complete diplomacy (and don't forget to congratulate him—he's a new dad!). The menu features tasty Louisiana ribs, blackened mahi mahi, and Georgia chicken—a grilled breast with mango sauce—all surprisingly good at less than $20 a plate.

Professional Sports in Montreal
The **Montreal Canadiens** are members of the National Hockey League. The team, founded in 1909, actually predates the NHL, which was formed in 1917. Their current home is the downtown Bell Centre. "The Habs" have won 24 Stanley Cups, more than any other team in NHL history. They last won the cup during the 1993–94 season. Visit them at www.canadiens.com.

The **Montreal Alouettes** have been members of the Canadian Football League since 1996, although the original team dates to 1946. They currently play to sold-out crowds at Molson Stadium on the grounds of McGill University. They won the coveted Grey Cup in 2002. Their official Web site is www.montrealouettes.com.

The **Montreal Impact** soccer team is a member of the United Soccer Leagues first division level of play. The loyal hometown fans look forward to enjoying Impact games at the new Saputo Stadium near Olympic Park in time for the 2008 season. Visit www.impactmontreal.com.

The **Montreal Expos** Major League Baseball team is now the Washington Nationals, as of the 2005 baseball season. *Adieu, Nos Amours. C'est la vie.*

Gay Village / Latin Quarter

Culture / Major Attractions / Architecture

Cinémathèque Québécois
514-842-9768
www.cinematheque.qc.ca

335 Blvd. de Maisonneuve Est, Montréal, QC H2X 1K1
What's nearby: UQAM Centre de Design, Berri/UQAM metro station
Price: Free

Movie aficionados and couch potatoes, here's a museum for you. Cinémathèque Québécois, billed Montreal's Museum of the Moving Image (although I've never heard anyone call it that), explores all aspects of the world of cinema and television. Recent exhibits have featured a collection of vintage televisions and a thorough and impressive look at the history of animation. There's usually a fun exhibit on movie posters from around the world on any given visit. Best of all, museum admission is free. Thematic film screenings, mostly in French but some in English, are held daily for a nominal fee. Closed Monday.

CineRobotheque

514-496-6887
www.nfb.ca/cinerobotheque
1564 Rue St-Denis, Montréal, QC H2X 3K2
Price: $
What's nearby: Berri/UQAM metro station, St-Denis Theatre

The place for film buffs. Operated by the National Film Board of Canada. Visitors can choose from 9,000 titles of animation, feature films, and documentaries for use at a personal viewing station. But the best part of the visit—your film is retrieved by an assembly-line-inspired robot.

Écomusée du Fier Monde is housed in a former public bath

Écomusée du Fier Monde

514-528-8444
www.ecomusee.qc.ca
2050 Amherst St., Montréal, QC H2L 3L8
What's nearby: St-Jacques Market, Usine C, Berri/UQAM metro station
Price: $

Dubbed a museum of industrial and working-class history, Écomusée du Fier Monde
(loosely translated as museum of a proud world) highlights the Centre-Sud neighborhood's legacy as the onetime heart of Montreal's industrial revolution. The museum is
appropriately housed in the former Genereux public bath, which was built in the 1920s to
improve the health of working-class Montrealers when apartments lacked their own
shower or bath facilities. Nowadays you can walk right into the pool area without getting
wet, as the space has served as an art gallery and museum since its rebirth in 1996. Wall
panels are written mostly in French.

Just for Laughs Museum

514-845-3155
www.hahaha.com
2111 Blvd. St-Laurent, Montréal, QC H2X 2T5
What's nearby: dozens of restaurants along Blvd. St-Laurent and Rue Prince Arthur just
    north of Rue Sherbrooke
Price: $

The Just for Laughs Festival offers stand-up comedy, special events, and an annual parade.

Some of Montreal's most unusual museum moments have been experienced at the Just for Laughs Museum since it opened in 1993. For example, in Dialogue in the Dark, a legally blind guide led visitors through the likes of a busy city street and a tranquil park—completely in the darkness. Yugo Next turned the iconic automobile/lemon into a variety of unique objets d'art like a piano or a giant toaster. Abracadabra taught kids the thrill of being a magician. Its current exhibit, on since 2003, features 100 funny clips from 100 very funny comics, but the visit is now by reservation only, with a 15-person minimum. You're only as good as your last exhibit, right? Hopefully the original luster will soon return to a museum that was once full of imaginative promise.

La Prison des Patriotes Exhibition Centre
450-787-9980
www.mndp.qc.ca
903 Ave. de Lorimier, Montréal, QC H2K 3V9
What's nearby: Papineau metro station, La Loïe restaurant
Price: $

It's not the most visited museum in the city, but you may notice the neoclassical-style building when catching the fireworks show under the Jacques Cartier Bridge during the summer and wonder: *Qu'est-ce que c'est?* The Centre pays tribute to the rebellious Quebec Patriotes who fought for French rights against British rule during the Lower Canada Rebellion of 1837–38. The building was formerly the Pied-du-Courant Prison, where more than 1,200 rebels were imprisoned and another dozen were hanged. It's a place to brush up on your Français, as the panels are written only in French.

La Grand Bibliothèque Nationale
514-873-1100
www.banq.qc.ca
475 Blvd. de Maisonneuve Est, Montréal, QC H2L 5C4
What's nearby: La Paryse restaurant, CineRobotheque, Berri/UQAM metro station
Price: Free to visit or for Quebecers to take out books; nonresidents have to pay a hefty fee for a temporary library card

Montreal's new, extensive, and popular public library has been a hit since it opened in 2005. Their Web site says it best: "The national collection contains everything published in Quebec, everything published about Quebec elsewhere in the world, and all publications whose production involves at least one Quebecer, from the days of New France to the present." In all there are 4 million documents published in a variety of formats. The open and airy building design features an exterior façade of 6,000 frosted green glass plates, with yellow birch-wood interiors on four floors. The generous international newspaper and magazine selection offers a great place for out-of-towners to catch up on their reading. A free exhibition space highlights the likes of the provincial history of schoolbooks.

UQAM Centre de Design
514-987-3385
www.centredesign.uqam.ca
1440 Rue Sanguinet, Montréal, QC H2X 3X9

What's nearby: Cinémathèque Québécoise, Berri/UQAM metro station
Price: Free

A small gallery space with design in mind. Centre de Design is part of the University of Quebec at Montreal (the UQAM acronym). Visits prove most fun when exhibits concentrate on one particular theme. For example, in the past the space has offered homage to the closet coat hanger and paid tribute to the household brush in all shapes, styles, and sizes. Yes, even the toilet brush got proper due. Can't wait to see what's next. It's always fun, and best of all, it's free. Open Wednesday through Sunday when school is in session.

FESTIVALS / SPECIAL EVENTS / GUIDED TOURS

Festival International Montréal en Arts—FIMA
www.festivaldesarts.org
Rue Ste-Catherine
What's nearby: Beaudry metro station, Sir Montcalm Bed & Breakfast

FIMA is a kilometer-long, open-air, pedestrian-only art gallery that features the creative wares of some 150 artists and artisans who sell everything from oil paintings to high-end crafts. It's located in Montreal's Gay Village but is open to all art lovers. The festival runs along Rue Ste-Catherine from Rue St-Hubert to Avenue Papineau. The four-day event coincides with the opening weekend of the Montreal Jazz Festival, the last weekend of June.

Gay Pride Festival
www.celebrations-lgbta.org
www.diverscite.org
Where: In the Gay Village along Rue Ste-Catherine from Rue Berri to Ave. Papineau

You don't have to be gay to play. Montreal's gay pride festival celebrates its Sweet 16 in 2008. Celebrations LGBTA hosts the parade—recently held the last Sunday in July. After the parade, stroll along Rue Ste-Catherine and join the throngs of partygoers for a drink. Or two. Or more. Divers/Cite handles the outdoor music and dance parties during the first weekend of August. There are free outdoor shows and ticketed club nights dedicated to disco, jocks, drag queens, cabaret, and men in uniform.

Just for Laughs Festival
514-845-2322, 1-800-244-3155
www.hahaha.com
Where: Various locations for paid events, Rue St-Denis in the Latin Quarter for free street events

The Just for Laughs Festival turned a milestone 25 years old in 2007 and is still going strong. The 10-day fest held in mid-July features hundreds of free and ticketed performances and fun activities. Traditional stand-up comedy routine galas are always popular draws, in the past hosted by Howie Mandell, William Shatner, George Lopez, and David Hyde-Pearce. Unique theater acts abound, too, like the insanely popular Family Guy Live, the quick-change artistry of Arturo Brachetti, or the cross-dressing antics of the Kids in the Hall. Free outdoor stuff along Rue St-Denis features roving street performers, boisterous buskers, and a colorful parade of twins.

Montreal International Fireworks Competition

514-397-2000

www.montrealfireworks.com

Where: Paid seating at La Ronde Amusement Park, free viewing on or under the Jacques Cartier Bridge

Montrealers take their pyrotechnics quite seriously—some 200,000 people attend each fireworks show. Now that's an oooooh and ahhhhh to remember. The show is hosted at La Ronde Amusement Park, but there are a number of places to watch the fireworks for free: Old Port of Montreal, Jean Drapeau Park, and in the Gay Village with its proximity to the Jacques Cartier Bridge, which is closed to vehicular traffic on fireworks nights. To get to the bridge, take the metro to the Papineau station and just follow the crowd. There are nine or 10 shows each summer in late June and throughout July—usually Wednesday and Saturday night at 10, rain or shine. It's a pretty solid bet, too. In the two decades of fireworks since 1985, never has the display been canceled due to bad weather.

SHOPPING

Archambault (Berri store)

514-849-6201

www.archambault.ca

500 Rue Ste-Catherine Est, Montréal, QC H2L 2C6

What's nearby: Berri/UQAM metro station, Gouverneur Hotel, St-Hubert Rotisserie Chicken

The Montreal Fireworks Festival is a summertime favorite. On or near the Jacques Cartier Bridge is the place to be

Archambault music is a Quebec institution that dates to 1896. This flagship store, which opened in 1930, currently features three well-stocked floors of CDs, DVDs, musical instruments, and sheet music, including a generous selection devoted to jazz and Francophone music. Fifteen locations throughout the province.

Rue Amherst Retro Antiques Shopping Tour

Hey, where ya goin' with that lampshade? 1975? Amherst Street in the Gay Village between Boulevard de Maisonneuve and Rue Sherbrooke boasts a fun selection of '70s retro-style antiques shops. It's fun to buy or browse. Here's a tour from south to north.

Seconde Chance looks like Grandma's gone wild. Well at least her attic has. At 1691 Rue Amherst, 514-523-3019.

The '80s is the new '70s at **Cité Déco**. Vintage furniture from the 1930s to the 1980s. At 1761 Rue Amherst, 514-528-0659.

Antiquités Curiosités features lamps and larger furniture pieces. At 1769 Rue Amherst, 514-525-8772.

Jack's is one of the most popular and packed stores on the street—2,500 square feet in all of vintage lighting, circa '60s carpets and chairs, and mod furniture. It's funky. It's friendly. But don't ask for Jack, he's not there (that's when it used to be a men's store). Ask for owner Jean Guy. At 1860 Rue Amherst, 514596-0060, www.jacks70.com.

Antiquités A-Z offers furniture, glassware, and small appliances. At 1840 Rue Amherst, 514-538-0144.

Le 1863 offers fabulous '50s pieces, signature '60s Scandinavian stuff, as well as barware and glassware. At 1863 Rue Amherst, 514-816-8111.

Zéphyr offers part antiques store and part art gallery space. At 2112 Rue Amherst, 514-529-9199.

The stuff at **Spoutnik** is out of this world. At 2120 Rue Amherst, 514-525-8478.

RUE STE-CATHERINE GAY VILLAGE TOUR

There's quite a mix of shopping to be found on Rue Ste-Catherine in the Gay Village. Here are a few suggestions from west to east.

Blank

514-313-6716
www.portezblank.com and www.wearblank.com
926 Rue Ste-Catherine Est, Montréal, QC H2L 2E7 (in the Gay Village)

and

514-849-6053
4276 Blvd. St-Laurent, Montréal, QC H2W 1Z3 (in the Plateau)

What American Apparel does for the U.S. (read more about them next), Blank does for Quebec—quality T-shirts and clothing made entirely in the province from start to finish, including the manufacture and dyeing of the fabric, as well as the cutting and sewing of the clothes. For retail and wholesale purchases.

American Apparel

514-526-3998

www.americanapparel.net
1205 Rue Ste-Catherine Est, Montréal QC H2L 2H1

Started by Montreal native Dov Charney, American Apparel features hip clothing made entirely at their Los Angeles plant. There are now hundreds of stores worldwide, with 10 in Montreal. Also downtown at 1455 Rue Peel, and in the Plateau at 4001 Rue St-Denis and 967 Ave. du Mont-Royal Est.

Albatroz

514-524-4505
1215 Rue Ste-Catherine Est, Montréal, QC H2L 2H1

Albatroz features a mix of clothing, jewelry, décor, gifts, masks, incense, and eclectic items from around the world.

Priape

514-521-8451
www.priape.com
1311 Rue Ste-Catherine Est, Montréal, QC H2L 2H4

A Montreal institution since 1974, with other Canadian locations in Toronto, Vancouver, and Calgary, Priape offers gay-themed movies, clothing, "toys," and dirty greeting cards.

Multimags

514-525-8976
1321 Rue Ste-Catherine Est, Montréal, QC H2L 2H4

There are about eight Multimags stores throughout the city. Like the rest, this one offers hundreds of magazine titles and international newspapers, but also a nice selection of goofy gifts, coffee table and art books, and some very funny gay-themed greeting cards.

Fétiche Store

514-529-0808
www.fetichestore.ca
1323 Rue Ste-Catherine Est, Montréal, QC H2L 2H4

Oh you naughty wicked monkey, you. Steps away from similarly themed Priape, Fetish Store, which opened in 2007, offers less books and cards, and more leather, rubber, and latex clothing. Baby powder sold separately.

THEATER/NIGHTLIFE/ENTERTAINMENT

GAY VILLAGE NIGHTLIFE

Montreal is a very gay-friendly, gay-tolerant city. While Gay Village bars and clubs readily come and go, a few have remained as the more well-established and popular hot spots. Traveling from north to south on Rue Amherst, start—or end—the evening at **Gotha Lounge**, a cozy venue complete with fireplace that's perfect for a martini or meeting new Montreal friends. At 1641 Rue Amherst, 514-526-1270. Closer to the main Ste-Catherine strip, **Parking** attracts a wide mix of revelers on two floors who want to dance the night away. It's most popular on Friday and Saturday nights. At 1296 Rue Amherst, 514-282-

1199. Farther south is **Bolo Club** for country music and line-dancing fans, 960 Rue Amherst, 514-849-4777. Back on the main drag, **Campus** provides male strip shows where men watch naked men Monday through Saturday while the ladies get to sneak more than a peek on Sunday. At 1111 Rue Ste-Catherine Est, 514-526-9867. Next, divas and drag queens sashay to the front of the line at **Cabaret Chez Mado,** the place to go if you have a soft spot for sequins. It's owned by Mado La Motte, Montreal's most famous drag queen. Evening gowns optional; 1115 Rue Ste-Catherine Est, 514-525-7566. Talk about disco inferno: Rising from the ashes of a recent fire, **Unity** stands for techno music, guest DJs, and young good-looking boys and girls who want to party all night long on Friday and Saturday nights. At 1171 Rue Ste-Catherine Est, 514-523-2777. **Club Date** has been a piano bar and karaoke staple for years, at 1218 Rue Ste-Catherine Est, 514-521-1242. **Black Eagle / Aigle Noir** attracts the leather and jeans crowd and features guy-on-guy porn screenings, at 1315 Rue Ste-Catherine Est, 514-529-0040. One of the larger venues, **The Drugstore** has six floors, pool tables, an outdoor terrace, and is popular with the lesbian crowd. At 1366 Rue Ste- Catherine Est, 514-524-1960. **Sky Complex** is a popular bar / nightclub / strip club / restaurant venue for young well-built Montreal professionals. It's for cocktails, dancing, and fireworks on the rooftop terrace, at 1474 Rue Ste-Catherine Est, 514-529-6969. Once the most popular spot in the Village, **Bourbon** Hotel and Bar Complex just ain't what it used to be. Warning, hustler alert. At 1574 Rue Ste-Catherine Est, 514-523-4679. **Bar Meteor** offers a friendly feel from its loyal older patronage, at 1661 Rue Ste-Catherine Est, 514-523-1481. Finally, **Bar le Stud** remains one of the most popular neighborhood joints for bears, daddies, and the guys who love them, specifically on Wednesday and Sunday nights. At 1812 Rue Ste-Catherine Est, 514-598-8243.

Still open after all these years. Montreal boasts a number of popular **gay saunas and bathhouses**. In fact, Montreal has more saunas and bathhouses than any other city in North America. The dress code of choice: white bath towels—or no clothes at all. Some of the more frequented establishments include **Sauna Centre Ville** in the village, at 1465 Rue Ste-Catherine Est, 514-524-3486; **Le 456**, located on the border of Old Montreal and downtown, at 456 Rue de la Gauchetière Ouest, 514-871-8341; and in the Plateau near Lafontaine Park at **Sauna du Plateau**, 961 Rue Rachel Est, 514-528-1679, or closer to the mountain at **Sauna 5018**, at 5018 Blvd. St-Laurent, 514-277-3555.

LATIN QUARTER NIGHTLIFE
The Latin Quarter boasts a youthful crowd from the nearby University of Quebec at Montreal—the legal drinking age here is 18. That said, these Latin Quarter bars cater to quite a mix of ages. **La Distillerie** likes to serve up a number of their colorful cocktail specialties in Mason jars, 300 Rue Ontario Est, 514-993-3454, www.pubdistillerie.com. Just down the block, **Jello Bar** offers a retro vibe with live music, pool tables, and 50 different martinis, 151 Rue Ontario Est, 514-285-2621, www.jellobar.com. **L'Absynthe** is popular for live jazz, 1738 Rue St-Denis, 514-285-1738. **Les 3 Brasseurs** Quebec microbrewery has a Latin Quarter location at 1658 Rue St-Denis, 514-845-1660.

The Latin Quarter also features a number of intimate venues for live music. Many well-known musical acts have performed at the likes of **Cabaret Just for Laughs**, 2111 Blvd. St-Laurent, 514-845-2014, www.hahaha.ca; **Medley** at 1170 Rue St-Denis, 514-842-6557, www.medley.ca; **Metropolis,** 59 Rue Ste-Catherine Est, 514-844-3500, www.metropolismontreal.ca; and **Olympia Theatre**, 1004 Rue Ste-Catherine Est, 514-845-3524. Tickets can be purchased at the box office or ahead at www.ticketpro.ca.

The Theatre St-Denis is a centerpiece of the Latin Quarter.

Theatre St-Denis

514-849-4211

www.theatrestdenis.com

What's nearby: Outdoor free festivities of the Just for Laughs Festival, Berri/UQAM metro
    station

Price: Depends on production

Theatre St-Denis in the Latin Quarter features mostly French productions but the occasional English music performance as well. It also hosts both the ticketed English and French gala stand-up performance shows of the Just for Laughs Festival every summer. Tickets available through Tel-Spec, 514-790-1111 or www.tel-spec.com.

Usine C

514-521-4198

www.usine-c.com.

1345 Ave. Lalonde, Montréal, QC H2L 5A9 (one block south of Rue Ontario between
    Visitation and Panet)

What's nearby: Porto restaurant, Au Petit Extra restaurant

Price: $$–$$$ for tickets

Take an old jam factory (*usine* translates to factory) in the Centre Sud or central south part of town once home to light industry, and transform the space into a modern venue for equally contemporary dance. Exposed brick walls, wood-planked ceilings, and a trademark smokestack define this 450-seat theater, while resident eclectic dance troupe Carbon 14 (say Carbon *quatorze*) highlight the stage.

Museums Pass

The Montreal Museums Pass offers access to 30 of Montreal's finest museums and cultural institutions as well as unlimited public transportation valid for three days in a row. You get one museum visit per pass, and it's a bargain at $45, taxes included. You can opt for the pass without public transportation for $35. The pass is available at most of the participating museums, the Old Montreal Tourist Welcome Centre at 174 Rue Notre Dame Est; the Infotouriste Center at 1255 Rue Peel, and a number of Montreal hotels. Visit www.museesmontreal.org.

Hochelaga/Maisonneuve

CULTURE / MAJOR ATTRACTIONS / ARCHITECTURE

Château Dufrense

514-259-9201

www.chateaudufresne.com

2929 Ave. Jeanne d'Arc, Montréal, QC H1W 3W2

Price: $

What's nearby: Pie-IX metro station

A lesser-known tourist cousin just across the street from Olympic Stadium and the Botanical Garden is Château Dufresne, one of Montreal's finest examples of 1920s Beaux

Arts style architecture. The grand mansion, built for wealthy bourgeois brothers Marius and Oscar Dufresne, consists of 22 rooms, but the household was split in two—one half for each brother. The ornate ceiling frescos impress with meticulous craftsmanship and are a feast for the eyes. Much of the building's interior was designed by immigrant artist Guido Nincheri, who also decorated a number of Montreal churches. The site remains a popular backdrop for brides and grooms and period television and movie shoots.

Maisonneuve Market

514-937-7754
www.marchespublics-mtl.com
4445 Rue Ontario Est, Montréal, QC
What's nearby: The Biodome, Pie-IX metro station

Founded in 1915, Maisonneuve Market has lived an illustrious and varied history in the east end of town. It once served as a political gathering place, boxing arena, community center, and—its most recent title since 1995—a working market and vital centerpiece of an up-and-coming Montreal neighborhood. Some 40 outdoor seasonal vendors and another 10 vendors inside year-round sell everything from Christmas trees to Halloween pumpkins and quite a lot in between. Architect Marius Dufresne designed the Beaux Arts–style building in 1912. His former residence, Château Dufresne, is another similarly designed area attraction. Although you may have to lug them back to your hotel, cans of locally produced light amber maple syrup available at a number of vendors make the best souvenirs!

Montreal Biodome

514-868-3000
www.ville.montreal.qc.ca/biodome
4777 Ave. Pierre-De-Coubertin
What's nearby: Olympic Stadium, Viau metro station
Price: $$

One of Montreal's busiest attractions is the Montreal Biodome, a kid-friendly place for birds, bats, flora, and other fauna. Built as the Velodrome bicycle racing circuit for the 1976 Summer Olympics, the site was converted to the Biodome in 1990 and now includes four re-created ecosystems: a tropical forest, a Laurentian forest, the St. Lawrence Seaway, and a polar world inhabited by lots of penguins. Along the way you'll pass through a bat cave home to 400 bats, and practically swim with the fishes near the 660,000-gallon water tank. Within each environment temperature and lighting are adjusted to mimic the changing of the seasons. For example, in the Laurentian forest the leaves fall in autumn and come back in spring.

Olympic Stadium and Olympic Park

514-252-4737, 1-877-997-0919
www.rio.gouv.qc.ca
Boulevard Pie-IX and Rue Sherbrooke
What's nearby: Pie-IX metro station, Montreal Biodome
Price: $–$$

Montreal's Olympic Stadium—The Big O—has enjoyed (or endured) a memorable career in its 30-odd-year history. Built for the 1976 Summer Olympic Games, the building was plagued with problems—specifically its retractable roof—from the very beginning. The most recent blow to the Big O was the departure of the Montreal Expos at the end of the 2004 baseball season. But visitors still flock to the area because of the nearby Biodome and Botanical Garden. The venue is still used for large rock concerts, gay circuit parties, and special sporting events. New tenants to the area promise to keep a flow of local and tourist traffic as the Montreal Impact soccer team moves into a nearby stadium in 2008. If the budget is approved, the Montreal Planetarium may come to the area as well. Visitors can still enjoy a funicular ride to the observatory for spectacular views of the area—the tower ranks as the tallest inclined tower in the world. You can also enjoy a year-round dip in the same swimming pool used during the Olympics. Bring the camera—the stadium ranks as one of Montreal's most recognizable landmarks.

PARKS AND PUBLIC GARDENS

Montreal Botanical Garden and Insectarium
514-872-1400
www.ville.montreal.qc.ca/jardin
4101 Rue Sherbrooke Est, Montréal, QC H1X 2B2
What's nearby: Pie-IX or Viau metro stations, Montreal Biodome
Price: $$

Flora and fauna abound at the Montreal Biodome.

Teacher and botanist Brother Marie Victorin established the Montreal Botanical Garden in 1931. It has since blossomed into one of the world's premier botanical gardens. A visit is highly recommended any time of year. A winter tour includes a stroll through the 10 exhibition greenhouses that duplicate the likes of a Spanish hacienda or a trip to the tropics—especially welcome when there's snow outside. From February through April some 15,000 butterflies take flight in the main exhibition greenhouse with the annual Butterflies Go Free rite of spring. They're very friendly if you wear bright colors. In May you can *smell* the 400 purple, pink, and white lilac trees before you can see them. In summer, tea tastings in the Japanese pavilion makes for a moment of Zen, and you can even take a blindfolded tour in the Courtyard of the Senses, a thoughtfully planned garden space of sensory delights geared for those who are visually impaired. In September and October, the Magic of Lanterns—the garden's most popular event—promises an illuminating experience as some 800 imported colorful silk lanterns light up the Chinese Garden during Montreal's crisp autumn nights. Admission includes access to the Montreal Insectarium, a museum devoted to the world of bugs. Every other year a guest chef serves up interesting critter concoctions in a wildly popular event called Insect Tastings. Bring your appetite and opt for anything that's covered in chocolate.

SHOPPING

Village des Valeurs
514-528-8604
www.villagedesvaleurs.com

The Magic of Lanterns is the most popular event at the Montreal Botanical Garden.

2033 Blvd. Pie-IX, Montréal, QC H1V 9Z7
What's nearby: Maisonneuve Market, Pie-IX metro station

Secondhand clothing for men, women, and children. Household goods, too. There are a number of Value Villages in Montreal, but this is the closest one to a metro station. Don't make a special trip unless you're in the neighborhood visiting the Botanical Garden or Biodome—or are a die-hard thrift-store shopper. Located downhill from Olympic Stadium.

HOCHELAGA/MAISONNEUVE FOOD OPTIONS

Restaurants are limited in this part of town, but here are a few suggestions while visiting the area's tourist attractions. At **Maisonneuve Market**, snack on locally produced Oka cheese from Fromagerie Maisonneuve, or sample a pastry treat from **Premiere Moisson Boulangerie** at 4445 Ontario St. Est. The colorful, cheerful, original **LuBu Livres Café** offers coffee, pastries, sandwiches, waffles, and a well-stocked collection of Quebecois literature, at 4556 Rue Ste-Catherine Est, 514-523-5828, www.lubu.ca. The theme restaurant **Moe's Deli and Bar**, just two blocks west of Château Dufresne, offers burgers and mixed grill for about $10 a plate. At 3950 Rue Sherbrooke Ouest, 514-253-6637.

Jean Drapeau Park

Visitors can explore Jean Drapeau Park by bike, in-line skates, or by foot. But remember, there is a lot of ground to cover—about 660 acres on both islands—so wear comfortable shoes and bring some water. There's plenty to do, from museum visits to ballroom dancing, swimming—in the pool or at the beach—or bring a picnic lunch and lounge the day away.

The Montreal Biosphere offers environmental science fun for kids of all ages. It's one of Montreal's most recognizable landmarks.

The Osheaga Festival offers two days of music at Jean Drapeau Park.

The metro will get you to the park, and a bus transfer will get you to the likes of La Ronde or the Casino. Ferry service is also available from the Old Port. Bathrooms and snack kiosks are on-site. For information call 514-872-6120 or visit www.parcjeandrapeau.com.

CULTURE / MAJOR ATTRACTIONS / ARCHITECTURE

Montreal Biosphere
514-283-5000
www.biosphere.ec.gc.ca
Jean Drapeau Park, Île Ste-Hélène
What's nearby: Jean Drapeau Park metro station, Stewart Museum
Price: $

Operated by Environment Canada, the Biosphere is a museum dedicated to the preservation of the St. Lawrence River, the Great Lakes ecosystem, and the world around us. The building, one of the most recognizable structures on the Montreal skyline, is the former American pavilion built for Expo 67. It's a geodesic dome that appropriately resembles a gigantic playground jungle gym—and why not? It is a fun place after all. Architect Buckminster Fuller designed the dome (actually almost a full globe) and is currently the subject of an exhibit called Planet Bucky, which explores Fuller's visionary inventions and sustainable development legacy. Other family-friendly colorful and interactive exhibitions include Moving Giant, which explores the Great Lakes ecosystem, and Water Worlds, where you can actually "walk" on water. On Earth Day 2007 the Biosphere installed two wind turbines, one a domestic model similar to what can be installed in your own home. Admission is free for children 17 years old and younger.

Montreal Casino

514-392-0909

www.casinos-quebec.com

Jean Drapeau Park, Île Ste-Hélène

What's nearby: Jean Drapeau Park metro station, Jean Drapeau Park beach. (If traveling by car or cab, slow down to catch a close-up glimpse of Montreal's iconic high-end apartment complex, Habitat 67.)

Price: How much money do you have?

From nickel slots to high rollers, the Montreal Casino, open 24 hours, promises excitement any time of day. Run by Loto Québec, the casino has been a popular tourist attraction and provincial cash cow since it opened in 1992. The two main buildings are remnants of Expo 67—the futuristic-looking former French pavilion and the box-shaped Quebec pavilion with its reflective gold-mirrored exterior. You'll find all the gambling staples: slots, dice games, keno, roulette, poker, and blackjack. My favorite, the Wheel of Fortune, is easy to learn and won't break the bank—bet a loonie, pick a number, and double your money! The on-site cabaret has hosted the likes of Liza Minnelli and Frank Sinatra Jr. The famed Nuances restaurant received a trendy makeover in 2007 and offers high-end fare with impeccable service. Parking is a bit tricky—opt for the free valet service and just give a tip. For those 18 and older.

You can almost touch the sky on the Goliath roller coaster at La Ronde Amusement Park—when you're not upside-down, that is.

Row, row, row your dragon boat—the races are held every summer on Olympic Basin at Jean Drapeau Park.
That's the Montreal Casino in the background.

La Ronde Amusement Park

514-397-2000
www.laronde.com
Jean Drapeau Park, Île Ste-Hélène
What's nearby: Jean Drapeau Park metro station
Price: $$$

Quebec families, cliques of local elementary and high school students, and tourists alike
have been making annual summer pilgrimages to La Ronde Amusement Park since its
debut during Expo 67. A popular summer draw from the start, La Ronde has been a mem-
ber of the Six Flags Theme Park family since 2001. During that time La Ronde has received
a generous makeover of park grounds, and, more important, some great rides have been
added. Among them, Goliath, a wild, twisting roller-coaster whose inaugural passengers
all had David as their first, middle, or last name (get it? Davids vs. Goliath). Familiar
favorites rule as well, like the log flume ride La Pitoune—it lasts an entire five minutes! It
doesn't go upside-down, there's nothing to strap you down, and there's plenty of leg room
to boot. You just float along under the Montreal summer sun. The traditional Grand
Carrousel should satisfy all amusement park romantics as well. The International
Fireworks Competition originates from La Ronde 10 times in June and July, so the view is
as close as you can get. Your Six Flags season pass is valid at La Ronde. Upgrade your
admission ticket by about $10 and go to the front of the line.

Stewart Museum
514-861-6701
www.stewart-museum.org
Jean Drapeau Park, Île Ste-Hélène
What's nearby: Jean Drapeau Park metro station
Price: $

Housed in an actual fort that dates to the 1820s, the Stewart Museum highlights the 30,000 objects amassed by founder David M. Stewart, whose family fortune comes from the Macdonald Tobacco Company once based in Montreal. Steadfast in its mission, the impressive collection features navigational instruments, antique arms, scientific apparatus, archival documents, original maps, historical artifacts, and vintage books. Ongoing activities include a daily noonday gun salute all summer long, and 18th-century military drills performed by the fort's two resident reenactment troops: the soldiers of La Compagnie Franche de la Marine, and the Olde 78th Fraser Highlanders. A fun winter activity is Trails by Night, an adventurous New France walk through the woods—on snowshoes.

Festivals / Special Events

Canada Grand Prix
514-350-0000
www.grandprix.ca
Jean Drapeau Park, Île Ste-Hélène
What's nearby: Jean-Drapeau metro station for the race, Crescent Street for the party
Price: How much money do you have?

High octane and hormones rule at the annual Grand Prix, Montreal's official kickoff to the summer tourist season and one of its largest annual tourist draws. The race takes place at Jean Drapeau Park on Circuit Gilles Villeneuve, named after the Quebec-born Formula 1 driver who died in a car crash in 1982. With upward of 100,000 people in attendance on any given day, do yourself a favor and take public transportation to get to the track. Meanwhile, downtown hotels, bars, and restaurants decorate with red carpet and checkered flags as the young, rich, beautiful—and all of the above—come out to enjoy the nonstop party. It centers on Crescent Street (www.crescentmontreal.com) as well as the popular eateries along St-Laurent Blvd., known as Montreal's Main, just north of Rue Sherbrooke.

Osheaga Music Festival
www.osheaga.com
Jean Drapeau Park, Île Ste-Hélène
What's nearby: Jean-Drapeau metro station
Price: $$$—about $80 for the one-day pass

After two very successful editions in 2006 and 2007, Osheaga hopes to one day rank with popular multiple-day outdoor music festivals à la England's Reading, California's Coachella, and Tennessee's Bonnaroo. Pronounced o-she-hah-ga—a reference to Montreal's geographic name made during a meeting between explorer Jacques Cartier and indigenous Mohawk peoples—the two-day fest is held on or around Labor Day weekend and features 60 acts on four stages. While the likes of forty-somethings like myself are way outnumbered by throngs of those a generation younger, it's an all-ages, well-behaved affair for the musically young at heart.

Other Events at Jean Drapeau Park

Fêtes des Neiges, Montreal's Winter Carnival, is held for three weekends in late January and early February. The snow tubing will make you feel like a kid again.

The **Dragon Boat Races** every July bring out a loyal following who embrace this ancient and colorful Chinese tradition—now an Olympic sport as of the 2008 Beijing Summer Olympics. At Olympic Basin.

With the Canada Grand Prix so popular, the need for speed continues with **Molson Indy CART** or **NASCAR** racing every August.

Care to dance? **Ballroom dancing** goes outdoors under the stars every summer from June to August, usually on Wednesday and weekend nights. Admission is free. Located near the metro entrance.

Outdoor concerts like the Vans Warped Tour and Osheaga Festival take to the stage as well. These concerts are always held rain or shine. But if you're not in the mood for a crowd of 10,000 plus, then it's wise to stay away from the park on these dates.

Parks and Public Gardens

The Jean Drapeau **Cultural Circuit** offers 11 large sculptures that adorn both islands—it's like an outdoor artistic treasure hunt. The most famous is Alexander Calder's *Man*, which was built for Expo 67. The on-site information kiosk near the metro entrance offers free maps that mark the location of each sculpture.

Seven buildings from Expo 67 remain as well, including the pavilions of the United States (the present-day Biosphere), France and Quebec (now the Montreal Casino), as well as the structures built by Canada, Korea, Tunisia, and Jamaica.

The Floralies Gardens and lagoons, built for the Floralies Internationales horticultural fair in 1980, boast 60 acres of annuals, perennials, and aquatic plants. It's located on Île Notre-Dame near the casino.

Sports / Biking / Activities / Beach and Water Sports

The public swimming pool at the Complexe Aquatique was renovated in 2005. The pool is open to the public from May through August. Admission is about $5 for adults. Located steps from the metro on Île Ste-Hélène.

A **beach** in Montreal? Yes there is. Complete with a sandy shore and filtered water from the St. Lawrence River, so it's clean for swimming. Open during summer. On Île Notre-Dame. About $8 for adults. Transfer from the metro station to the nearby bus for easiest access.

Other water-sports fun includes sailboat, windsurfer, kayak, canoe, and paddleboat rentals. Prices start at $14. At the Water Sports Pavilion near the beach.

L'École Provinciale de Ski Nautique offers water-skiing lessons, and the Montreal Rowing Club offers rowing lessons at the Olympic Basin for about $35 an hour.

Old Montreal and the Old Port

CULTURE / MAJOR ATTRACTIONS / ARCHITECTURE

Bonsecours Market

514-872-7730
www.marchebonsecours.qc.ca
350 Rue St-Paul, Montréal, QC H2Y 1H2
What's nearby: Pierre du Calvet restaurant and hotel, Old Port Clock Tower, Champ-de-Mars metro station

Old Montreal's majestic Bonsecours Market dates to 1847. It once played home to Parliament for about two weeks in 1849. The market now houses upscale, mostly made-in-Quebec souvenirs and high-end crafts. Very clean public restrooms, just in case. The souvenirs are nice, but missing is the authentic market-style hustle and bustle of food kiosks.

Centre d'Histoire de Montréal / Montreal History Center

514-872-3207
www.ville.montreal.qc.ca/chm
335 Place d'Youville, Montréal, QC H2Y 3T1
What's nearby: Cluny ArtBar, Old Port of Montreal, Square-Victoria metro station
Price: $

CHM is chock-full of historical treasures and chronicles city history from day one. Successful exhibitions in the past have paid tribute to Montreal's majestic urban horse and

The Bonsecours Market in winter.

carriage, a lighthearted history of the city's playgrounds and parks, and the music that defines the city—jazz. It's appropriately housed in the refurbished Place d'Youville fire station that dates to 1903.

Château Ramezay Museum

514-861-3708
www.chateauramezay.qc.ca
280 Rue Notre Dame Est, Montréal QC H2Y 1C5
What's nearby: City Hall, Champ-de-Mars metro station
Price: $

Built in 1705, the house once belonged to Claude de Ramezay, a former New France governor of Montreal. Now serving as Montreal's oldest private museum, which dates to 1895, the collection reflects the history of Montreal's strategic place in Canadian—and American—history. The Château acted as an American headquarters during the Revolutionary War when Montreal was occupied by the Americans from fall 1775 to summer 1776 (see that, you came *this* close to not waiting at the border to show your passport). The artifacts include books, coins, photographs, and documents, including a signed letter from Benjamin Franklin, who visited Château Ramezay for a reception in 1776 to drum up support for the Revolution. The small temporary exhibition space features two or three new exhibits a year and has explored everything from 18th-century New France crimes and punishments to a history of Quebec license plates. Every summer the Governor's Garden re-creates a New France—style working Montreal residence farm.

City Hall / Champ de Mars

514-872-3101
275 Rue Notre Dame Est, Montréal, QC H2Y 1C6
What's nearby: Tourist Office at 174 Rue Notre Dame Est, Place Jacques-Cartier
Price: Free guided tours during weekdays

The building dates to the 1870s and was designed in the time-appropriate Second French Empire style. Today the building is home to the offices of the mayor of Montreal. The lobby is open daily, but the white limousines line up outside for weekend weddings (folks are married at another city building just down the block but come here for the photos). It's always colorfully lit through all four seasons and a favorite Montreal photo opportunity. Just behind the building is the Champ de Mars public square, where visitors can still see remnants of the New France—era fortified wall of Ville-Marie.

Clock Tower

www.quaysoftheoldport.com
Clock Tower Quay
What's nearby: Bonsecours Basin, Champ-de-Mars metro station
Price: Donation

A beacon for visiting Old Port ships since 1922, the Clock Tower was built as a memorial to World War I sailors who perished at sea. If you've got the energy, climb all 192 steps to the top for great views of the Old Port and St. Lawrence River. Along the way the inner workings of the clock are visible. Bring the camera. Open mid-May through Labor Day.

You can climb all 192 steps to the top of the Old Port Clock Tower.

Marguerite Bourgeoys Museum and Notre Dame de Bonsecours Chapel

514-282-8670
www.marguerite-bourgeoys.com
400 Rue St-Paul Est, Montréal, QC H2Y 1H4
What's nearby: Champ-de-Mars metro station, Restaurant Pierre du Calvet, Bonsecours
    Market
Price: $

Located in the eastern end of Old Montreal, this museum and working chapel combine to
tell the story of Marguerite Bourgeoys, one of Montreal's first settlers and considered
Montreal's first teacher. The current chapel dates to 1771 and boasts an archaeological dig
site, which reveals remnants of the original chapel built in 1675. From the museum you can
access the tower for great views of Old Montreal. Those on the tall side may need to duck
when accessing the chapel from the side hallways (folks were a bit shorter back then).

Montreal Science Centre

514-496-4724, 1-877-496-4724
www.centredessciencesdemontreal.com
At the King Edward Quay (pier) near St-Laurent Blvd. and Rue de la Commune
What's nearby: Pointe-à-Callière, Place Jacques-Cartier, Jardin Nelson restaurant, Place-
    d'Armes metro station
Price: $$

For low- or high-tech science enthusiasts of all ages. The very kid-friendly Montreal
Science Centre has been an Old Port top draw since it opened in 2000. It received a com-
plete makeover, featuring all new exhibition space, in autumn 2007. Past exhibits have
highlighted Body Worlds, those plastic-looking cadavers from Germany, and a criminally
fun whodunit called Autopsy of a Murder. The space also presents original IMAX produc-
tions. Bring the kids or grandkids and have some good clean fun in the process.

Notre Dame Basilica

514-842-2925
www.basiliquenddm.org
110 Rue Notre Dame Ouest, Montréal, QC H2Y 1T2
What's nearby: Place-d'Armes metro station, Place d'Armes Hotel, Centaur Theatre
Price: $

This is Old Montreal's iconic and ornate neo-Gothic-style church that charges admission
to get in—about $4. But it's well worth the visit. The building dates to 1829, but the first
tower wasn't completed until a decade later, and the interiors weren't complete until the
1870s. The design elements include intricate wood-carvings, stained-glass windows, and a
Casavant Frères organ that will truly take your breath away. Some famous people have
passed through these doors: Pope John Paul II visited in 1984. It's also where Celine Dion
got married and where Montreal Canadiens hockey great Maurice "Rocket" Richard and
Prime Minister Pierre Elliot Trudeau were laid to rest. It now offers a colorful multimedia
program called "And Then There Was Light."

Notre Dame de Bonsecours Chapel offers a museum, a chapel, and an archaeological dig.

Notre Dame Basilica in Old Montreal.

Place d'Armes
Where: Bordered by Rue Notre Dame to the south and Rue St-Jacques to the north

A public square of Old Montreal where working Montrealers, visiting tourists, and grand horse-drawn carriages converge. A quick inventory: Start at the statue and face the church on Rue Notre Dame; that's the Notre Dame Basilica—you must take a peek inside (it's worth the $4). Just to the right is the St-Sulpice Seminary. Almost make an about-face to the domed building with six stately columns—that's the Bank of Montreal, which runs along Rue St-Jacques, once home to the country's financial district. The building dates to 1847 and currently houses a small free museum that highlights coins, money, and banking. Just to the right you'll find the Royal Trust Building; then face the northeast corner of the square and the Place d'Armes Hotel—quite nice digs in town. Now face east to the New York Life Insurance Building—you can't miss it, it's the edifice with the beautiful clock. Then just to the right, the art deco era is evident in the Aldred Building, which was built in 1931 and was indeed inspired by the likes of the Empire State Building and Chrysler Building. Now have a look at the centerpiece Maisonneuve Statue, which pays tribute to Paul Chomedey de Maisonneuve, one of the founders of the city. The statue also memorializes other early settlers Jeanne Mance, Lambert Closse, Charles LeMoyne, and an Iroquois Indian to represent the Iroquois nation.

Place Jacques Cartier
Where: Extending between Rue Notre Dame and Rue de la Commune, diagonally across from City Hall

Here you'll find street performers entertaining the crowds, pricey restaurants for tourists, and artists with easels painting portraits and caricatures. There's also a party and fireworks every Halloween and New Year's Eve. The space was once an outdoor public market square that dates to the mid 1800s—you can still buy flowers. Incidentally, the statue in Place Jacques Cartier obviously pays homage to . . . Lord Nelson? Yes, the statue was erected in 1808 by local British merchants and predates London's Trafalgar Square monument by about 35 years.

Pointe à Callière, the Montreal Museum of Archaeology and History
514-872-9150
www.pacmuseum.qc.ca
350 Place Royale (corner of Rue de la Commune), Montréal, QC H2Y 3Y5
What's nearby: Centaur Theatre, Olive et Gourmando café, Square-Victoria metro station
Price: $$

Dig this! Local archaeologists consider Pointe à Callière the birthplace of Montreal—they believe this is where Paul Chomedey de Maisonneuve and Jeanne Mance founded Ville-Marie in 1642. The museum even houses the remains of the first Catholic cemetery of Montreal's earliest settlers. By 1695 the site was the former residence of Montreal's third governor, Chevalier Louis-Hector de Callière, the museum's namesake. During the late 1980s, just before construction of the museum, archaeologists discovered about 700,000 artifacts on or near the site. The museum officially opened its doors in 1992. Past exhibits have highlighted ancient Japanese treasures as well as local themes like the St. Lawrence Iroquoians, the Lachine Canal, and "the Main"—Montreal's St-Laurent Boulevard. The Dead Sea Scrolls even once paid a visit. Pointe à Callière has big plans to expand with an ambitious tunnel that will follow the now-obsolete William collector sewer, which was built in 1832. The tunnel will extend from the museum's current address to the Canada Customs building on Rue McGill—a quarter mile away.

Sir George-Étienne Cartier National Historic Site

514-283-2282
www.pc.gc.ca/lhn-nhs/qc/etiennecartier
458 Rue Notre Dame Est, Montréal, QC H2Y 1C8
What's nearby: Hostellerie Pierre du Calvet, Champ-de-Mars metro station
Price: $

They like to play Victorian-era dress-up at George's house. Enhanced by an opulent upper-crust setting complete with authentic period furnishings, live costumed actors re-create Montreal circa the 1870s when Sir George was a prominent lawyer, businessman, politician, and one of the founding fathers of the Canadian Confederation. The presentations explore the social classes and graces of the time, with themes like "Montreal: Magnificent and Miserable, Confessions of a 19th-century Servant." Huh! Good help was hard to find even back then!

Festivals / Special Events / Guided Tours

Calèche horse-drawn carriage rides are available throughout Old Montreal. Prices cost $45 for a half-hour ride and $75 for the hour. Calèches can always be found along Rue de la Commune near Place Jacques-Cartier and in front of the Notre Dame Basilica at Rue Notre Dame near the Place d'Armes public square.

Le Balade is an open-air shuttle that offers guided bilingual tours along the Old Port promenade. May through September. $5 for adults. Departs from the Jacques Cartier Quay, 514-496-7678, www.quaisduvieuxport.com.

Spooky, good-natured fun can be had with a lantern-lit ghost tour through the streets of Old Montreal hosted by **Montreal Ghosts**. You never know who you'll meet along the way. Tours start at 8:30 PM and last 90 minutes. Buy tickets at the departure point, 469 Rue St-François-Xavier. About $16.50 for adults; 514-868-0303, www.fantommontreal.com.

Old Montreal Walking Tours are held daily during the summer from the end of June through the end of September. Weekend tours available mid-May through mid-June and the first half of October. The tour lasts 90 minutes and stops at all major Old Montreal points of interest. English tours depart at 11 AM and 1:30 PM from the Notre Dame Basilica boutique at Rue Notre Dame; $16.50 for adults. Reserve at 514-844-4021 or visit www.guidatour.qc.ca.

Sports/Biking/Activities

Quadricycle

514-849-9953
www.quadricycleintl.com, www.quaysoftheoldport.com
Old Port of Montreal—Jacques Cartier Quay
Price: $–$$

The quadricycle is a four-wheeled, pedal-powered covered contraption that seats four and sometimes more if the kids are along for the ride. In fact, it's an absolute hoot and most fun when you let the kids steer. We're talking good-old-fashioned family time here. Daily rentals during summer; weekends in April, May, September through mid-October. Rates are per person for a half-hour rental, about $7 for adults.

Vélo Aventure Bicycle and In-line Skate Rentals
514-288-8356
www.quaysoftheoldport.com
Old Port of Montreal—Conveyors Quay
Price: $$

You can tell the tourists from the locals at the Old Port because the tourists walk while the locals bike ride and in-line skate. So act like a local. Vélo Aventure offers bike and skate rentals from May through October for about $10 an hour.

MONTREAL BY SEA—OLD PORT CRUISES
When in the Old Port of Montreal along the St. Lawrence River, do what comes naturally—go for a boat ride. There are a number of options from which to choose. **AML Cruises** offers hour-and-a-half excursions from Montreal to the nearby islands of Boucherville just to the north. About $26. Dinner cruises also available. They set sail from the King Edward Quay (514-842-3871, www.croisieresaml.com). **Le Bateau Mouche** is an Old Port staple and offers St. Lawrence River sightseeing in a glass-enclosed boat. Day cruises start at $21. Romantic evening dinner cruises also available. Departs from Jacques Cartier Quay (514-849-9952, www.bateau-mouche.com). **Le Petit Navire** offers 45-minute nautical jaunts of the Old Port waterways. About $15. Also from the Jacques Cartier Quay (514-602-1000, www.lepetitnavire.ca). The **Amphi-Bus** amphibious vehicle starts on land and floats right into the St Lawrence River. About $26. Departs from King Edward Quay (514-849-5181, www.amphi-bus.com). The St. Lawrence River shuttles or **navettes** are the biggest bargain of all. The cost is only about $6 for a one-way trip from the Old Port's Jacques Cartier Quay to Jean Drapeau Park or Longueuil on the South Shore. You can bring your bike, too (514-842-1201, www.navettesmaritimes.com). Child and senior discounts available for all cruises. Also visit www.quaysoftheoldport.com. Finally, **Croisières Évasion Plus** lets you set sail from Montreal to Quebec City from July through September. The six-hour cruise costs about $120 one-way (514-364-5333, www.evasionplus.com).

Saute Moutons Jet Boating and Rafting
514-284-9607
www.jetboatingmontreal.com.
Clocktower Pier, Old Port of Montreal (Quays of Montreal)
What's nearby: Champ-de-Mars metro station, Montreal Science Centre
Seasonal: May until October
Price: $$$, about $60

Saute Moutons is a wet and wild jet-boat ride along the St. Lawrence River rapids best enjoyed on a hot summer day. The fun starts with the outfit—visitors don lifejackets, aqua boots, and bright yellow rain ponchos (a must souvenir photo). The 15-minute trip to the rapids by flat-bottomed jet boat includes a fun history lesson—told via bullhorn. Soon you're riding the Lachine Rapids—the same rapids explorer Samuel de Champlain had a difficult time navigating 400 years ago during the summer of 1608. The boat tackles the rapids in complete safety. But be prepared—you're in for a giddy soaking. It's a pricey

Care to dance? The Old Port offers summer tango and salsa.

tourist show that's worth the adventure. Reservations a must. Bring a change of clothes and sunscreen.

THEATER/NIGHTLIFE/ENTERTAINMENT

Centaur Theatre
514-288-3161
www.centaurtheatre.com
453 Rue St-François-Xavier, Montréal, QC H2Y 2T1
What's nearby: Ora Restaurant, Notre Dame Basilica, Place-d'Armes metro station
Price: $$–$$$

Montreal's premier English-language theater has been offering innovative productions for four decades. Housed in the former Old Stock Exchange building, the theater offers six plays on two stages annually, a combination of world premieres by talented local play-wrights and time-honored stage classics. Past award-winning works have included *Wit*, *The Beauty Queen of Leenane*, and English-language translations of a number of works by acclaimed local playwright Michel Tremblay. But it was another Montreal playwright, Steve Galluccio, who broke all house box office records with his wildly popular coming-out tale, *Mambo Italiano*, which was later released as a feature film.

Old Montreal Nightlife

Old Montreal never met a happy hour it didn't like. Young, boisterous, good-looking Montrealers flock to **Suite 701** and the rooftop **AIX La Terrasse** at the Hotel Place d'Armes for fun martinis in swanky digs. At 55 Rue St-Jacques Ouest, 514-842-1887, www.hotelplacedarmes.com. While equally touted as a restaurant, the **Modavie** wine bar and live jazz experience makes a worthy Old Montreal stop, 1 Rue St-Paul, 514-287-9582, www.modavi.ca. Colorful cocktails are the main concern at **W Bartini** at the ultra chic W Hotel, 901 Square Victoria, 514-395-3100, www.starwoodhotels.com.

Tango and Salsafolie

www.tangolibre.qc.ca, www.salsafolie.com, www.quaysoftheoldport.com

Old Port of Montreal—Place des Vestiges (near Bonsecours Basin) for tango, King Edward
   Quay for Salsafolie

Price: Free or $

Care to dance? Summer sizzles at the Old Port with tango and salsa dancing open to all. The camaraderie is genuine, the setting spectacular, and the music is hot, hot, hot! The venue: under the stars along the St. Lawrence River. Free tango lessons are held every Friday in August for all levels. The lessons are sometimes accompanied by a live Argentinean tango orchestra. It's one wonderful Montreal summer moment. Salsafolie features DJ and live music, lessons, and hundreds of salsa dance-loving fans every Sunday from 4 PM to 11 PM from late June through mid-September. Only $5.

The Plateau

Parks and Public Gardens

Lafontaine Park

In the Plateau bordered by Rue Sherbrooke, Ave. du Parc Lafontaine, Rue Rachel, and Ave.
   Papineau

What's nearby: Sherbrooke metro station, Maison des Cyclistes

Pull up a park bench, you're in for a relaxing afternoon—Montreal-style. Lafontaine Park is where the local residents of the Plateau and Village neighborhoods come to play—and unwind—in a big way. You'll find soccer fields and softball diamonds, picnic tables and play-grounds. And sometimes the dogs outnumber the people. During summer, tennis courts are available for a nominal fee, while in winter the ice skating is free, but bring your own skates. The park, Montreal's third largest, also features landscaped gardens, public statues and sculptures, and two man-made ponds where summer sunbathers flock to catch some rays and bare almost everything. It's quite a people-watching show. Other shows to catch every summer are under the stars at the park's outdoor Théâtre du Verdure, which offers a stellar line-up of free outdoor performances. Perennial favorites Les Grands Ballets Canadiens presents the most popular show every year. Space is limited, so get there early—especially when Les Grands is performing. It's a must-see Montreal summer moment.

Wintertime fun in Mount Royal Park.

Mount Royal Park

514-843-8240

www.lemontroyal.qc.ca

Where: Access from downtown at the corner of Rue Peel and Ave. des Pins Ouest, or from
the Plateau at the corner of Ave. du Mont-Royal and Ave. du Parc; public transportation
available from Mont-Royal metro station and transfer to bus number 11 west

Price: Free or nominal for sports equipment rental fees (skates, snowshoes, paddleboats)

Mount Royal Park was designed by Frederick Law Olmstead, also the designer of New
York's Central Park. The summit's belvedere offers perhaps the best photo opportunity of
your Montreal trip: a panorama of downtown and beyond, including the St. Lawrence River
and Mont St-Bruno 20 miles away. The parking area along Camillien Houde Drive offers
eastern views of the city, including the Olympic Stadium. There is something to do during
every season at Mount Royal Park—summer bike rides and strolls or paddleboating on
Beaver Lake, fall foliage treks, winter fun on snowshoes, skates, or inner tube-sleds, and
hikes at the first hint of spring. The Smith House located near the main parking lot closest
to the Chalet and lookout offers a small museum, café, and boutique with maps of the park.
Every Sunday, young percussionists assemble near the Sir George-Étienne Cartier monument along Avenue du Parc for an impromptu, uniquely Montreal peculiarity known as the
tam tam. It's full of music, free spirits, and the lingering scent of marijuana.

Downtown view of Montreal from the Mount Royal Park belvedere.

Shopping

Au Papier Japonais
514-276-6862
www.aupapierjaponais.com
24 Ave. Fairmount Ouest, Montréal, QC H2T 2M1
What's nearby: Fairmount Bagels

This Mile End specialty shop offers delicate Japanese papers and art supplies. One-day workshops are held fall, winter, and spring. Topics include kite-making on *washi* paper, and painting in watercolors on Japanese papers. The store's business cards are the most beautiful you've ever seen—no two are alike.

Le Colisée du Livre (2 locations)
514-521-6118
1809 Ave. du Mont-Royal Est, Montréal, QC
What's nearby: Ave. du Mont-Royal shopping

or

514-845-1792
908 Rue Ste-Catherine Est, Montréal, QC
What's nearby: Berri/UQAM metro station, retro antiques shopping on Rue Amherst

Fun-to-browse Le Colisée du Livre mostly deals with used books at their two locations—one in the Plateau and one in the Village. You'll easily recognize each building by the trademark bright orange circular sign and burnt orange façade. Either location is nothing fancy to look at—no big-chain bookstore with café here. Instead you'll find garish overhead fluorescent lighting and overstuffed wooden bins of books. While most titles are in French, make your way downstairs at the Plateau store or upstairs at the Village location for a small but worthy selection of English hardcovers and paperbacks priced to sell. Simply a booklover and bargain hunter's dream come true.

Rue Laurier Ouest Shopping Tour
Rue Laurier Ouest, located in Outremont and Mile End, offers a stretch of high-end restaurants and upscale shopping for the home. Select restaurants are listed in the Montreal food chapter. Here are a few suggestions on where to shop from west to east.

La Maison d'Émilie
514-277-5151
www.lamaisondemilie.com
1073 Ave. Laurier Ouest, Montréal, QC H2V 2L2
A colorful collection for bath and kitchen.

Casa
514-279-7999
1101 Ave. Laurier Ouest, Montréal, QC H2V 2L3
Accessories for the home, including glassware, candles, and kitchenwares.

Au Papier Japonais offers handmade Japanese paper and a variety of art supplies.

Home

514-279-4545
www.home-store.ca
1061 Ave. Laurier Ouest, Montréal, QC H2V 2L2
Home features beautiful high-end furniture, lighting, and accessories.

Tilley Endurables

514-272-7791
www.tilley.com
1050 Ave. Laurier Ouest, Montréal, QC H2V 2K8

Did you know that Tilley Endurables is a Canadian original? The flagship store is in Toronto. This one has all your favorite Tilley products—men's and women's hats, travel gear, and bags.

Maison La Cornue

514-277-0317
365 Ave. Laurier Ouest, Montréal, QC H2V 2K5
Exclusive items and appliances for kitchen and dining.

Mémoire des Sens

514-270-8830
220 Ave. Laurier Ouest, Montréal, QC H2T 2N8
The nose knows. For essential oils and candles.

Comme la vie, avec un accent

514-278-5421
251 Ave. Laurier Ouest, Montréal, QC H2V 2K1

The store name translates to "Like life, with an accent." Here you'll find fun décor for kitchen and bath, everything from colorful napkins to decorative picture frames.

Les Touilleurs

514-278-0008
www.lestouilleurs.com
152 Ave. Laurier Ouest, Montréal, QC H2T 2N7

For high-end kitchen appliances and gadgets. The space also offers a cooking workshop/atelier that features local guest chefs. This store design, which won local commerce awards, is straightforward in approach—no clutter and not a box to be found. Everything is displayed simply on wooden shelves and tables.

Jet-Setter

514-271-5058
www.jet-setter.ca
66 Ave. Laurier Ouest, Montréal, QC H2T 2N4

Leavin' on a jet plane? Jet-Setter offers luggage, travel essentials and accessories, and fun mini travel games.

Sports/Biking/Activities

Maison des Cyclistes / Vélo Québec
514-521-8356, 1-800-567-8356
www.velo.qc.ca
1251 Rue Rachel Est, Montréal QC H2J 2J9
What's nearby: Lafontaine Park, Auberge de la Fontaine

The resource and rest stop for bicycling enthusiasts. Maison des Cyclistes features biking-related books, maps, and even a bike tour travel agency. The on-site café offers light breakfast and lunch fare including croissants, sandwiches, fresh fruit, and a variety of coffees and espressos for that extra jolt of energy. And there's plenty of parking, too—for bikes, of course. In addition, Vélo Québec hosts the annual Montreal Bike Fest, a weeklong fete that includes tours of Montreal at night and the Tour de l'Île, a popular neighborhood bike tour held in late May or early June.

Theater/Nightlife/Entertainment

Barmacie Baldwin
514-276-4282
www.baldwinbarmacy.com
115 Ave. Laurier Ouest, Montréal, QC H2T 2N6
What's nearby: It's about 10 blocks west of Laurier metro station

For posh happy-hour cocktails in Outremont.

Plateau Nightlife
The Plateau offers live music venues, neighborhood bars, jazz clubs, and the like. **Café Campus**, a popular Montreal staple, caters to a young crowd who enjoys DJ music, theme nights, and live shows, 57 Rue Prince Arthur, 514-844-1010, www.cafecampus.com. **Champs** offers three floors of sports-bar fun—and it's packed every Super Bowl Sunday, 3956 Blvd. St-Laurent, 514-987-6444. **Dièse Onze** offers live jazz performances, 4115A Rue St-Denis, 514-223-3543. More live music can be had at **Quai Des Brumes**, 4481 Rue St-Denis at the corner of Mont-Royal Ave., 514-499-0467.

Lively neighborhood bar ambience can also be found along Mont-Royal Avenue. Heading east from the Mont-Royal metro station, try **Barraca** for rum specialties and tapas, 1134 Ave. du Mont-Royal, 514-525-7741, www.barraca.ca. **Edgar Hypertaverne** is like it sounds. At 1562 Ave. du Mont-Royal Est, 514-521-4661. There's also a lighthearted vibe at **La Verre Bouteille**, 2112 Ave. du Mont-Royal Est, 514-521-9409.

Tango Libre
514-527-5197
www.tangolibre.qc.ca
2485 Ave. du Mont-Royal Est, Montréal, QC H2H 1L4
What's nearby: Mont-Royal bus 97, Mont-Royal Ave. shopping
Price: $

The place for tango aficionados. All levels welcome. While Tango Libre offers multiple-week dance lessons for locals, dance sessions are open to all Thursday through Saturday evenings for about a $10 admission fee. Bring a date, or meet one there. Located in the eastern end of the Plateau district.

Whisky Café

514-278-2646

www.whiskycafe.ca

5800 Blvd. St-Laurent, Montréal, QC H2T 1T3

What's nearby: Corner of Rue Bernard

For the whisky connoisseur. Whisky Café in Mile End features more than 150 varieties of Scotch whiskys and a generous selection of wines, ports, and champagnes as well. Contemporary music, lively happy hour, upscale bar food, and separate cigar bar. Open nightly.

Surrounding Neighborhoods

NORTH: LITTLE ITALY / ST-LAURENT BOROUGH / ST-MICHEL

SOUTHWEST: LACHINE / LACHINE CANAL / LITTLE BURGUNDY AND ST-HENRI / POINTE ST-CHARLES

WEST: CÔTES DES NEIGES / SNOWDON

Little Italy

SHOPPING

Plaza St-Hubert

514-276-8501

www.plaza-st-hubert.com

Addresses range from 6201 to 7141 Rue St-Hubert, Montréal, QC

What's nearby: Beaubien or Jean-Talon metro stations

Going to the chapel and gonna get married? Your first stop should be Plaza St-Hubert, four city blocks of shopping under a canopied sidewalk in Little Italy. There are about 400 stores and services with an emphasis on men's and women's formal wear, tuxedos, evening gowns, wedding gowns, shoes, and jewelry.

St-Laurent Borough

CULTURE / MAJOR ATTRACTIONS / ARCHITECTURE

Musée des Maîtres et Artisans du Québec

514-747-7367

www.mmaq.qc.ca

615 Ave. Ste-Croix, Montréal, QC H4L 3X6

What's nearby: Du Collège metro station

Price: $

It's a bit out of the way and most easily accessed by metro, but if you're a fan of fine Quebec craftsmanship, then this is the place for you. The permanent exhibition highlights antique

The Musée des Maîtres et Artisans du Québec is housed in a church.

furniture, tools, textiles, ceramics, metalwork, and religious artifacts from the 17th century and later. It's appropriately housed in a church that boasts its own unique tale. The church, which dates to 1867, was once located in downtown Montreal. In 1931 the church was slated to be destroyed to make room for a train station. The Fathers of Ste-Croix bought the building for $1 and had it moved stone by stone to its new location in two months' time. How's that for can-do attitude! Open Wednesday through Sunday; free admission on Wednesday.

St-Michel

THEATER/NIGHTLIFE/ENTERTAINMENT

Tohu Circus Arts City
514-376-8648, 1-888-376-8648
www.tohu.ca
2345 Rue Jarry Est, corner Rue Iberville, Montréal, QC H1Z 4P3
What's nearby: Autoroute 40 (Metropolitan Highway)
Price: $$ for theater tickets; free for gallery entrance

Tohu Circus Arts City celebrates Montreal's passion for the big top. Co-founded in 1999 by hometown faves Cirque du Soleil and the Montreal National Circus School, the eco-friendly building was specifically built with circus performance in mind, so every seat is a good one. Tohu presents unique circus acts from around the world and locally—including the annual show presented by the National Circus School graduates every June. It's one hot ticket in town. A permanent exhibit features circus history, with artifacts that include vintage circus posters, costumes, and wigs. It's a little bit out of the way and most conveniently accessed by a 10-minute cab ride from the eastern border of the Plateau.

Lachine

PARKS AND PUBLIC GARDENS

René-Lévesque Park
514-634-3471, extension 346
www.ville.montreal.qc.ca
1 Chemin du Musée
What's nearby: the Lachine Canal, Musée de Lachine; take Rue St-Patrick as far west as you
    can go
Price: Free

René-Lévesque Park, located on the western end of the Lachine Canal where the canal empties into Lac St-Louis, is a magnificent outdoor sculpture garden that boasts 50 monumental works of art. It's the largest of its kind in Canada. It's accessible by car—about 20 minutes from downtown—and there's plenty of parking. Or you can get there by bike. Take the Lachine Canal bike path from Old Montreal and ride the entire length of the canal, about 8.5 miles.

Lachine Canal / Little Burgundy and St-Henri

CULTURE / MAJOR ATTRACTIONS / ARCHITECTURE

Atwater Market
514-937-7754
www.marchespublics-mtl.com
138 Ave. Atwater, Montréal, QC H4C 2G3
What's nearby: Rue Notre Dame antiques shopping, Lachine Canal, Lionel-Groulx metro
station

Good taste reigns at bustling, colorful Atwater Market, where boisterous vendors offer samples of fruit and cheese and compete for your culinary purchase. Located in the St-Henri neighborhood southwest of downtown, the art deco structure was built in 1933 and remains a Montreal landmark. Today six dozen vendors call Atwater Market home. Specialty shops of note include Les Douceurs du Marché on the main floor, for a wonderful selection of teas, spices, and olive oils (514-939-3902). And just next door, some of the best pizza in town by the pie or the slice can be sampled at Pizz'ancora.

PARKS AND PUBLIC GARDENS

Lachine Canal
The Lachine Canal provided safe passage for ships that needed to avoid the unnavigable Lachine Rapids. Plans for building a canal date to the 1600s, but it was industrialist and sugar

Atwater Market is full of good taste.

magnate John Redpath who helped see the canal to fruition. The result paid off when the canal officially opened in 1825 and Montreal soon became a major seaport. The heyday lasted until 1959, when the canal was replaced by the St. Lawrence Seaway. Today the warehouses that line the banks have been renovated into condominiums boasting trendy Montreal living spaces with great views of downtown. The bike paths on the banks of each side of the canal stretch from Old Montreal to the town of Lachine, about 8.5 miles away. The site features five working locks that accommodate small passenger boats; the canal reopened to pleasure craft in 2002. The Lachine Canal is now a National Historic Site of Canada.

Sports/Biking/Activities

H2O Adventures Kayak / Boat Rentals

514-842-1306

www.h2oadventures.com

2985 Rue St-Patrick near the Atwater pedestrian bridge on the Lachine Canal bike path

What's nearby: Atwater Market, Rue Notre Dame antiques shopping, Lionel-Groulx metro station

Price: $$–$$$

When the Lachine Canal reopened to pleasure boating in 2002, H2O Adventures soon opened shop, providing kayak, paddleboat, and motorized boat rentals that let you cruise the canal in style. OK, the electric boats only move at a speed of about 3 knots, but they seat up to five people and are completely eco-friendly. While the boats are way outpowered by their bigger and faster speedboating cousins, a wake speed-limit is enforced, so no *Poseidon*-style adventures here! But it doesn't matter the size of the ship, from one seafaring crew to another—everybody waves to each other. Kayak lessons also available. Open daily from May through mid-September.

Pointe St-Charles

CULTURE / MAJOR ATTRACTIONS / ARCHITECTURE

Maison St-Gabriel
514-935-8136
www.maisonsaint-gabriel.qc.ca
2146 Place Dublin in Montreal, QC H3K 2A2
Price: $

Maison St-Gabriel, Montreal's oldest farmhouse, dating to 1668, is home to the Sisters of the Congregation of Notre Dame. The congregation was led by settler Marguerite Bourgeoys, Montreal's first educator, who supervised and taught the *filles du roy,* or King's Wards, young orphaned girls from Europe who ventured to New France to help offset the disproportionately high male population of the 17th century. The house remains in immaculate condition, with everything put in its proper place. You truly get the feeling that no time has passed. A nearby barn offers temporary exhibits that feature religious artifacts

A New France garden at Maison St-Gabriel.

and Quebec crafts. A re-created working garden adds to the authentic New France feeling. It's a bit out of the way in the Pointe St-Charles residential neighborhood southwest of downtown and south of the Lachine Canal, but it is accessible by public transportation.

Côtes des Neiges / Snowdon

CULTURE / MAJOR ATTRACTIONS / ARCHITECTURE

Montreal Holocaust Memorial Centre and Museum

514-345-2605
www.mhmc.ca
5151 Chemin de la Côte-Ste-Catherine, Montréal, QC H3W 1M6
What's nearby: Segal Centre for Performing Arts, Côte-Ste-Catherine metro station / Bus 129
Price: $

A somber but inspirational reminder of dark days past. The only one of its kind in Canada, the Holocaust Museum contains artifacts including photographs, documents, concentration camp uniforms, and video accounts told by survivors. Incidentally, after World War II Montreal became the third-largest Holocaust survivor community in the world. Closed Saturday.

St. Joseph's Oratory—L'Oratoire St-Joseph du Mont-Royal

514-733-8211, 1-877-672-8647
www.saint-joseph.org
3800 Chemin Queen Mary, Montréal, QC H3V 1H6
Price: Free or donation

While he would probably never take credit, the story of St. Joseph's Oratory is the legacy of Brother André, whose vision it was to build a shrine to St. Joseph. The first impression is a grand, almost imposing structure with an exterior dome that measures 367 feet tall. The subtleties of the visit make for a most reflective Montreal experience and linger in your travel memory long after your stay, like the physical rise in temperature when entering the votive chapel, the display of worn canes and crutches left by visitors healed by their trip, pilgrims who still visit and ascend the exterior steps on their knees deep in prayer, a pristine Way of the Cross garden that envelops the senses, and the basilica's endless ascent by escalator—heavenly. You'll also witness one of the most diverse groups of visiting tourists from all around the world, with conversations that take place in French, English, Spanish, Italian, Korean, Japanese, and more. The site features a museum space that offers photo documentation of Pope John Paul II's 1984 trip to Montreal, and information on Brother André, as well as his coffin and separately buried heart.

THEATER/NIGHTLIFE/ENTERTAINMENT

Segal Centre for Performing Arts at The Saidye

514-739-2301
www.saidyebronfman.org
5170 Chemin de la Côte-Ste-Catherine, Montréal, QC H3W 1M7
What's nearby: Côte-Ste-Catherine metro station, Montreal Holocaust Museum
Price: $$–$$$

St. Joseph's Oratory celebrated its 100th anniversary in 2004.

Backed by a dedicated team of theater professionals, the Segal Centre for Performing Arts at The Saidye (formerly the Saidye Bronfman Centre for the Arts) features an intimate 306-seat English-language theater that produces six plays a season. The result: performances that consistently entertain—and wow—Montreal audiences (their recent production of *I Am My Own Wife* was simply amazing!). The season always culminates with an additional play presented in Yiddish with English and French subtitles that's produced by the center's Dora Wasserman Yiddish Theatre, the only permanent Yiddish theater in North America. The result here: usually a rollicking good time had by all, specifically by the immensely loyal local patrons who double as semiprofessional cast members. In fall 2007 the complex reinvented itself into the Segal Centre for Performing Arts at The Saidye, which added The Studio, a new 177-seat theater that can easily transform itself into a dance studio, lecture hall, or cabaret, as well as the new CinemaSpace and ArtLounge, a high-definition digital screening room with 77 seats. The Segal Centre is a bit out of the way but usually worth the trip.

Montreal Festivals 101

In Montreal a festival is never far away. Here are some of the best fests and special events the town has to offer.

The **Montreal International Auto Show** rolls into town every January at Palais des Congrès (514-331-6571, www.montrealautoshow.com).

The **Wildside Festival** features original theatrical productions at the Centaur Theatre every January (514-288-3161, www.centaurtheatre.com).

Fêtes des Neiges is Montreal's wintertime bash on Jean Drapeau Park held weekends in late January and early February (514-872-6120, www.fetedesneiges.com).

The **Montreal High Lights Festival** offers theater, dance, music, but mostly it's a foodie's dream come true, with more than 350 culinary events about town every February (514-288-9955, www.montrealenlumiere.com).

Blue Metropolis is a weeklong mostly English literary fest every April (514-932-1112, www.bluemetropolis.org).

The **Montreal Chamber Music Festival** sounds great every May (514-489-7444, www.festivalmontreal.org).

Festival TransAmériques offers provocative theater late May through early June (www.fta.qc.ca).

Montreal Museums Day offers free admission to some 30 area museums. Usually the last Sunday in May (www.montrealmuseums.org).

The **Montreal Bike Fest** offers a week of two-wheeled fun highlighted by the Tour de l'Île, a 25-mile bike ride around Montreal in early June (1-800-567-8356, www.velo.qc.ca).

Cheers! **The Beer Festival** features tastings of more than 300 beers, ciders, and Scotches from around the world. Beginning of June at the Windsor train station and courtyard downtown (514-722-9640, www.festivalmondialbiere.qc.ca).

The **Montreal Fringe Festival** offers eclectic and fun independent theater mid-June (514-849-3378, www.montrealfringe.ca).

The **Canada Grand Prix** races into town every June at the Circuit Gilles Villeneuve at Jean Drapeau Park (514-350-0000, www.grandprix.ca).

Also in June, the **Montreal First Peoples' Festival** celebrates Amerindian and Inuit cultures through dance, music, and visual arts (514-998-8837, www.nativelynx.qc.ca).

The **Montreal International Fireworks Competition** can only mean summer has truly arrived in Montreal. There are 10 pyrotechnic displays from June through July. On or near the Jacques Cartier Bridge offers the best view (1-800-797-4537, www.internationaldesfeuxloto-quebec.com).

Main Madness celebrates "The Main"—St-Laurent Blvd.—with two pedestrian-only street fairs in mid-June and late August (www.boulevardsaintlaurent.com).

The **Montreal Baroque Festival** offers a touch of class every June (514-845-7171, www.montrealbaroque.com).

Fête National du Québec is Quebec's big provincial holiday that's better known to the locals as St-Jean-Baptiste Day. The colors of choice for the day: blue and white, the colors of the Quebec flag. Lots of special events and indigenous Quebecois-style music at every corner bar on and around June 24 (514-849-2560, www.cfn.org).

The **Montreal International Jazz Festival** ranks as the biggest and most well-known fest of them all. More than 350 free outdoor concerts late June through early July (1-888-515-0515, www.montrealjazzfest.com).

Festival International Montréal en Arts—FIMA turns Montreal's gay village into an outdoor art gallery in late June (514-525-4545, www.festivaldesarts.org).

Célafête is the official celebration of Canada Day, Canada's national holiday on July 1 (514-866-9134, www.celafete.ca).

Mondial des Cultures des Drummondville offers colorful displays of traditional folk music and dance from around the world every July in nearby Drummondville, about halfway between Montreal and Quebec City (819-472-1184, www.mondialdescultures.com).

The Montreal Beer Festival: Á votre santé!—Cheers!

The **Fantasia Film Festival** is fantastic. For the latest fantasy, martial arts, comedy, drama, and animated movies from throughout Asia and the world every July (514-490-9354, www.festivalfantasia.com).

The **African Nights Festival** offers African music, cuisine, activities, and workshops in mid-July (514-499-9239, www.festivalnuitsdafrique.com).

The **Montreal International Reggae Festival** is a long weekend of music from Jamaica, Africa, and around the world held mid-July in the Old Port (514-637-2886, www.montrealreggaefestival.com).

The **Just for Laughs Festival** is a true Montreal original, with lots of unique and funny free events on Rue St-Denis in the Latin Quarter (514-790-4242, www.hahaha.com).

The **Montreal International Dragon Boat Race Festival** is a colorful boat competition held at the Olympic Basin at Jean Drapeau Park in late July (514-866-7001, www.montrealdragonboat.com).

Divers/Cite hosts **Montreal's Gay and Lesbian Pride Celebration.** The weeklong festivities run late July and early August (514-285-4011, www.diverscite.org).

Les FrancoFolies de Montréal offers Francophone music from around the world. Downtown near Place des Arts late July and early August (514-876-8989, www.francofolies.com.)

The **Montreal Highland Games** features Scottish music, dance, athletics, and men in kilts, late July in the Pierrefonds suburb (514-332-5242, www.montrealhighlandgames.qc.ca).

The St-Jean-sur-Richelieu **Hot Air Balloon Festival** proves an uplifting experience every August in St-Jean near Montreal's South Shore (450-347-9555, www.montgolfieres.com).

The **Montreal World Film Festival** takes to the big screen late August through early September (514-848-3883, www.ffm-montreal.org).

What's **Osheaga**? Think Coachella in California and Bonnaroo in Tennessee. It's a two-day outdoor music fest that features 60 musical acts. Usually the first or second weekend in September at Jean Drapeau Park (www.osheaga.com).

Black and Blue is a gay/straight circuit party for the young and beautiful in mid-October during the Canadian Thanksgiving / Columbus Day weekend (www.bbcm.org).

6

Montreal Area Side Trips

If you thought there was a lot to do in the city, wait until you visit the countryside. These listings encompass the Eastern Townships, the Laval suburbs, Mont-Tremblant and the Laurentians to the north, the Montérégie region and Montreal's suburban South Shore, and west to Oka and Hudson. Included are select museums, historic sites, food tours, resorts, sports activities, bike tours, lodging, spas, and important regional Web sites.

Eastern Townships

CULTURE / MAJOR ATTRACTIONS / ARCHITECTURE

Musée J. Armand Bombardier
450-532-5300
www.museebombardier.com
1001 Ave. J. A. Bombardier, Valcourt, QC J0E 2L0
Price: $

This museum pays tribute to Joseph Armand Bombardier, the man who invented the snowmobile. Themes include an international snowmobile exhibit, info about the inventor, Bombardier's original garage, which dates to 1926 and was his first work space, and temporary exhibits on the world of transportation science and technology.

FESTIVALS / SPECIAL EVENTS / TOURS

Eastern Townships Wine Route
1-800-355-5755
www.easterntownships.org

OK, so who's the designated driver this time? The Eastern Townships Wine Route is a collective of 14 vineyards in the region. There's a lot of ground to cover, about 80 miles in all, through seven villages. Guided visits at each winery last about an hour and a half, so pick two or three for the day. Reservations are recommended. Most vineyards feature a gift shop and wine tastings. Addresses, Web links, and maps are available through the Eastern Townships Tourism Bureau.

Now that's a train set! Exporail, the Canadian Railway Museum, is home to 150 train cars and engines.

Festival Orford

819-843-3981, 1-800-567-6155

www.arts-orford.org.

Where: Orford Arts Centre, 3165 Chemin du Parc, Orford, QC J1X 7A2. Take Autoroute 10 to exit 118 and Road 141 through Mont Orford Park.

At Festival Orford the Eastern Townships come alive with the sound of music. The festival features classical music concerts, master classes for students of all ages, and relaxing and artistic walks through the woods. This musical retreat has been a local tradition since 1951. The Rising Stars Concert series features up-and-coming young musicians who attend the summer music academy and then get to perform at the intimate 500-seat amphitheater and at nearby churches and venues. The site also features an Artistic Path, which combines a relaxing stroll through the woods with 20 outdoor sculptures. Dining, lodging, and music studios are also available on-site for students. Festival Orford runs mid-June through mid-August.

Mondial des Cultures Drummondville

819-472-1184

www.mondialdescultures.com

226 Rue St-Marcel, Drummondville, QC J2B 2E4

Price: A mix of free and ticketed events

Mondial des Cultures Drummondville is a popular celebration of folk dance and music that's held every July at a number of venues in the town of Drummondville, which is about halfway between Montreal and Quebec City. The dancers and performers come from all over the world. The festival celebrated a milestone 25th anniversary in 2007. It's a colorful, magical, energetic display of goodwill and camaraderie.

Tour des Arts

www.tourdesarts.com

If they make the art, you will come. Tour des Arts offers self-guided visits to three dozen artist studios in the Eastern Townships villages of Knowlton, Sutton, and Brome. You get to visit the studios, watch demonstrations, talk to the artists, and buy magnificent one-of-a-kind art including oil paintings, watercolors, jewelry, knitwear, designer clothing, furniture, braided rugs, pottery, and folk art. While the studios are open year-round by appointment, they are open daily for visits during Tour des Arts week held mid-July. Information is available through the Sutton Tourist Bureau at 1-800-565-8455 and the Lac Brome Chamber of Commerce at 1-877-242-2870.

Week-ends Gourmands Rougemont

450-469-3790, 1-866-335-5731

www.rougemont.net (in French)

Where: At various orchards in Rougemont, the apple of Quebec's eye. From Montreal take Autoroute 10 East, exit 29.

It's apple pickin' time. Week-ends Gourmands' annual rite of autumn in Rougemont celebrates the apple harvest season with tastings, recipe sharings, guided tours, and special events held weekends from mid-September until mid-October. The three dozen participants include orchards, cider makers, and even a vinegar producer. One hot product in recent years is ice cider, which is made when apples are left on the tree to freeze and picked during the coldest parts of December and January. The apples are then thawed, pressed, bottled, and transformed into ice cider. It's the perfect wine accompaniment to cheese and dessert. Some growers offer pick-your-own-apple activities as well as specialty products like homemade pies, jams and jellies, and cider vinegars.

LODGING

Auberge aux Deux Pères
819-769-3115, 514-616-3114
www.auxdeuxperes.com
680 Chemin des Pères, Magog, QC J1X 5R9

Auberge aux Deux Pères is a comfy gay-owned B&B on the shores of Lake Memphremagog. The accommodations feature four rooms—three with private bath—as well as a heated swimming pool and a full breakfast. It's the perfect getaway from it all. Your hosts are the affable two dads Bruce and Normand.

Aux Jardins Champêtres
819-868-0665, 1-877-868-0665
www.auxjardinschampetres.com
1575 Chemin des Pères, Magog, QC J1X 5R9

Aux Jardins Champêtres combines a charming country inn with a gourmet restaurant. The menu ingredients are locally grown and produced in the Eastern Townships.

Eastman Spa
450-297-3009, 1-800-665-5272
www.spa-eastman.com
895 Chemin des Diligences, Eastman, QC J0E 1P0

A lovely spa option in the Eastern Townships located on about 300 tranquil acres. The facilities include an indoor and outdoor pool, 10 miles of hiking trails, and views of Mount Orford. All spa services are offered, including hair and beauty treatments, massage therapy, psychological and spiritual consultations, and naturopathic and nutritional evaluations. About an hour east of Montreal. If you can't make it to the Townships, they have day-spa accommodations in Montreal at 666 Rue Sherbrooke Ouest, 514-845-8455.

PARKS AND PUBLIC SPACES

Mont-Mégantic National Park
819-888-2941, 1-866-888-2941
www.sepaq.com, www.astrolab-parc-national-mont-megantic.org
189 Route du Parc, Notre-Dame-des-Bois, QC J0B 2E0

Stargazers to the front of the line. Mont-Mégantic National Park is operated by Parcs Québec. At about 3,600 feet, it's the highest summit in Quebec that is accessible by car. You'll find hiking trails, camping facilities, snowshoe and cross-country ski trails—and look at that view! Not only can you see the Green Mountains of Vermont and the White Mountains of New Hampshire and Maine, you can almost touch the heavens above. The mountain's main attractions are Astrolab, an astronomy interpretation center at the base of the mountain, and the Mont-Mégantic Observatory located at the summit. The park is open year-round, but Astrolab is open daily in summer and weekends in fall and the spring. Half-hour guided tours are available at the observatory—but call to check the schedule. Reservations required for astronomy evenings at the public observatory.

SPORTS/BIKING/ACTIVITIES—GOLF AND SKI

Le Parcours du Vieux Village Golf Course
450-534-1166, 1-888-793-3392
www.golfduvieuxvillage.ca
50 Rue du Bourgmestre, Bromont, QC J2L 2R8

Owl's Head Resort Golf Course
450-292-3666, 450-292-3318 (hotel)
www.owlshead.com
181 Chemin du Mont Owl's Head, Mansonville, QC J0E 1X0

Ski Bromont
450-534-2200
www.skibromont.com
150 Rue Champlain, Bromont, QC J2L 1A2
Autoroute 10, exit 78

There are four seasons of fun to be had at Ski Bromont. Winter, of course, offers skiing on 104 trails on seven slopes, as well as a snow park and a ski school. Springtime offers mountain biking trails, and in summer get wet and wild at the Ski Bromont Water Park, which features swimming pools and water slides. Come autumn, enjoy leaf-peeping at its finest.

Sugar Shacks
Cabane à sucre or sugar-shack season is an official rite of Quebec spring. About 20 miles to the south of Montreal in Mont-St-Gregoire, the Gingras family has been producing maple syrup for three generations, since 1948, at their Érablière La Goudrelle cabane à sucre. The traditional sugar-shack menu includes hearty pea soup, slabs of ham and bacon, crepes, omelets, boiled potatoes, and baked beans. Drizzle as much maple syrup as you wish over your entire plate. You can also sample creton, a pâté-like spread made from minced pork and light spices that is best served on bread, toast, or crackers. Also try oreilles de crisse— deep-fried strips of salt pork. The menu is typically all-you-can-eat, so bring your appetite, but don't overdo it. The authentic Quebec camaraderie is the best part of all. Prices range from about $12 to $25, depending on sugar shack and day and time of visit. Sugar shacks are open daily during peak season, from late February through mid-April. Mont-St-Gregoire is something of a sugar-shack alley. For a complete list visit L'Association des Restaurateurs des Cabanes à Sucre du Québec, www.laroutedessucres.com. The site is in French, but click "cabane à sucre" and select a region to get an idea of the vicinity.

Érablière La Goudrelle
450-460-2131
www.goudrelle.com
136 Chemin du Sous-Bois, Mont-St-Gregoire, QC J0J 1K0

Érablière au Sous-Bois
450-460-2269
www.cabaneasucre.com
164 Chemin du Sous-Bois, Mont-St-Gregoire, QC J0J 1K0

Sucrerie des Gallant
450-459-4241
www.gallant.qc.ca
1160 Chemin St-Henri, Ste-Marthe-de-Rigaud, QC J0P 1W0
Also offers lodging and spa facility.

Au Gré des Saisons
450-479-1010
www.augredessaisons.com
288 Rang Ste-Germaine, Oka, QC J0N 1E0

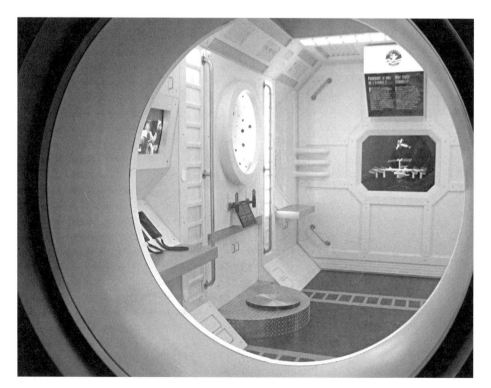

The Cosmodome in Laval is out of this world.

Laval

CULTURE / MAJOR ATTRACTIONS / ARCHITECTURE

Cosmodome

450-978-3600
www.cosmodome.org
2150 Autoroute des Laurentides, Laval, QC H7T 2T8
Price: $

The Cosmodome is out of this world! Part science museum and space camp for children 9 to 13, the Cosmodome offers exhibitions that colorfully explore the solar system, past lunar voyages, and telecommunications and satellites. The space camp offers a replica of the space shuttle Endeavour, complete with full-size flight deck.

FESTIVALS / SPECIAL EVENTS / TOURS

Mondial Choral—World Choral Festival

450-680-2920
www.mondialchoral.org

Everybody sing! Mondial Choral offers dozens of free and paid concerts at area churches, theaters, and parks. The monthlong choral music event features 100 choirs from all around the world, some who come to compete in national and international choral competitions. The events are held throughout Laval from mid-June through mid-July.

Mille Îles River Park offers a relaxing getaway less than half an hour from downtown Montreal.

SPORTS/BIKING/ACTIVITIES

Mille Îles River Park

450-622-1020

www.parc-mille-iles.qc.ca

345 Blvd. Ste-Rose, Laval, QC H7L 1M7—Take Autoroute 15 North to exit 16 and follow the signs. Price: $$

Outdoor enthusiasts with time constraints, here's a nearby piece of paradise for you. Mille Îles River Park offers boating and fishing activities for the entire family. Best of all, it's only a 25-minute drive from downtown Montreal. The park encompasses 6 miles of waterways from Terrebonne to Deux Montagnes and all points in between. Nearby islands—accessible only by boat—offer picnic tables and restrooms. Mille Îles River Park has 250 watercraft for rent, including paddleboats, canoes, single and double kayaks, rowboats with motors, 10-person canoes, and pontoon boats. Hourly or daily rentals and guided or nonguided tours are available. Reservations are necessary except for the smaller craft rentals. Prices start at about $10 per hour for a single kayak rental. Special evening guided tours include a Beaver's Epic, a kayak at dusk tour, and a bug tour called On the Trail of Insects. These tours start at $15 for adults, $8 for children. While we're talking bugs, long sleeves and long pants are highly recommended. Open spring through October.

Regional Web Sites

Eastern Townships Region—Cantons de l'Est —Tourism Eastern Townships

1-800-355-5755

www.easterntownships.org

La Montérégie Region—Tourisme Montérégie

1-866-469-0069

www.tourisme-monteregie.qc.ca

Quebec Cheese Route—La Route des Fromages Fins du Québec

514-381-5331

www.routedesfromages.com

Laurentides Region—Tourisme Laurentides

(includes the Laurentians)

450-224-7007, 1-800-561-6673

www.laurentides.com

Laval Region—Tourisme Laval

1-877-465-2825

www.tourismelaval.com

Montérégie / South Shore

CULTURE / MAJOR ATTRACTIONS / ARCHITECTURE

Coteau-du-Lac National Historic Site of Canada

450-763-5631

www.pc.gc.ca/coteau

At 308A Chemin du Fleuve, Coteau-du-Lac, QC JOP 1BO
Price: $

Operated by Parks Canada, Coteau-du-Lac was a passageway for the Amerindians, the French, and the British. It's the site of the very first canal built in North America. Visitors can explore remnants of the original canal—you can actually walk through it—which was built between 1779 and 1781. The site also features an interpretive center and an archaeological garden. The replica of an octagonal blockhouse built by the British is also quite impressive and features historical exhibitions and artifacts. The site is open May through October. Nearby is the Soulanges Bike Path, 22 miles of clearly marked paved bike path along the Soulanges Canal. The path starts in Rivière Beaudette and ends in Pointe-des-Cascades near the St. Lawrence River.

Droulers/Tsiionhiakwatha Archaeological Site

450-264-3030
www.sitedroulers.ca
1800 Leahy Rd., St-Anicet, QC JoS 1Mo
Price: $

Droulers/Tsiionhiakwatha Archaeological Site reconstructs an authentic Iroquoian settlement on the actual spot where Iroquois once lived a few miles from the St. Lawrence River. The site features a striking oval-shaped tall wooden fence barrier, a mazelike entrance that was meant to confuse unwanted visitors, recreated longhouses that accommodated 10 families, a shell midden or garbage pile, and a small museum. Open Tuesday through Sunday from May through August, weekends in September and October.

A re-created longhouse at Droulers/Tsiionhiakwatha Archaeological Site.

Exporail, the Canadian Railway Museum

450-632-2410

www.exporail.org

110 Rue St-Pierre, St-Constant, QC J5A 1G7. Take Autoroute 15 south of Montreal to exit.
Price: $$

All Aboarrrrrrrrrrrrrrrrrrd! The next stop is Exporail, the Canadian Railway Museum.
Exporail is a museum devoted to trains—very big trains. The site hosts 150 locomotives,
passenger cars, freight cars, and streetcars, which were all made in Canada. The trains are
cared for by the 900-member Canadian Railroad Historical Association, the owners of the
museum and a very sincere and passionate group who adore these historic treasures and
aren't afraid to show it. The 125 active volunteers do everything from drive the streetcar to
lay the track. The pavilion, updated and restored in 2003, holds 45 pieces of equipment.
These include a restored Sydney & Louisburg car from the Maritimes, which was once used
by wireless inventor Guglielmo Marconi to help perform his radio experiments. There's
even a photo of Marconi on the platform of the car to prove it. A popular locomotive is the
8905 Fairbanks-Morse Trainmaster, which is built with submarine engines from World
War II. There's also a rolling school car, which has a classroom with desks and living quar-
ters for the teacher. The site also features a library, exhibition space, and special events
like weekends devoted to model trains. A tour of the grounds is offered by authentic
streetcar. Best of all—Exporail brings out the kid in all of us. Seasonal hours: open daily
during the summer, weekends in winter.

Fort Chambly on the Richelieu River.

The Chambly Canal.

Fort Chambly National Historic Site of Canada

450-658-1585

www.pc.gc.ca/lhn-nhs/qc/fortchambly

2 Rue de Richelieu, Chambly, QC J3L 2B9

Price: $

Located on the Richelieu River, Fort Chambly explores a number of historical themes, including the life of its caretaker, the settlement of the area, and the story of two New France military regiments—the Carignan-Salières Regiment and the Compagnie Franches de la Marine. The fort was built by the British but abandoned by 1860. At the end of his career as a Montreal journalist, Chambly native Joseph Octave Dion returned home to find the fort in disrepair. He soon became the fort's first curator and caretaker and lived there for 35 years until he died in 1916. The museum also explores the region's seigneurial system, the allotment of land parcels by the King of France. Coincidentally, the officers of the Carignan regiment who received these land grants—Sorel, Varennes, Verchères, Lavaltrie, Chambly—are also the names of nearby towns in the region. The area also offers the Chambly Canal, a number of restaurants, ice cream parlors, gift shops, bike paths, and bike and paddleboat rentals nearby along Rue Bourgogne. Bike rentals are available at Vélo Chambly, 1731 Ave. Bourgogne, 450-447-3450, www.velochambly.com. Paddleboat and Sea-Doo rentals are offered at Location Motomarine, 1737 Ave. Bourgogne, 450-447-0617. For original gifts, visit Kado Deko, 1846 Ave. Bourgogne, 450-715-1597.

Fort Lennox is less than 10 miles from the U.S. border.

Fort Lennox National Historic Site of Canada

450-291-5700

www.pc.gc.ca/lhn-nhs/qc/lennox

1 61st Ave. St-Paul-de-l'Île-aux-Noix, QC J0J 1G0. About 15 minutes north of the U.S. border. Take Autoroute 15 to exit 6 and follow the brown and white tourist signs.

Price: $

A short five-minute ferry ride on the Richelieu River to Île-aux-Noix is a voyage back in time
almost 200 years. Fort Lennox is a hidden treasure that's chock-full of Canadian and
American history. The island was the perfect place for a British fort: It was close to the U.S.
border, which is only 8 miles away; it was located on a natural transportation hub of the day,
the Richelieu River (remember, there were no highways back then); and it linked two strategic bodies of water—the St. Lawrence River to the north and Lake Champlain to the south.
The ramparts offered a panoramic view of the river, which meant plenty of time to see the
enemy, and most important, plenty of time to get ready. While the location was great, the fort
was not without some design flaws. For example, the gun holes, called loopholes—the open-
ings through which the weapons would shoot—would not clear the casemates, the area where
the food was stored and cooked. Now I've never been in the army, but I sure wouldn't want to
shoot the cook! The site of the fort changed hands from the French, then to the British, on to
the Americans, back to the British, and finally, the Canadians. Americans took control during
the American Revolution, and the fort was used as a base to attack Montreal in 1775. But upon
retreat from a failed Quebec City attack, many American soldiers fell ill and about 1,000 of
them died and were buried on the island in a mass grave. The exact location of the grave is
still unknown. There are two British cemeteries and a plaque to commemorate the American
soldiers buried here. The British built the current fort between 1819 and 1829, and six original buildings remain, including the officers' quarters, soldiers' barracks, guardhouse, prison,
and ammunition magazines. Inside the barracks, rows of straw mattresses, redcoat uniforms,
and storage boxes display the actual names of members of the 24th Regiment of the British
army. Many of these soldiers could bring their families. In 1833 Fort Lennox was home to 57
soldiers, 33 wives, and 69 children. Between 1858 and 1862 the fort served as a youth reform
school, and during World War II it was used as a refugee camp for 400 German Jews. An on-
site canteen offers snacks, or it's a perfect place to pack a picnic lunch. Live costumed
demonstrations are held weekends in July and August. The site is open daily during the summer until Labor Day, weekends until Canadian Thanksgiving / Columbus Day. Guided tours
are available. Allow two and a half hours for your visit.

Hydro Quebec Electrium

450-652-8977

www.hydroquebec.com

2001 Rue Michael Faraday, Ste-Julie, QC

Simply electrifying! Hydro Quebec, the provincial electric company, offers Electrium, an
interpretation center open year-round that explores the world of electricity and science.
Hydro Quebec also offers free guided tours of its generating stations, dams, and other
facilities throughout the province. The generating stations are open May through Labor
Day. Visitors age 18 years and over must present an ID card. Reserve at 1-800-365-5229.
Here are three Montreal-area locations.

Beauharnois Generating Station

Located southwest of Montreal near Lakes St-Louis and St-François, the Beauharnois generating station is one of the largest power plants in the world. It boasts 38 generating units in a station that extends about two-thirds of a mile.

Carillon Generating Station

This generating station is located on the Ottawa River near Oka Park.

Rivière des Prairies Generating Station

The generating station was built in the 1930s and is located on Rue du Barrage in Laval about 25 minutes from Montreal. Tours include visits to the turbine pits and spillway.

Museum of Costume and Textile of Quebec

450-923-6601
www.mctq.org
349 Rue Riverside, St-Lambert, QC J4P 1A8
Autoroute 132/20 East, exit 6, corner of Notre Dame, the first traffic light after the exit
Price: $

With about 500 square feet of exhibition space, the MCTQ resembles a living room and an upstairs bedroom. In fact, that's probably what the space once was—the building is the former residence of André Marsil, the founder of St-Lambert. While small in size, the MCTQ is big in spirit and steadfast in its passionate mission to present innovative exhibitions that highlight the world of textiles. Past themes have explored Chinese embroideries, handmade star quilts, and a history of the iron. Accessible by public transportation from Montreal: Take the Longueuil metro station on the yellow line and transfer to bus 6, 13, or 15.

Archéo-Québec

www.archeoquebec.com

Finally, you can get your hands dirty without getting in trouble. Every August Archéo-Québec hosts Quebec Archaeology Month, some 70 archaeologically themed activities held at 50 sites throughout Montreal, Quebec City, and the entire province. Activities include tours, workshops, seminars, and actual archaeological digs—some are authentic and some are just for fun, to teach budding archaeologists the stages of a real dig. Visit the Web site starting late July for a complete list of activities.

Pointe-du-Buisson Archaeological Park

450-429-7857
www.pointedubuisson.com
333 Rue Émond, Melocheville, QC J0S 1J0
Price: $

For budding archaeologists of all ages. You supply the curiosity, Pointe-du-Buisson Archaeological Park will supply the gloves, a knee pad, a trowel, a bucket, and a working archaeological dig on the banks of the St. Lawrence River that was once a fishing and portage site for the Amerindian people who occupied it for 5,000 years. Guided walks through the woods lead to well-mapped checkerboard patterns of yard-size squares of earth where visitors join in the archaeological hunt for artifacts like arrowhead fragments, primitive jewelry, and pieces of pottery. If you don't find anything, that's OK, too. It just means to look somewhere else. You don't get to keep any treasures discovered—the artifact remains property of the site—but you do get bragging rights. There are 2 miles of nature trails in all. Long sleeves, long pants, and bug repellent come in handy during mosquito season.

FESTIVALS / SPECIAL EVENTS / TOURS

The Beer and Flavor Festival—La Fête Bières and Saveurs
450-447-2096
www.bassinenfete.com
Price: $

Every Labor Day weekend, Fort Chambly hosts the Beer and Flavor Festival, an end-of-summer culinary bash with good taste in mind. The site features 100 vendors who offer homegrown artisanal Quebec products like cider, wine, microbrews, chocolate, bread, and sausage. The weekend includes culinary demonstrations (usually in French), jugglers, musicians, singers, clowns, and face painting for the kids.

St-Jean-sur-Richelieu International Balloon Festival
450-347-9555
www.montgolfieres.com.
Where: The St-Jean Municipal Airport—Autoroute 10 to exit 22, then Route 35 south, exit 9
Price: $$ for grounds admission, about $15; evening balloon flights start at about $190

When pigs fly! The sky's the limit at the St-Jean-sur-Richelieu International Balloon Festival, an annual summertime staple held during the middle of August. The site features concerts, rides, and more than 100 balloons every year, with many offering special fun shapes. In the past the balloons have resembled everything from a giant black and white panda, a colorful yellow daisy, a red devil, a busy bee, and a pink pig. To see the balloons take off, you have to get there early or in the evening, around 6 AM or 6 PM. One of the more popular events of the festival is Night Glows, where the balloons are lit from inside to create giant colorful lanterns. The Night Glows are usually held on the weekends of the festival at around 8:45 PM. Balloon flights are available if the conditions are right: cool temperatures, light winds, and a sunrise or sunset departure. Your final destination? Wherever the wind takes you.

SPORTS/BIKING/ACTIVITIES

Pulsations
514-567-0638
www.pulsations.ca
Where: At various parks throughout the greater Montreal vicinity

Pulsations offers four-season outdoor fun for those 21 and older. Choose from hiking, biking, camping, golfing, and kayaking excursions spring, summer, and fall; and ice skating, cross-country skiing, and snowshoeing during winter. Montrealer Daniel Dansereau created Pulsations a few years ago to help hardworking Montrealers enjoy a rejuvenating back-to-nature break every weekend. The activities vary in skill level, and many sessions are devoted to beginners. One to two dozen outdoor enthusiasts attend each activity, a nice mix of women, men, mostly singles, and some couples. The age range is 20s to 50s. All the activities are bilingual. Equipment rentals and carpooling are available as well. Come prepared with a good pair of boots, a backpack with whatever necessities you may need, and your own lunch. The sessions aimed at beginners last about two to three hours. Pulsations charges $5 to $30 for each activity; visitors must pay for park admission fees as well.

Route Verte Bicycle Paths
514-521-8356, 1-800-567-8356
www.routeverte.com
1251 Rue Rachel Est, Montréal, QC H2J 2J9 (Same location as Maison des Cyclistes)

Inaugurated in summer 2007 by Vélo Québec, Route Verte offers 2,400 miles of provincewide well-marked bicycle paths that link 18 regions of Quebec, from the Gaspé Peninsula in the north to the Abitibi-Témiscamingue Ontario border to the west, and all points in between. The network offers a link to Bienvenue Cyclistes establishments—bed-and-breakfasts, campsites, and hotels along the route where you can stay overnight and safely store your bicycle. The lodgings offer a variety of tools for minor repairs and info on nearby bike repair shops and retailers. Suggested itineraries, newsletters, maps, and special-event listings are also available through Vélo Québec.

North / Laurentides / Mont-Tremblant

FESTIVALS / SPECIAL EVENTS / TOURS

1001 Pots
819-322-6868
www.1001pots.com
2435 Rue de l'Église, Val David, QC
Take Autoroute 15 North to exit 76, Route 117
Price: Admission $2

The village of Val David in the Laurentians hosts 1001 Pots, a monthlong event that highlights the art of ceramics from mid-July through mid-August. On hand are more than 100 exhibitors who sell their pottery wares—10,000 original ceramic works in all. Items include everything from a single cup and saucer to a full service for eight guests. There are many one-of-a-kind pieces as well, including teapots, sculptures, kitchenware, and decorative pottery.

Mont-Tremblant
Mont-Tremblant is a world-renowned ski resort that actually offers four seasons of fun. For golf, resorts, fall foliage, skiing, special events, and a fairy-tale-like pedestrian village. Continental Airlines offers nonstop service from Newark International Airport (EWR) to Mont-Tremblant Airport (YTM). The flights run during the peak winter ski season from mid-December until early April. Visit www.tremblant.ca.

LODGING

Le Château Montebello
819-423-6341, 1-888-333-6078
www.fairmont.com/Montebello
392 Notre Dame, Montebello, QC J0V 1L0
This Fairmont property offers golf, a spa, and luxury accommodations.

SPORTS/ACTIVITIES/GOLF/SKI

Gray Rocks
819-425-2771, 1-800-567-6767
www.grayrocks.com
2322 Rue Labelle, Mont-Tremblant, QC J8E 1T8
This resort offers a golf course, accommodations, and skiing.

Le Diable Golf Course
1-800-461-8711
1000 Chemin des Voyageurs, Mont-Tremblant, QC J8E 1T1

Le Géant Golf Course
1-800-461-8711
1000 Chemin des Voyageurs, Mont-Tremblant, QC J8E 1T1

Mont Blanc
819-688-2444, 1-800-567-6715
www.skimontblanc.com
1006 Route 117, St-Faustin-Lac-Carré, QC J0T 1J2
Mont Blanc offers skiing, a ski school, a spa, and accommodations.

West: Hudson/Oka

THEATER/NIGHTLIFE/ENTERTAINMENT

Hudson Village Theatre
450-458-5361
www.villagetheatre.ca
28 Wharf Rd., Hudson, QQ

Hudson Village Theatre is a popular 148-seat regional theater that is housed in a former train depot. The professional productions run all season long and include plays, concerts, musicals, film festivals, and children's productions. About 40 minutes west of Montreal.

CULTURE / MAJOR ATTRACTIONS / ARCHITECTURE

Oka Abbey

450-479-8361
www.abbayeoka.com
1600 Chemin d'Oka, Oka, QC J0N 1E0

The Abbey of Notre-Dame-du-Lac at Oka is a working monastery that belongs to the Order of Cistercians, which was founded in France in 1098. They are also known as Trappists. Currently 30 monks reside in the Oka Monastery. The abbey offers day visits (except Sunday) as well as midweek and weekend retreats. Silent spiritual retreats cost a suggested $40 donation a night. The guesthouse accommodations include a meal, a private room, linens, and towels. Washroom facilities are shared. A variety of products made by local monasteries are available at the on-site store, including chocolate, jellies, Oka cheese, honey, caramel, and fruitcake. The store is closed Sunday.

PARKS AND PUBLIC GARDENS

Oka Park

450-479-8365, 1-800-665-6527
www.sepaq.com
2020 Chemin Oka, Oka, QC J0N 1E0

Oka Park, run by Parcs Québec, is situated along Lac des Deux Montagnes about 40 minutes west of Montreal. The park offers camping and hiking, as well as kayak, canoe, and paddleboat rentals. There's also a beach. A nude beach. The Web site offers beautiful photos and lots of info, but not a word about the nude beach, which is renowned in the area. I know. I've been there. And I got sunburned (only because I'm fair skinned!).

Parcs Québec

1-800-665-6527
www.sepaq.com
Quebec provincial parks and reserves are operated by Société des Établissements de Plein Air du Québec, or Sépaq. The Sépaq banner encompasses two dozen parks, 20 reserve sites, and another dozen resorts or attractions including campgrounds, Montmorency Falls, and the Aquarium near Quebec City. It's a wonderful resource for Quebec's great outdoors.

Fall Foliage

Attention leaf peepers: The Tourism Quebec Web site offers Symphony of Colours, a fall foliage resource that tracks the peak colors of autumn in the province. Visit www.tourisme.gouv.qc.ca, and click or search "fall foliage."

Go for a stroll or just relax on the Dufferin Terrace.

7

QUEBEC CITY TRANSPORTATION AND PRACTICAL INFORMATION

GEOGRAPHY AND GENERAL ORIENTATION

Upper Town, Lower Town, inside the wall, outside the wall—what's a tourist to do? Here's everything you need to know to navigate Quebec City like a local.

Quebec City is more compact than Montreal. That means the majority of hotels, restaurants, and attractions are all nearby one another. Walking is the easiest way to get around, but be prepared to give your legs a workout—there are quite a few hills to climb. There is good news as well—in Quebec City, half the time you get to walk downhill!

Quebec City is situated where the St. Charles River to the north empties into the St. Lawrence River. The city is named after the Algonquian word *kebec*, which means "where the river narrows." Northeast of the city along the St. Lawrence, at the eastern tip of Île d'Orléans about 20 miles away, the river is about 7 miles wide. From Quebec City to the city of Lévis on the south shore, the river is less than 3/4 mile wide. It's close enough that you could canoe across—a feat that many revelers do in an annual wild boat race held during Quebec Winter Carnival. Quebec City is about 160 miles northeast of Montreal, less than three hours' drive. Traveling south on Quebec's Route 73/173 will take you into Maine.

Downtown in Quebec City usually refers to points outside the fortifications or walled part of the city. This includes the St-Jean-Baptiste *faubourg*, a city suburb or district. Old Quebec refers to points inside the wall. These parts of downtown and Old Quebec are both part of Upper Town. The Lower Town half surrounds Upper Town to the east in the Old Port and to the north in the St-Roch neighborhood. West of the city you'll find the suburbs of Sillery and Ste-Foy, which now use Quebec as their city address after amalgamation on January 1, 2005. The region is more French than Montreal, but most who work in the tourist industry are fully bilingual.

Many streets lead into downtown and Old Quebec, but as much as you study a map beforehand and think you will know where you're going, I guarantee that once you pass those gates of the walled city, you will get lost. But don't fret; there are enough pedestrians, tourists, and horse-drawn carriages around who can offer help with directions. Many streets run one-way.

The major east-west (although on a compass, the arrow would point northeast or southwest) thoroughfares include Rue St-Jean, Boulevard Réne-Lévesque, Rue Ste-Anne, and Rue St-Louis. Rue St-Jean is one-way in the St-Jean district outside the wall, but runs east-west for a portion inside the wall. Rue St-Louis actually enjoys a number of names: in

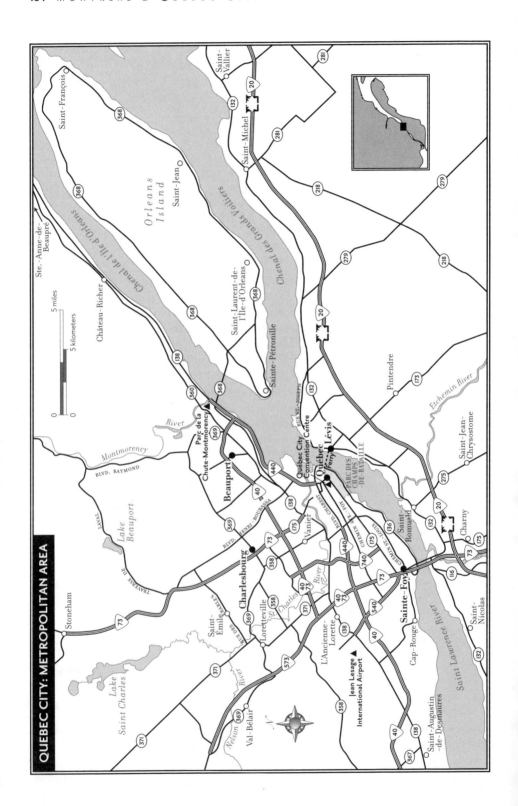

QUEBEC CITY: METROPOLITAN AREA

the Ste-Foy suburb as Boulevard Laurier or Route 175, in the downtown area it's known as the Grande Allée, and inside the walled city, where it runs one way, it's Rue St-Louis. Got it? I told you that you'd get lost!

There are a number of ways to get from Upper Town to Lower Town by car or by foot. Côte de la Montagne offers access near Rue Buade not far from the Château Frontenac. It will take you directly into the Old Port to Rue Dalhousie. But Côte de la Montagne is sometimes closed for special events like the New France Festival. And steep! You will feel calf muscles in your legs that you've never felt before. There are a number of staircases that offer access between Upper Town and Lower Town near here, including the Breakneck Stairs. Do what I do—take the Quebec Funicular for $2 and enjoy the view!

Suburbs include Charlesbourg to the north of the St. Charles River and Beauport to the northeast. Charlesbourg is home to the Pepsi Colisée, once the arena to the NHL's Quebec Nordiques, and now the home ice of the Quebec Remparts of the Quebec Major Junior Hockey League. It's also home to Les Galeries de la Capitale shopping mall, which features an indoor mini amusement park. To the northeast of the city along the St. Lawrence River you'll find the Montmorency Falls, the pastoral Île d'Orléans, and Ste-Anne-de-Beaupré, with its famed basilica that still draws pilgrims from all over the world.

Quebec Winter Carnival
866-422-7628 Info-Carnaval
www.carnaval.qc.ca

The Quebec Winter Carnival midwinter bash has been helping residents and tourists survive the long cold winter since 1955. The fun includes two parades, dogsled races, and a colorful canoe race across the frigid St. Lawrence River. The Plains of Abraham hosts a number of outdoor activities, including a snow slide and a fun human foosball game. Dress accordingly—you'll be outdoors most of the day. The warm-up of choice: a shot of warm Caribou wine. The dress of choice: the iconic bright red arrow sash, tied once around your winter coat at the waist.

The Ice Palace plays home to Bonhomme, the carnival ambassador (please don't call him a mascot). The Palace sits across from the Parliament Building and receives a new look every year. A team of 20-strong constructs the sleek frozen structure using 6,000 blocks of ice imported from Montreal. At night the palace is lit by vibrant mood lighting while DJ music fills the air.

Admission is by Bonhomme effigy passport, a coveted Winter Carnival collectible that costs $10 for access to all sites. The carnival runs 17 days, usually the last weekend in January through the second weekend in February. Next dates are January 30–February 15, 2009, and January 29–February 14, 2010.

Population

Quebec City has a population of about 505,000. It is the second-largest city in the province after Montreal and the seventh-largest city in Canada. Quebec City attracts about 9 million visitors a year. The population of the metropolitan area is 712,000, according to the Quebec Metropolitan Community, which comprises 28 municipalities, including Charny and Lévis on the south shore.

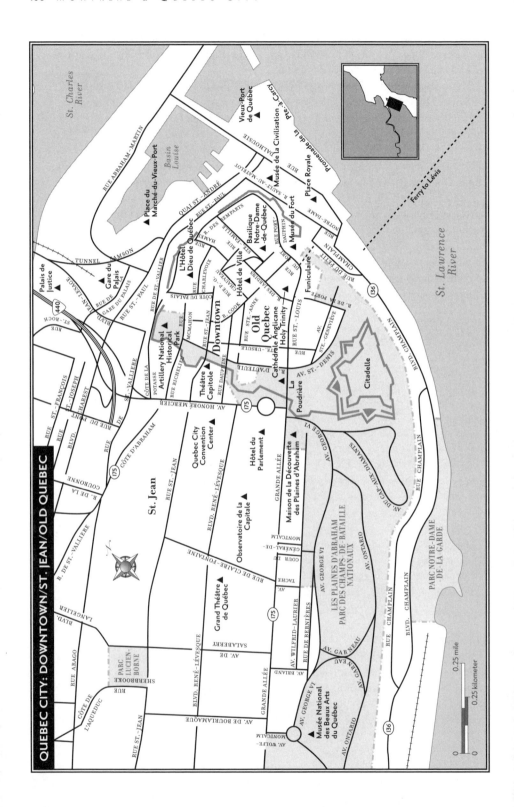

QUEBEC CITY: DOWNTOWN/ST. JEAN/OLD QUEBEC

Districts/Neighborhoods

UPPER TOWN: DOWNTOWN

Downtown Quebec is nestled between the suburbs to the west and the walled city to the east. Just to the north is the St-Jean district. To the south is Battlefields Park or the Plains of Abraham, which overlooks the St. Lawrence River. The area includes Parliament Hill, home to the government buildings that make up the provincial capital, and the trendy Grande Allée, a busy avenue for tourists and locals alike that features a variety of restaurants and hotels.

UPPER TOWN: ST-JEAN FAUBOURG

Just to the north of the downtown Parliament Hill area is the St-Jean-Baptiste Faubourg city district, a working-class neighborhood that offers plenty of restaurants, shops, bars—and spirit! Its main thoroughfare is Rue St-Jean.

UPPER TOWN: OLD QUEBEC

Once inside the wall you are in the area known as Old Quebec (Vieux-Québec). You can access the walled city at the St-Jean Gate and the St-Louis Gate. Everywhere you turn there are magnificent, centuries-old structures that date as far back as the 1600s—the oldest building in the city dates to 1675 and is now Aux Anciens Canadiens restaurant. Quebec is the only walled city in North America north of Mexico, and in 1985 the city was designated a UNESCO World Heritage Site. The centerpiece of Old Quebec is indeed the Château Frontenac, but you will also find the Dufferin Terrace, which overlooks the St. Lawrence River; Hôtel de Ville or City Hall; the Basilica-Cathedral of Notre-Dame de Québec; and the Musée de l'Amérique Française. In addition there are dozens of boutiques, hotels, and restaurants—it's basically tourist central.

LOWER TOWN: OLD PORT

The Old Port was where Samuel de Champlain first established a permanent New France settlement. The area includes Place Royale and Quartier Petit-Champlain, the New France hub of commerce that centuries ago bustled with settlers, traders, and merchants. The merchants and shops remain—this time for the tourists—as do many historical houses and buildings. Toward the St. Lawrence River you'll find Rue Dalhousie, which hugs the pier where visiting cruise ships from around the world dock every spring, summer, and fall. Many streets in the Old Port run one way. Some, like Rue du Sault-au-Matelot, are closed to traffic during the summer. The Old Port is bordered in the north by Bassin Louise (Louise Marina), which runs along Rue St-André. Rue St-Paul runs parallel to Rue St-André for a stretch and offers more than a dozen antiques shops. Continuing along Rue St-Paul north and west of the train station will lead directly into Boulevard Charest in the heart of the St-Roch district. The Old Port is chock-full of tacky souvenir shops, fancy art galleries, dozens of restaurants, and boutique hotels. It's also home to Musée de la Civilisation, the train station, and the Old Port Market.

LOWER TOWN: ST-ROCH

First, say rock. St. Rock wasn't the most appealing Quebec City district to live in or visit a few decades ago. But all that changed in the early 1990s. Today the area remains a working-class section of town but now boasts businesses and light industry, dozens of restaurants and retailers, a few hotels, and the centerpiece Jardin St-Roch. The main east-west

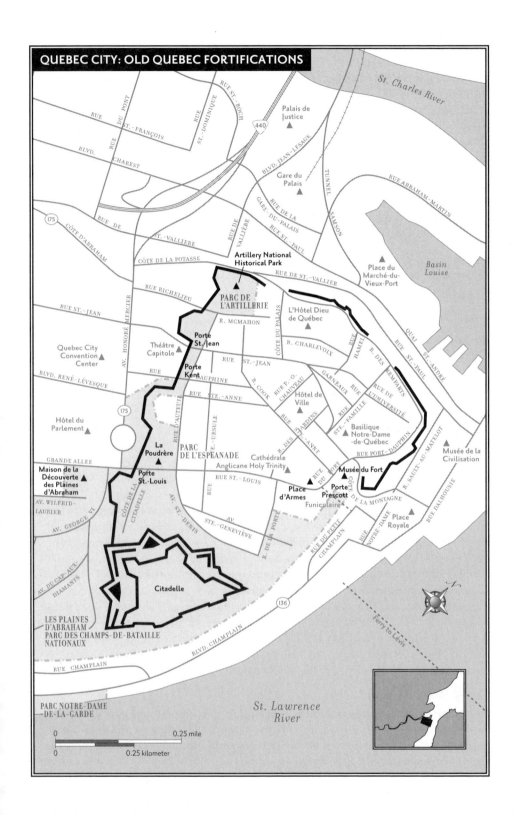

QUEBEC CITY: OLD QUEBEC FORTIFICATIONS

St. Charles River

RUE ST.-ROCH

RUE DU PONT ST.-FRANÇOIS

RUE ST.-DOMINIQUE

RUE

440

Palais de Justice ▲

BLVD. JEAN-LESAGE

BLVD. CHAREST

Gare du Palais ▲

TUNNEL

RUE ABRAHAM-MARTIN

175

CÔTE D'ABRAHAM

RUE DE

RUE DE LA

GARE-DU-PALAIS

RUE ST.-PAUL

Basin Louise

RUE ST.-VALLIER

RUE DE VALLIÈRE

CÔTE DE LA POTASSE

Artillery National Historical Park

RUE DE ST.-VALLIER

Place du Marché-du-Vieux-Port ▲

QUAI ST.-ANDRÉ

RUE RICHELIEU

PARC DE L'ARTILLERIE ▲

L'Hôtel Dieu de Québec ▲

RUE ST.-JEAN

R. MCMAHON

R. CHARLEVOIX

RUE HAMEL

R. DES REMPARTS

RUE ST.-PAUL

AV. HONORÉ-MERCIER

Porte St.-Jean

Théâtre Capitole ▲

CÔTE DU PALAIS

RUE ST.-JEAN

RUE DE L'UNIVERSITÉ

Quebec City Convention Center ▲

Porte Kent

RUE DAUPHINE

R. COOK

RUE P.-O.-CHAUVEAU

GARNEAUX

RUE DES REMPARTS

BLVD. RENÉ-LÉVESQUE

RUE

RUE STE.-ANNE

Hôtel de Ville ▲

RUE STE.-FAMILLE

Hôtel du Parlement ▲

175

RUE D'AUTEUIL

RUE STE.-URSULE

RUE DES JARDINS

Basilique Notre-Dame -de-Québec ▲

R. SAULT-AU-MATELOT

Musée de la Civilisation ▲

GRANDE ALLÉE

La Poudrère ▲

PARC DE L'ESPLANADE

RUE STE.-ANNE

Cathédrale Anglicane Holy Trinity ▲

RUE PORT-DAUPHIN

Musée du Fort ▲

RUE DALHOUSIE

Maison de la Découverte des Plaines d'Abraham ▲

Porte St.-Louis

CÔTE DE LA CITADELLE

AV. ST.-DENIS

RUE ST.-LOUIS

RUE DU FORT

Place d'Armes

Porte Prescott

CÔTE DE LA MONTAGNE

RUE NOTRE-DAME

Place Royale ▲

AV. WILFRID-LAURIER

AV. GEORGE VI

AV. STE.-GENEVIÈVE

R. DE LA PORTE

Funiculaire

RUE DE PETIT-CHAMPLAIN

AV. DU CAP-AUX-DIAMANTS

Citadelle

136

LES PLAINES D'ABRAHAM PARC DES CHAMPS-DE-BATAILLE NATIONAUX

BLVD. CHAMPLAIN

Ferry to Lévis

N

RUE CHAMPLAIN

St. Lawrence River

PARC NOTRE-DAME -DE-LA-GARDE

0 — 0.25 mile

0 — 0.25 kilometer

streets are Rue St-Joseph and Boulevard Charest, which leads directly into Rue St-Paul in the Old Port near the train station, a 10-minute walk away. Access to Lower Town St-Roch from Upper Town St-Jean is available at the du Soleil staircase near Rue St-Claire as well as by a free public elevator. This takes you to Rue de la Couronne, which leads you past the garden directly into the heart of the St-Roch downtown core. One word of note: Some maps still refer to pedestrian-only party-central Rue du Parvis as Rue d'Église.

SUBURBS: STE-FOY

Ste-Foy is the suburban neighborhood that's located east and west of Autoroute 73 near the Pierre Laporte Bridge and west of downtown. It is home to Laval University and a number of shopping malls.

SUBURBS: MONTCALM

The Montcalm district is nestled between Ste-Foy and Sillerey to the west and downtown to the east. The area includes lovely homes, the western end of the Plains of Abraham, and the Musée National des Beaux-Arts du Québec.

Safety

If you think Montreal is one of the safest cities you'll ever visit, than wait until you get to Quebec City. The city is so safe to visit that this entry is stumping me a bit.

Worth noting: The St-Roch neighborhood is still-an-up-and-coming place to live and visit, so just be alert to your surroundings. Local street people congregate in the small courtyard near the church on Rue St-Joseph. As for downtown, youngsters hang out atop the fortification wall near the St-Jean Gate. There is the occasional panhandler as well.

Physical safety should be addressed, especially when visiting Quebec during winter. Be cautious when ascending and descending the appropriately named Breakneck Stairs—or any street for that matter—when snow and ice are present.

Airport and Shuttles

Quebec is serviced by Jean Lesage International Airport. The airport code is YQB. Call 418-640-2600 or visit www.aeroportdequebec.com.

The airport does not have a shuttle service to downtown. A taxicab ride from the airport to Old Quebec costs a flat rate of $30. Check with your hotel to see if they provide airport shuttle service.

Unlike Montreal, when you depart from Quebec City to the United States by airplane, U.S. Customs is handled upon your arrival in the States.

Old-Quebec architecture is everywhere you look.

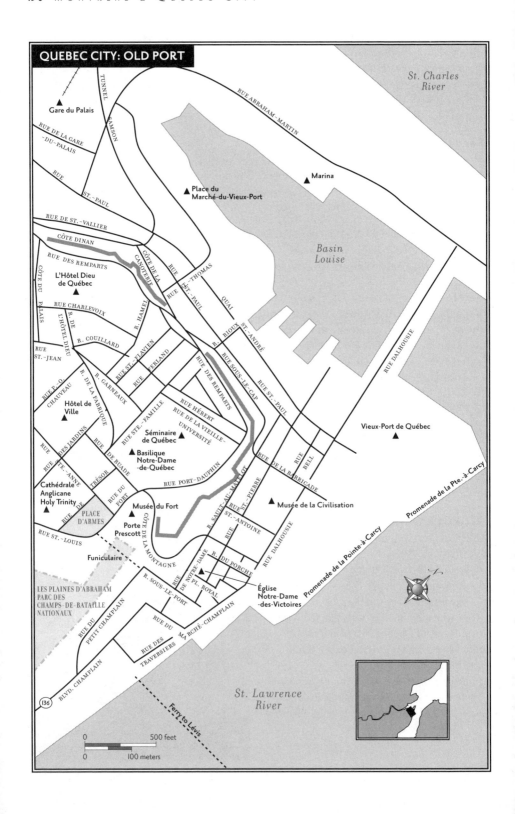

QUEBEC CITY: OLD PORT

St. Charles River

TUNNEL

SAMSON

▲ Gare du Palais

RUE DE LA GARE
~DU~PALAIS

RUE

ST.~PAUL

RUE DE ST.~VALLIER

RUE ABRAHAM~MARTIN

▲ Marina

Place du
▲ Marché-du-Vieux-Port

CÔTE DINAN

RUE DES REMPARTS

CÔTE DE LA

CANOTERIE

Basin
Louise

CÔTE DU PALAIS

▲ L'Hôtel Dieu
de Québec

RUE CHARLEVOIX

R. HAMEL

RUE ST.~THOMAS

RUE ST.~PAUL

QUAI ST.~ANDRÉ

R. RIOUX

RUE DALHOUSIE

L'HÔTEL DIEU

R. DE

RUE
ST.~JEAN

R. COUILLARD

RUE ST.~FLAVIEN

RUE FERLAND

RUE DES REMPARTS

RUE SOUS~LE~CAP

RUE ST.~PAUL

RUE P.-O.
CHAUVEAU

R. DE LA FABRIQUE

R. GARNEAUX

RUE STE.~FAMILLE

RUE HÉBERT

RUE DE LA VIEILLE~
UNIVERSITÉ

Vieux-Port de Québec ▲

▲ Hôtel de
Ville

Séminaire
▲ de Québec

RUE DE LA BARRICADE

RUE BELL

Promenade de la Pte.~à~Carcy

RUE DES JARDINS

RUE DE BUADE

▲ Basilique
Notre-Dame
-de-Québec

RUE STE.~ANNE

RUE TRÉSOR

RUE PORT~DAUPHIN

RUE DU FORT

RUE SAULT~AU~MATELOT

RUE ST.~PIERRE

▲ Musée de la Civilisation

Cathédrale
Anglicane
Holy Trinity ▲

RUE DE

PLACE
D'ARMES

▲ Musée du Fort

CÔTE DE LA MONTAGNE

RUE ST.~ANTOINE

RUE DALHOUSIE

Promenade de la Pointe-à-Carcy

RUE ST.~LOUIS

Porte
Prescott

Funiculaire

LES PLAINES D'ABRAHAM
PARC DES
CHAMPS~DE~BATAILLE
NATIONAUX

R. SOUS~LE~FORT

RUE DE NOTRE~DAME

RUE DE PL. ROYAL

R. DU PORCHE

Église
Notre-Dame
-des-Victoires

RUE DU
PETIT CHAMPLAIN

RUE DU MARCHÉ~CHAMPLAIN

RUE DES
TRAVERSIERS

136

BLVD. CHAMPLAIN

Ferry to Lévis

St. Lawrence
River

0   500 feet

0   100 meters

Train Station / Bus Station

The Quebec City train station—Gare du Palais— is located in the Old Port at 450 Rue de la Gare-du-Palais.

Service from Quebec City to Montreal and other points in Canada is handled by **VIA Rail**, 1-888-842-7245, www.viarail.ca.

The main bus station shares the terminal with the train station, although its official address is the side entrance at 320 Rue Abraham-Martin, 418-525-3000.

Orléans Express offers bus service from Quebec City to Montreal and throughout the province, 418-525-3043 or www.orleansexpress.com.

Intercar provides bus service from Quebec City to points north and east in the province, including Ste-Anne-de-Beaupré and the Charlevoix Casino, 418-627-9108 or www.intercar.qc.ca.

Carpooling

Allo Stop *Covoiturage*—Carpooling
418-522-0056
www.allostop.ca
665 Rue St-Jean, Québec, QC G1R 1P7

Mush, mush, woof, woof. Quebec Winter Carnival dogsled races run along Rue St-Louis.

Allo Stop is a popular carpool service that offers inexpensive travel between Montreal and Quebec City. You can drive your own car and get some gas money, about $30 if you chauffeur three passengers, or you can be the passenger and chip in $16 for gas, one-way. (Also in Montreal at 4317 Rue St-Denis, 514-985-3032.)

Car Rentals
At Jean Lesage Airport:

National Alamo
418-877-9822, 1-800-462-5266
www.nationalcar.com

Avis
418-872-2861, 1-800-879-2847
www.avis.com

Enterprise
418-861-8820, 1-800-261-7331
www.enterprise.com

Hertz
418-871-1571, 1-800-263-0600,
www.hertz.com

A sign in Old Quebec. Excusez-moi, but how do I get to . . . ?

The St-Roch-du-Soleil staircase bridges the St-Roch and St-Jean neighborhoods.

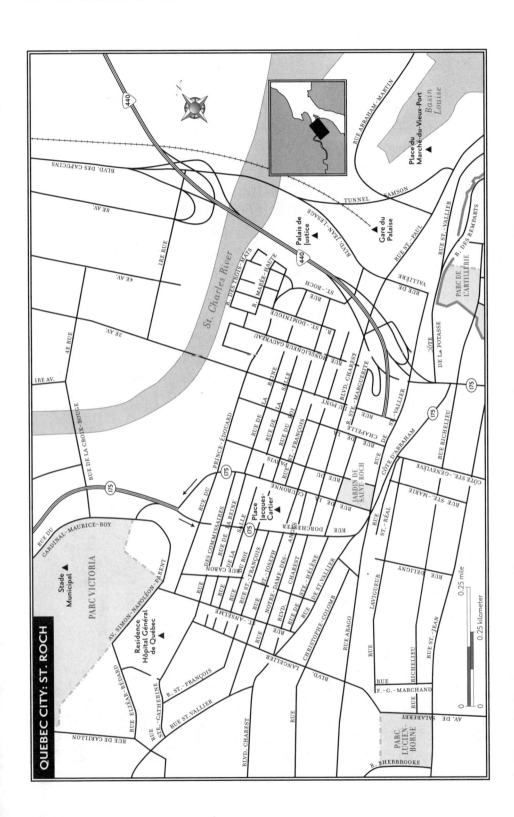

QUEBEC CITY: ST. ROCH

The Quebec City train station is easy to spot in the Old Port.

Taxis

Like in Montreal, cabs are driven by registered drivers who use their own cars. Cabs can be any make, model, or color—look for the illuminated sign on the roof. Hailing a cab in Quebec City is very safe. Call 418-525-5191 or visit www.taxicoop-quebec.com. Also call Taxi Quebec at 418-525-8123.

Public Transportation—Buses

Quebec City's public transit bus system is operated by Réseau de Transport de la Capitale, or RTC. Quebec City does not have a subway system. Bus stops are indicated by a sign, which offers the bus number and general direction of the route.

Bus routes can take you to points throughout the city, including popular tourist spots outside of the Old Quebec area like the Aquarium, Musée National des Beaux-Arts du Québec, Montmorency Falls, the Colisée Pepsi, and the Ste-Foy shopping malls. The main Old Quebec bus stop / transfer point is at Rue des Jardins just next to City Hall.

Bus tickets, passes, and schedules are available at more than 200 convenience stores that display the RTC symbol. A one-way exact fare currently costs $2.50. A bus ticket fare costs $2.30. A one-day pass costs $5.95. The museum card, which is valid for three days of visits to area museums and two days of unlimited bus service, costs $40. Call 418-627-2511 or visit www.rtcquebec.ca

Roads and Highways / Bridges / Ferry / Rush Hour

The major east-west highway from Montreal to Quebec City north of the St. Lawrence River is Autoroute 40, or the TransCanada Highway. Autoroute 20 approaches Quebec City from Montreal along the south shore of the St. Lawrence. Travel time is just a bit quicker on Autoroute 20.

Autoroute 73 connects Autoroute 40 in the north to Autoroute 20 on the south shore near Charny. Autoroute 73 traverses the Pierre Laporte Bridge, one of two bridges that connect Quebec City to the south shore.

To get into Old Quebec and the Old Port, take Boulevard Laurier (Route 175), which runs east-west through the Ste-Foy suburb. At Chemin St-Louis, Boulevard Laurier becomes the Grande Allée. The name again changes, into Rue St-Louis, when the Grande Allée reaches the St-Louis Gate in Old Quebec.

For one of the most scenic drives in town, take the Boulevard Champlain exit directly after crossing the Pierre Laporte Bridge from the south shore. Boulevard Champlain was completely repaved in 2007 and upgraded with bike paths and landscaping. It runs along the St. Lawrence River and is highly recommended, especially if you're staying at any hotel in the Old Port.

The Québec-Lévis ferry operates year-round and takes only about 10 minutes to cross the river. The boat is a passenger and car ferry and is recommended more for an inexpensive mini river cruise than it is for access into the city with your car. Call 418-643-8420 or visit www.traversiers.gouv.qc.ca.

Quebec enjoys a minor rush hour along the major highways and roads near the bridge and also along Boulevard Laurier.

Parking/Signage

To park in Quebec City is to pay in Quebec City. Most streets in the city have metered parking—fees apply for use during the day and early evening. Some meters have maximum time limits for parking, so you'll have to keep coming back to deposit more change.

There are a number of paid parking lots throughout the city. Overnight lots are available indoors at City Hall, about $16 for 24 hours. Outdoor parking is available in the Old Port along Rue Dalhousie across from Museé de la Civilisation, about $16 a day, and two Rue St-Paul lots across from the Old Port Market, about $12 a day.

Downtown parking outdoors includes the lot on Avenue Wilfrid-Laurier one block south of Grande Allée between Battlefields Park and the Château Laurier Hotel, for about $16 a day. Many hotels offer parking on site. Parking fees vary, but expect to pay about $20 for the day at the Hilton or Delta Hotels. You'll pay most for parking at Château Frontenac—about $28 a night if you're not a guest.

Parking signs and street signs are in French.

Emergency Contacts

For emergencies dial 911.

Service de Police de la Ville de Québec handles local police matters in the city. The main office is at City Hall at 2 Rue des Jardins, 418-641-6010. Also visit www.ville.quebec.qc.ca.

Sûreté du Québec is equivalent to highway or state police. For emergencies dial 310-4141 or *4141 on your cell phone. Also visit www.suretequebec.gouv.qc.ca.

The Royal Canadian Mounted Police Quebec City detachment is at 925 9th Airport St. Call 418-648-3733 or visit www.rcmp-grc.gc.ca.

Hospitals and Dental Emergencies

The most convenient hospital and emergency room is Hôtel Dieu de Québec, located in Old Quebec inside the wall at 11 Côte du Palais just off Rue St-Jean. Call 418-525-4444.

For dental emergencies call 418-524-244 weekdays, 418-656-6060 weekends. Leave a message and they will return your call.

Consulates

The United States Consulate General is at 2 Place Terrasse Dufferin, across from the Governor's Garden not far from the Château Frontenac. Business hours are Monday through Friday from 9 AM to 4:30 PM. Call 418-692-2095.

Tourism Offices

Quebec City Tourism

418-641-6290, 1-877-783-1608

www.quebecregion.com

Quebec City Tourism has all the citywide tourist info you'll need, including maps and brochures. The Museum Card may be purchased there as well. Open daily at these locations:

835 Ave. Wilfrid-Laurier, Québec, QC G1R 2L3, in Old Quebec one block south of Grande Allée near the Plains of Abraham.

12 Rue Ste-Anne, Québec, QC G1R 1A1, across from Château Frontenac.

3300 Ave. des Hôtels, Ste-Foy, Québec, QC G1W 5A8, in the Ste-Foy suburb.

This Quebec City street sign says one way, except for horse-drawn carriages.

Bonjour Québec
1-877-266-5687
www.bonjourquebec.com
Tourism information for the entire province.

Post Offices
The main Canada Post location in Quebec City is at 5 Rue du Fort, 418-694-6103. The site features full mailing services and stamps for collecting as well. A full-service Canada Post counter is available in the St-Jean Faubourg at Baron Pharmacy, 698 Rue St-Jean, 418-529-2171. And in St-Roch at the Brunet Pharmacy, 605 Rue St-Joseph Est, 418-529-5741.

Pharmacies and Health and Beauty Aids
The Brunet Pharmacy name has been a Quebec fixture since 1855. The chain offers a number of Quebec City locations. Downtown at Rue 1019 Cartier, 418-524-0230. In the Old Port at 57 Rue Dalhousie, 418-694-1262. And in St-Roch at 605 Ave. St-Joseph Est, 418-529-5741.

Grocery Stores and Supermarkets
Large supermarkets aren't readily available in the tourist parts of town, but these should do the trick. Inter-Marché is a midsize grocery store with the basics, 850 Rue St-Jean—outside the wall not far from the Hilton Hotel, 418-522-4889. And Metro in St-Roch at 860 Blvd. Charest Est, 418-648-8794.

Old Port skyline.

Area Codes

Quebec City's area code is 418. The area code covers a large region—as far north as the Gaspé Peninsula. The 819 area code serves much of the rest of the province to the west as well as the Eastern Townships—basically everything outside the Montreal (514 and 450) metropolitan area.

Media

The *Chronicle-Telegraph* is Quebec City's English-language community newspaper and dates to 1764—it's considered the oldest newspaper in North America. Other English newspapers readily available include the *National Post*, the *Globe & Mail*, and the *Montreal Gazette*. The local French daily newspapers in town are *Le Soleil* and *Journal de Québec*. *Le Devoir* is published in Montreal but is available throughout the province and the country. *Voir* is a free weekly alternative paper published in French.

Tourism Radio is offered in English and French. It's like a Quebec history lesson while you're driving. For English, tune in to station CING at 89.7 FM. English-language programming is also available on CBC Radio One at 104.7 FM.

Useful Web Sites and Info
City of Quebec
www.ville.quebec.qc.ca
Quebec Plus
www.quebecplus.com
Quebec City Tourism
www.quebecregion.com
Petit-Champlain Quarter
www.quartierpetitchamplain.com
Quebec City Museums
www.museocapitale.qc.ca

A colorful concierge welcomes you to Le Port-Royal Hotel.

8

QUEBEC CITY LODGING— *S'HÉBERGER*

Quebec City accommodations are divided here into Upper Town, Lower Town, and suburbs, and grouped according to neighborhoods, such as the Old Port, where you'll find boutique-style hotels as well as more moderately priced stays near the train station; Old Quebec, with lodgings found inside the wall; and downtown outside the wall near the St-Jean neighborhood and the Grande Allée. While the lower town St-Roch district enjoys an up-and-coming restaurant scene, a few hotels are offered in this area as well. In addition, there are a few Ste-Foy options not far from the airport. Quebec City offers a nice mix of boutique hotels, big-name brands, midsize gems, and quaint B&Bs. Similar to Montreal, the price guide is listed in Canadian dollars for a one-night stay. Also like Montreal, there are bargains to be found in Quebec City, so shop around.

$	up to $75
$$$	76 to $150
$$$$	151 to $250
$$$$$	251+

Upper Town: Downtown / Outside the Wall / Grande Allée / Faubourg St-Jean

Auberge Louis-Hébert
418-525-7812
www.louishebert.com
668 Grande Allée Est, Québec, QC G1R 2K5
Price: $$

A comfortable guesthouse with seven gracious rooms located on the busy Grande Allée. Their room and table d'hôte dinner special for two people at the on-site Louis-Hébert restaurant is a good deal at $195. The Capitole Observatory and the Plains of Abraham are a block and a half away.

Château des Tourelles
418-647-9136, 1-866-346-9136
www.chateaudestourelles.qc.ca
212 Rue St-Jean, Québec, QC G1R 1P1
Price: $$

The five-room Château des Tourelles may get overshadowed by its Old Quebec B&B counterparts for location—it's toward the west end of Rue St-Jean outside the wall in the St-Jean district, but it easily ranks among them in style—the building dates to 1898 and features details like exposed brick and a winding staircase. As for the location, I think it's great. St-Jean is a real working neighborhood where the locals live and play. You'll find fun shops, lively bars, and some great affordable restaurants. All the rooms have a private bath, and there's an inviting rooftop terrace that offers spectacular views of the city. The price is right starting at $99 a night.

Château Laurier
418-522-8108, 1-800-463-4453
www.vieux-quebec.com/en/laurier
1220 Place George-V Ouest, Québec, QC
   G1R 5B8
Price: $$–$$$

Château Laurier recently built a new wing to its hotel, which added dozens of stylish, contemporary, and classy rooms. The rooms feature a spacious dark-wood built-in that hugs the wall and offers space for everything—an ample closet, plenty of easy-sliding drawers, in-room safe, mini-refrigerator, work desk, modern leather ergonomic office chair, and flat-screen TV.

The bed is comfortable and inviting, and the modern bathroom features a splendid gray slate ceramic walk-in shower. Some rooms face a small city parking lot—and then the historic Plains of Abraham and the St. Lawrence River. There's ample window area, and one window pane opens to the world outside—you can sometimes hear a horse-drawn carriage passing by. The nearby city parking lot fees are a bit less expensive than the hotel's indoor parking. A dozen and a half Grande Allée restaurants are just around the corner. Great staff and lively working lobby.

Delta Hotel
418-647-1717, 1-888-884-7777
www.deltaquebec.com
690 Blvd. René-Lévesque Est, Québec, QC
   GIR 5A8
Price: $$$

The Delta Hotel.

Business travelers to the front of the line. This is a typical classically decorated large-size brand-name hotel with 377 rooms. Many of the rooms received an update and makeover in summer and fall of 2007. The Delta features a swimming pool and gym, but there is also a nearby full-service Nautilus Plus Gym. The Delta also offers parking (about $20 a night) and is close to Parliament Hill, Grande Allée restaurants, and many fun neighborhood bars and restaurants along nearby Rue St-Jean. Panoramic views of the city as well. Very friendly staff. Avoid the desolate Place Quebec connector mall to the convention center if you can—too depressing. Summer season rates from about $200 to $240. Fall rates as low as $160.

Hilton Quebec

418-647-2411, 1-800-447-2411
www.hiltonquebec.com
1100 Blvd. René-Lévesque Est, Québec, QC
   G1R 4P3
Price: $$$

This downtown property of 700 rooms offers spectacular views of the entire city— you can even follow the outline of Quebec's walled fortification. The convenient location is adjacent to the convention center, across the street from Parliament Hill, near trendy Rue St-Jean, and minutes from the train station by taxi. There are also many restaurant options nearby on the Grande Allée. There's also an outdoor swimming pool open year-round. Yes, you can even take a dip during winter—but don't worry, it's heated. Bathrooms feature adjustable showerheads—great for tall folks like me.

Loews Concorde Hotel

418-647-2222, 1-800-463-5256
www.loewsleconcorde.com
1225 Cours du General de Montcalm,
   Québec, QC G1R 4W6
Price: $$–$$$$

The Loews Concorde Hotel is perhaps the oddest-looking building in the city—it's an angled tower of concrete and glass that looks as if a top-hat-shaped flying saucer has landed on the roof (it's actually their revolving restaurant l'Astral). There are 400 tasteful and modern rooms in all, and the views are fantastic in any direction.

Marriott Courtyard

418-694-4004, 1-866-694-4004
www.marriott.com/yqbcy
850 Place d'Youville, Québec, QC G1R 3P6
Price: $$–$$$

The Marriott Courtyard bridges old and new. The location is great—it's just outside the St-Jean Gate. In all, there are 111 rooms on eight floors of a historic building—some rooms overlook the Place d'Youville skating rink during the annual Winter Carnival. The accommodations are clean, classic, and comfortable. Fall rates from $149 to $309. Spring and summer rates start between $189 and $229.

The Hilton Hotel swimming pool is open year-round

Palace Royal Hotel
418-694-2000, 1-800-567-5276
www.hotelsjaro.com
775 Ave. Honoré-Mercier, Québec, QC
    G1R 6A5
Price: $$–$$$

It's a great location—in the same vicinity as
the Marriott Courtyard, but near a busier
intersection. The rooms and décor feature a
lavish innocent elegance, starting at about
$150 for a standard or about $380 for the
nuptial suite.

Upper Town: Old Quebec—Inside the Wall

Auberge Place d'Armes
418-694-9485, 1-866-333-9485
www.aubergeplacedarmes.com
24 Rue Ste-Anne, Québec, QC G1R 3X3
Price: $$–$$$

Auberge Place d'Armes is located on busy
pedestrian-only St-Anne along a row of
hotels and restaurants. Château Frontenac
is steps away. There are currently 12 colorful rooms, some with exposed brick, and
there are plans to expand. Sharing the
building is the recommended Le Pain Béni
restaurant—hotel guests receive complimentary breakfast there. Room rates start
at $115. Minimum stays apply.

Champlain Hotel
418-694-0106, 1-800-567-2106
www.champlainhotel.com
115 Rue Ste-Anne, Québec, QC G1R 3X6
Price: $$–$$$

The Champlain Hotel boasts 50 spacious
rooms housed in two of its side-by-side
buildings, one of which dates from the
'60s—yes, the 1960s (I didn't know a building inside the wall could be that young).
Formerly an apartment house, the building
was transformed into a hotel and now features colorful modern accommodations.

There is coveted parking on-site for a few
cars, a hearty continental breakfast
included, and you're close to the hustle and
bustle of Rue St-Jean. There are dozens of
restaurants within a 10-minute walk. If
your room faces Rue Ste-Anne and you
leave your windows open, you can sometimes hear the clip-clop of a horse-drawn
carriage leisurely strolling by—it doesn't get
more Quebec than that! The reason for your
visit may be clean and comfortable lodgings, but what you'll remember most is the
genuine hospitality offered by owner
Michele Doré.

Château Bellevue Hotel
418-692-2573, 1-800-463-2617
www.vieux-quebec.com/en/bellevue
16 Rue de la Porte, Québec, QC G1R 4M9
Price: $$–$$$

Château Bellevue offers midsize affordable
accommodations in a quiet residential area
steps to all the action. There are 56 rooms
in a guesthouse setting—actually three
houses in a row. The hotel overlooks the
Governor's Garden, which overlooks the
Dufferin Terrace, which overlooks the St.
Lawrence River. Just to the east is the
Château Frontenac, and just up the hill to
the west is the citadel. Early summer rates
for the standard room start at about $110;
high-season July-through-October rates
begin at about $140.

Château Frontenac
418-692-3861, 1-888-274-0404
www.fairmont.com
1 Rue des Carrières, Québec, QC G1R 5J5
Price: $$$$

The center of the Quebec City universe is
indeed the Château Frontenac. The Château
was built as a luxury stopover when the
Canadian Pacific Railway joined one end of
Canada to the other. Back in the late 1800s,
it took five and a half days to travel by train
from the east to west coast. But the train

The Château Frontenac rises above the nearby Old Quebec architecture.

could not accommodate passengers overnight. The solution: build a string of hotels along the way where the passengers could lodge. CP built its first hotel in Banff in 1888; the Château Frontenac was the second property in the CP family—the location was perfect, as Quebec was the first stop for cruise ships arriving from Europe. It officially opened its doors on December 20, 1893, with 170 rooms. The cost for the room: $3 for the one-night stay. The Château's iconic tower wasn't added until 1924. Since its opening, many famous visitors have stayed at the hotel. In the summer of 1943, at the height of World War II, President Franklin Roosevelt, Prime Minister Winston Churchill, and Canadian Prime Minister Mackenzie King met at the Château to discuss plans for the D-Day invasion, among other things. Charlie Chaplin, Charles Lindbergh, and Celine Dion have stayed here as well. Today there are 618 rooms, all tastefully decorated and very clean, but not all rooms come with a view. The view on the less expensive inner courtyard is basically a parking lot. Nonetheless, the iconic turrets and copper roof peaks, green with age, as well as the St. Lawrence River, are visible from most of the corridors on any given floor. The rooms usually start in the $300 to $600 range, but there are deals to be found—like those small inner-courtyard rooms booked online that start at $199. Hey, if a class of seventh-grade French students from the States can stay here, so can you, if you time it right. It all comes down to this: You can say you stayed at the Château Frontenac. If you can't afford to stay, you can take a fun guided tour for about $10; enjoy afternoon tea at Le Champlain restaurant, which costs about $35; or at the least have a drink at the St-Laurent Bar and Lounge, which overlooks the Dufferin Terrace. Go for one of their house specialty martinis: the Winston Churchill or the F. D. Roosevelt. Cheers!

Clarendon Hotel

418-692-2480, 1-888-554-6001
www.hotelclarendon.com
57 Rue Ste-Anne, Québec, QC G1R 3X4
Price: $$–$$$

The Clarendon is one of the most beautiful hotels in the city, and the oldest as well—it opened its doors to lodging in 1870. Art deco style reigns here, evident in the clean lines of the façade, the stunning entrance doors made of glass and iron that look too heavy to open, and the most elegant front desk in town, with a marble counter and ornate wood and iron accents. You could lounge the day away in the inviting lobby. There are 143 sumptuous rooms, with high-season rates that start at $149 for standard rooms and $239 for deluxe rooms. The central location leaves you steps to dozens of restaurants along Rue St-Jean and Rue St-Louis.

Le Coureur des Bois

418-692-1117, 1-800-269-6414
www.gayquebec.net
15 Rue Ste-Ursule, Québec, QC G1R 4C7
Price: $–$$

This is a gay-owned bed-and-breakfast with three rooms to rent. The baths are shared, but the place is very clean. The building offers rich wood floors, exposed brick walls, an inviting community area, and a cozy outdoor terrace. A hearty breakfast is included. The location is great—just inside the walled city. It's also very close to the wonderfully romantic restaurants Le St. Amour and Le Patriarche. You can't beat the price—rooms range between $70 and $130. It's one of the best values in town.

Gîte Côte de la Montagne

418-694-4414, 1-888-794-4414
www.gitedelamontagne.com
54 Côte de la Montagne, Québec, QC
    G1K 4E2
Price: $$–$$$

The first clue is the address—Côte de la Montagne—montagne translates to mountain. This B&B with four rooms and one loft apartment is on a very steep street that connects Upper Town to Lower Town. The historic building is at the top of the Breakneck Stairs. Four of the rooms offer exposed stone or brick, a fireplace, ample windows, and lots of space. Two rooms share a bath, and breakfast is included. In addition, the third-floor apartment features an open loft bedroom, two sofa beds, spiral staircase, full kitchen, fireplace, and perhaps the best private terrace in town, with views of the Quebec Funicular, Rue du Petit-Champlain, and the St. Lawrence River. Wow! You could have a small party up there. Rooms with shared bath start at $170 a night. The loft apartment costs $300 a night year-round. The entire B&B can be rented out to accommodate a small group—call for prices.

Hôtel du Vieux Québec
418-692-1850, 1-800-361-7787
www.hvq.com
1190 Rue St-Jean, Québec, QC G1R 1S6
Price: $$–$$$

When you see the red roof, you've arrived. Hôtel du Vieux Québec gets the job done with an affordable no-nonsense style. This 44-room hotel runs along busy Rue St-Jean and is convenient to shopping, parking, dining (the busy and cozy Les Frères de la Côte Restaurant shares the lobby), and lots to do—the Musée de l'Amérique Française is a short walk away. The clean rooms satisfy with full amenities; some feature rustic exposed brick walls. The continental breakfast, which comes in a picnic basket that's hung on your door, is a nice touch. The lounge area, with fireplace, piano, and board games, offers the perfect place for groups to gather.

Hôtel Ste-Anne
418-694-1455, 1-877-222-9422
www.hotelste-anne.com
32 Rue Ste-Anne, Québec, QC G1K 4A8
Price: $$$

You wouldn't know it from the outside—the building dates to the 17th century—but the Hôtel Ste-Anne offers 28 very modern and updated rooms—you could call it boutique-style. It opened in 2004, so the rooms, baths, and furnishings are clean and contemporary; some rooms are accented with vaulted ceilings and exposed brick. There is little view to speak of—especially the rooms in back; but those are quiet. Some rooms in front have a view of the Château Frontenac come fall when the leaves have fallen from the trees. The lobby is small and a bit hurried—it shares the space with an adjacent restaurant, and you are in the thick of action along busy Ste-Anne's stretch of outdoor cafés. Standard rooms start at about $145 in low season and $180 during high season.

Le Manoir D'Auteuil Hotel
418-694-1173
www.manoirdauteuil.com
49 Rue d'Auteuil, Québec, QC G1R 4C2
Price: $$–$$$

This small but stylish and very affordable 16-unit guesthouse is located just inside the wall. The rooms are spacious and clean, and the location leaves you truly in the center of everything—a short walk to Parliament Hill and the Grande Allée restaurants in one direction, and just around the block to the restaurants along Rue St-Louis. High season rates start between $99 and $199.

Manoir Victoria Hotel
418-692-1030, 1-800-463-6283
www.manoir-victoria.com
44 Côte du Palais, Québec, QC G1R 4H8
Price: $$$–$$$$

The Manoir Victoria offers 156 rooms in a lavish setting. Highly touted is its on-site spa that offers a variety of indulgences and treatments including body scrubs, body wraps—the newest is a cranberry wrap—facials, massages, manicures, and pedicures. The facility includes an indoor swimming pool, sauna, and gym. The location is across from the hospital, just off busy Rue St-Jean. The classic and spacious rooms start at $159 to $325 a night during high season.

Best of Gay Quebec City

Gay life in Quebec City is not as busy as in Montreal, but there are a few gay establishments in town.

Bar Le Drague is a popular place, with a busy outdoor summer terrace and a year-round nightclub and cabaret. At 815 Rue St-Augustin, just off Rue St-Jean, behind the Hilton and Delta Hotels. Call 418-649-7212 or visit www.ledrague.com.

Taverne 321 is a pub-style bar in the St-Roch neighborhood. At 321 Rue de la Couronne, 418-525-5107.

Quebec City offers a few saunas, including **Sauna Hippocampe** at 31 Rue McMahon just inside the wall. Call 418-692-1521 or visit www.clubsauna.com. **Bloc Sauna** shares a space with **Empire Lyon** adult store at 225 Rue St-Jean. Call 418-523-2562 for the sauna, 418-648-2301 for the store.

Two gay-operated B&Bs are recommended—**Le Coureur des Bois**, 15 Rue Ste-Ursule, 418-692-1117, www.gayquebec.net; and **727 Chambres & Pension**, 727 Rue d'Aiguillon, 418-523-7705.

Domaine de l'Arc en Ciel is a gay campground 30 minutes from Quebec City. At 1878 Rang 5 in Joly, 418-728-5522, www.dom-aec.com.

Celebrations for **Pride Quebec** (Fierté Québec) are usually held in mid-August. Visit www.fiertequebec.net.

Lower Town: Old Port

Auberge St-Antoine
418-692-2211, 1-888-692-2211
www.saint-antoine.com
8 Rue St-Antoine, Québec, QC G1K 4C9
Price: $$$–$$$$

These are sumptuous Old Port boutique digs. There are 90-plus rooms in all, some with views of the St. Lawrence River as well as the visiting cruise ships when they're in town. The classic rooms are simple and spacious, ranging from $159 to $279; the larger modern rooms and stunning luxury suites are a splurge that will start at $299 and up. You're near Rue du Petit-Champlain for strolling and shopping, exclusive Old Port art galleries, and just next door to the Musée de la Civilisation. Their on-site upscale Panache restaurant has been making waves in town as well.

Hôtel 71
418-692-1171, 1-888-692-1171
www.hotel71.ca
71 Rue St-Pierre, Québec, QC G1K 4A4
Price: $$$–$$$$

The Old Port in Quebec City is home to a half-dozen upscale boutique hotels; Hôtel 71 is one of them. There are 40 rooms that employ ultramodern décor in a building complete with thick stone façade that dates to the 19th century. Very clean, very contemporary, and with full amenities. High-season rates start at $235 a night.

Hôtel des Coutellier
418-692-9696, 1-888-523-9696
www.hoteldescoutellier.com
253 Rue St-Paul, Québec, QC G1K 8C1
Price: $$–$$$

There are 24 tastefully decorated rooms at Hôtel des Coutellier, which start at about $150 a night. The Old Port location is just across from the train station and nearby Rue St-Paul antiques shops and restaurants.

Hôtel Dominion 1912

418-692-2224, 1-888-833-5253
www.hoteldominion.com
126 Rue St-Pierre, Québec, QC G1K 4A8
Price: $$$–$$$$

The Dominion 1912 is a ritzy contemporary Germain property, the folks who put the boutique in boutique hotels. The rooms feature full amenities, Aveeda bath products, windows everywhere you look, and new linens as of fall 2007. This is the premier boutique property; you can buy the linens if you wish—you can even buy the bed. The décor employs a modern urban style, but the Dominion 1912 kept historic and charming early 20th-century features, like the doors to the safes when the edifice played home to the stock exchange. The space offers an inviting working lobby with grand fireplace, comfy sofas, and bookcases. The staff is wonderful, and there is coveted on-site Old Port parking. The hotel is just across the street from highly acclaimed Laurie Raphaël restaurant, and a dozen other restaurants are nearby. Rooms start at about $200.

Hôtel le Priori

418-692-3992, 1-800-351-3992
www.hotellepriori.com
15 Rue du Sault-au-Matelot, Québec, QC
   G1K 3Y7
Price: $$–$$$$

Le Priori offers urban boutique chic design in an Old Port building that dates to 1734. Some of the 21 rooms and 5 loft-style suites employ vivid color schemes like deep purple carpeting and mustard-colored chairs, while exposed brick walls meet stainless steel conical sinks. Design function meets form, too, with comfy mattresses, impeccable bed linens, and perfect pillows. There are lovely Thalassa eco spa soaps as well. And I dare you not to take a bath if your room comes with the inviting antique clawfoot tub. Very friendly and accommodating reception staff. Adjacent to highly recommended Restaurant Toast! The Musée de la Civilisation and coveted Old Port parking are nearby as well.

Hôtel le Saint-Paul

418-694-4414, 1-888-794-4414
www.lesaintpaul.qc.ca
229 Rue St-Paul, Québec, QC G1K 3W3
Price: $$–$$$

A very friendly staff runs Hôtel le Saint-Paul. The building's exterior—specifically its tin mansard roof—was refurbished in 2006. The rooms are basic but clean and comfortable. There is no view in back, and in the front, if you look past the gas station, there is a scenic view of the port and mountains to the east. The location is great, especially for those who arrive by train—the station is a three-minute walk. Also across the street is the Old Port Market, the perfect place for fresh Quebec produce and products. A convenient and affordable city parking lot is nearby as well (about $12 for the 24-hour period). Rue St-Paul boasts a dozen fun, affordable eateries and plenty of antiques shops. The hotel is an economical value, with high-season rates starting from about $115 to $200.

Le Port-Royal Hotel

418-692-2777
www.hotelportroyalsuites.com
144 Rue St-Pierre, Québec, QC G1K 8N8
Price: $$$

You are first met by a very friendly and well-dressed reception and concierge staff. The lobby is barely navigable it's so small, but the positive is accentuated with funky metallic wallpaper, two red velvet swivel chairs, and opulent lighting. The building dates to 1845 and was originally an Old Port warehouse—the reason for exposed ceiling pipes in some rooms. The 39 rooms/suites are quite ample in size, as the warehouse was originally converted into condo space

Hôtel Dominion 1912 offers Old Port class.

before opening as a hotel in 2005. Each room features a pull-out couch or a separate bedroom, living area, dinette, and kitchenette complete with service for four. Perfect for four folks or families (if two don't mind the pull-out sofa), or longer stays in town. Parking on-site, and full breakfast is offered at the adjacent Le 48 Restaurant.

Lower Town: St-Roch

Appartements Hôtel Bonséjours
418-681-4375, 1-866-892-8080
www.bonsejours.com
237 Rue St-Joseph Est, Québec, QC
    G1K 3A9
Price: $–$$$

This St-Roch lodging offers 14 suite-style rooms. The décor is nothing new, but per-

fect if you're in the market for affordable suites that come fully equipped with kitchen, dining nook, living area, and bathroom. Studio with kitchenette starts at $85 a night. Two-room suites range between $139 and $225.

Hotel Pur
418-647-2611
www.hotelpur.com
395 Rue de la Couronne, Québec, QC
    G1K 7X4
Price: $$–$$$

First the good news: The renovations are complete. What used to be a standard-looking Holiday Inn is now the oh-so-chic Hotel Pur. Now the better news: The 238 rooms, renovated in 2007, feature modern minimalist décor—quite funky. Now the best news: There are a dozen fantastic

Accommodations at Hôtel le Priori.

restaurants along up-and-coming Rue St-Joseph to feed your vacationing appetite—foodies to the front of the line. Now the not-so-best-part: Besides the restaurants and some boutiques, there are few attractions in the immediate area—you're not in Old Quebec or downtown—they're about a 15-minute walk uphill. But you're a very quick cab ride to the train station. Room rates from $150 to $190.

Royal William Hotel
418-521-4488, 1-888-541-0405
www.royalwilliam.com
360 Blvd. Charest Est, Québec, QC
    G1K 3H4
Price: $$–$$$

Don't be fooled by their Web site. Their photo of downtown is downtown St-Roch, which is a great neighborhood for foodies, but as previously mentioned, a 15-minute walk—*uphill*—to get into Old Quebec (there is a public elevator at the end of Rue de la Couronne nearby St-Roch Garden). That said, the 44 rooms feature more-than-average amenities for the property size: minibar, restaurant, bar, meeting rooms, and small fitness club. Rates from $149 to $189.

Ste-Foy Hotel Options
You're a bit out of the Old Quebec loop in Ste-Foy, but closer to the shopping malls—practically across the street—and the airport, which is a 10-minute drive. Here are some hotels options in the area. While the

Hôtel le Saint-Paul is steps from the train station.

addresses state Quebec as the city, the district is definitely suburban Ste-Foy. If you are planning a Ste-Foy visit, **Ristorante Michelangelo** is renowned for its Italian food. It's at 3111 Chemin St-Louis, 418-651-6262, www.lemichelangelo.com.

Hôtel Germain des Pres

418-658-1224, 1-800-463-5253
www.germaindespres.com
1200 Ave. Germain des Prés, Québec, QC G1V 3M7
Price: $$–$$$

A Germain boutique property with 126 modern rooms.

Hôtel Sépia

418-653-4941, 1-888-301-6837
www.hotelsepia.ca
3135 Chemin St-Louis, Québec, QC G1W 1R9
Price: $$–$$$

Hôtel Sépia offers 80 rooms with contemporary design and a free shuttle to Old Quebec during high season.

Hôtel Universel Québec

418-653-5250, 1-800-463-4495
www.hoteluniversel.qc.ca
2300 Chemin Ste-Foy, Québec, QC G1V 1S5
Price: $–$$

Hôtel Universel features an indoor saltwater swimming pool, a sauna, and 127 rooms.

Times Hotel & Suites

418-877-7788, 1-888-902-4444
www.timeshotel.ca
6515 Blvd. Wilfrid-Hamel, Québec, QC G2E 5W3
Price: $$–$$$$

There are 112 trendy modern rooms and an indoor pool at the Times Hotel.

Best of Quebec: Shopping Malls

The best malls are always in the suburbs, right? Quebec City is no exception. Ste-Foy offers three in a row.

Place Laurier
418-651-5000, 1-800-322-1828
2700 Blvd. Laurier, Québec, QC G1V 4J9
www.laurierquebec.com
There are 350 stores—it's considered the largest mall in eastern Canada. Stores include Sears, the Bay, Old Navy, Linen Chest, Tristan/America clothing, and HMV music.

Place de la Cité
418-657-7015
2600 Blvd. Laurier, Québec, QC G1V 4T3
www.placedelacite.com
Place de la Cité offers 150 smaller boutiques, including Roots Canadian-style clothing.

Place Ste-Foy
418-653-4184
www.placestefoy.shopping.ca
2452 Blvd. Laurier, Ste-Foy, QC G1V 2L1
The more upscale mall on the strip, with 130 stores including Tommy Hilfiger, Holt Renfrew, Buffalo, Simons, Gap, Guess, San Francisco, Nine West, Lacoste, Bombay, and Birks jewelers.

Les Bossus is a friendly French bistro in St-Roch.

9

QUEBEC CITY DINING— *MANGER*

There are some wonderfully inspiring places to eat in Quebec City, from corner cafés to bustling bistros to refined restaurants. Each eatery infuses its own unique culinary style. Here are some recommended places to enjoy Quebec City cuisine that I know and love best. Cafés, bakeries or patisseries, bread shops, ethnic food stores, quick bites, and gourmet shops will also be included.

Price Guide
(for a dinner entrée)

$1 to $15	$
$16 to $30	$$
$31 to $45	$$$
$46+	$$$$

Upper Town: Downtown / Outside the Wall / Grande Allée / Faubourg St-Jean

Blu Bar & Grill
418-522-6789
www.blubargrill.com
845 Rue St-Jean, Québec, QC G1R 1R3
What's nearby: Hilton Hotel, Nautilus Gym
Price: $$

It seems that where the nearby Grande Allée caters more to summertime tourists, Rue St-Jean adds more locals to the mix who live in the St-Jean Faubourg city district. One of the area's trendiest digs is Blu. The place looks great in off-white leather booths, dark wood, and blue mood lighting. The menu has a little something for everyone: burgers, pizza, pasta, mussels, and tasty appetizers. Open daily for lunch and dinner.

Chez Victor
418-529-7702
145 Rue St-Jean, Québec, QC G1R1N4
What's nearby: Delta Hotel, Colisée Bookstore
Price: $

Perhaps the best burger joint in town. Juicy creations served atop a hearty bun with your choice of cheese and condiments. Salads and sandwiches, too. A glass of wine with your burger? But of course! It's open daily for lunch and dinner and often very busy. The locals love this place.

Choco-musée Érico

418-524-2122
www.chocomusee.com
634 Rue St-Jean, Québec, QC G1R 1P8
What's nearby: Rue St-Jean boutiques and bars

Part chocolate museum, part chocolate factory—all good. Sample inventive flavors like the classic Dominicana white chocolate with vanilla, the liquor-infused Grand Duc with Grand Marnier, or the spicy *poivre rose* chocolate with pink peppercorn. You can stick around and watch them make the chocolate as well.

Commensal

418-647-3733
www.commensal.com
860 Rue St-Jean, Québec, QC G1R 1R3
What's nearby: Hilton Hotel, Rue St-Jean boutiques
Price: $

With six locations in Canada, Commensal has made a name for itself as the place for vegetarian buffet. Hot and cold dishes. Open daily for lunch and dinner.

Cosmos Café

418-640-0606
575 Grande Allée Est, Québec, QC G1R 2K4
What's nearby: the glitz of Grande Allée; Château Laurier Hotel
Price: $$

Colorful Cosmos Café is one popular Grande Allée spot. The space is tight—you could sample your neighbor's seafood ravioli for the asking—and it was offered. But the mood is right, with a lively young crowd who come to eat inexpensively and dress appropriately—shorts and sandals are the acceptable summer attire. Don't expect the fastest service when the place fills up—and it fills up fast—but do expect friendly service at any hour. Also visit the most beautiful bathrooms in town featuring slate walls,

no-touch waterfall-style faucets, and an aquarium with views to the dining area (that means guests can look in, right?). The food runs the gamut, like creamy lobster manicotti or Oriental-inspired pork with sautéed vegetables. All plates reasonably priced at less than $20. Quebec City's young and beautiful stick around when dinner is through to listen to live DJ music and have a drink at the bar.

Diana

418-524-5794
849 Rue St-Jean, Québec, QC G1R 1R2
What's nearby: Hilton Hotel
Price: $

The locals know about this place, and so should you. Diana's is a small resto on Rue St-Jean that's been open since 1945. It seems that every time you walk by, there is someone inside reading the newspaper and enjoying an authentic home-cooked Mediterranean meal. The food is consistently good and priced right, too—breakfast starts at about $6. Daily specials, salads, and hearty Mediterranean fare like souvlaki and brochettes.

Ginko

418-524-2373
www.ginko-japonais-cuisine.ca
560 Grande Allée Est, Québec, QC G1R 2K1
What's nearby: Plains of Abraham, Parliament, Château Laurier Hotel, Loews Concorde Hotel
Price: $$–$$$

Upscale Japanese cuisine on the popular Grande Allée. Ginko features soothing Japanese décor, complete with sushi bar, sake wine bar, and private grills where the chef cooks your meal right at your table. Inventive tempuras and tartares, sushi and stir-fry, and sizzling grilled steaks, chicken, and seafood.

Il Teatro

418-694-9996
www.lecapitole.com
972 Rue St-Jean, Québec, QC G1R 1R5
What's nearby: Capitole Theatre and Hotel,
     Place d'Youville, the St-Jean Gate
Price: $$

Tasty Italian fare at some of the best prices
in town—especially for lunch. Located in
the heart of it all just before the walled city,
Il Teatro is immensely popular with locals
for lunch and locals and tourists for dinner.
The almost two dozen pasta specialties
include linguini pastorella with goat
cheese, pancetta, and rosé sauce with oys-
ter mushrooms; and duck ravioli with but-
ter and Parmesan. Open daily for breakfast,
lunch, and dinner.

J. A. Moison

418-522-0685
www.jamoisan.com
699 Rue St-Jean, Québec, QC G1R 1P7
What's nearby: Delta Hotel

This working grocery store dates to 1871. It's
a feast for the eyes, complete with heavy
wooden and glass display counters and
shelves stocked to the ceiling—you'll feel
transported back in time a century or so. It's
also a feast for the palate. Epicurean special-
ties include candy, spices, groceries, cheese,
takeout sandwiches, sit-down coffee, and a
generous selection of Quebec microbrews.
Fun for a foodie to browse and buy.

L'Astral

418-647-2222
www.lastral.com
1225 Place Montcalm, Québec, QC G1R 4W6
What's nearby: Inside the Concorde Hotel;
     Plains of Abraham, Grande Allée
Price: $$$–$$$$

Famous for quality French fare, seafood,
and steaks. I haven't made it to L'Astral yet,
but I do know it's a pricey affair—a $25 to
$40 table d'hôte, a $28 Sunday brunch, a
$45 evening buffet, and nightly specialties
in the $40 to $50 range. Your most eco-

The J. A. Moison grocery store in St-Jean dates to 1871.

nomical best bet is the early bird dinner for about $21, served from 4:15 to 6:15 PM, or late-night dessert and coffee. So why so pricey? At 540 feet in the air, would you look at that view! L'Astral hugs the stratosphere with a full panorama of Quebec City and the stars beyond. It's the best view in town. The restaurant makes a complete rotation every hour and a half.

Le 47ième Parallèle

418-692-4747
www.le47.com
333 Rue St-Amable, Québec, QC G1R 5G2
What's nearby: Grand Théâtre
Price: $$–$$$

Inventive world cuisine that highlights a different culinary destination every month. The tasting menu comes in at about $50 and embarks you upon a gastronomic journey to the likes of California, Portugal, India, and Australia and New Zealand. The dishes are always fancifully presented. A very well-stocked wine list and nice terrace, as well.

Le Hobbit

418-647-2677
700 Rue St-Jean, Québec, QC G1R 1P9
What's nearby: J. A. Moison artisanal grocery store
Price: $$

Another fun Rue St-Jean eatery that's been generously supported by loyal locals over the years. For breakfast and the morning paper, a lunchtime croque-monsieur open-face melted ham and cheese sandwich, or inexpensive dinner fare.

Le Pain Grüel

418-522-7246
375 Rue St-Jean, Québec, QC G1R 1N8
What's nearby: Museovelo bike store and rentals

This is one serious artisanal bakery for lovers of bread—it's basically all they sell.

There are 40 varieties in all, including fruit and nut breads, wheatless spelt flour bread, and the bestselling St-Séverin multigrain wheat. Storefront on one side, bakery visible from the sidewalk on the other. Perfect for a culinary souvenir or the makings of a picnic along the Plains of Abraham. Closed Sunday and Monday.

Le Sultan Café

418-525-9449
467 Rue St-Jean, Québec, QC G1R 1P3
What's nearby: Museovelo bike store and rentals
Price: $–$$

A small café that specializes in Tunisian fare. Specialties include merguez sausage, chich taouk chicken skewers, and gigot d'agneau, or roasted leg of lamb. Middle Eastern pastries as well. Popular for lunch and very affordable.

Le Veau d'Or

418-525-7371
801 Rue St-Jean, Québec, QC G1R 1R2
What's nearby: Hilton Hotel
Price: $$

The name means the golden calf. So naturally the specialty of the house is veal. Try the likes of veal marsala or veal cordon bleu for about $16. Fun outdoor terrace. Hearty pasta, steaks, and fish dishes.

Tutto Gelato

418-522-0896
716 Rue St-Jean, Québec, QC G1R 1P9
What's nearby: Museovelo bike store and rentals, Delta Hotel

For homemade Italian gelato frozen treats in a variety of flavors, from mascarpone to mango, cantaloupe to caramel. Soy-based ice creams, too, so even the lactose intolerant are invited.

Voo Doo Grill

418-647-2000
www.voodoogrill.com
575 Grande Allée Est, Québec, QC G1R 2K4
What's nearby: Château Laurier, Capitole
    Observatory
Price: $$–$$$

One of the current hot spots of the trendy
Grand Allée, Voo Doo Grill is at times an
energetic, busy, and boisterous restaurant
that's not the place for a quiet meal. The
international/fusion-inspired food
strengths include an Oriental trio sampler
appetizer and velvety mushroom and truffle
soup. Desserts rank high, as well. The thin
mandarin chocolate pie is a delight, and the
sorbet topped with maple swizzle candy
adds a sweet authentic crunch. The tam tam
performers and belly dancers offer a fun
interlude when present, but the techno
music may be a bit too loud for some.
Continue the evening's fun at the on-site
Maurice Nightclub.

SAQ

Liquor stores in Quebec are run by the
provincial Société des Alcools du Québec, or
SAQ. Liquor is more expensive in Quebec
than in the States, so you may want to wait
until you get to duty-free for a better alcoholic bargain. That said, the stores are uni-
formly attractive, and SAQ's Signature stores
are worth a stroll. In Montreal at Complexe
Les Ailes, 677 Rue Ste-Catherine Ouest,
514-282-9445, and in Quebec City at the
Château Frontenac, 1 Rue des Carrières, 418-
692-1182. The most popular time of year at an
SAQ? The arrival of Bordeaux season every
spring. It's akin to the coming of Christmas.

Upper Town: Old Quebec—Inside the Wall

Au Parmesan

418-692-0341
www.parmesan.restoquebec.com
38 Rue St-Louis, Québec, QC G1R 3Z1
What's nearby: Musée des Ursulines
Price: $$–$$$

An intimate, friendly, casual Italian bistro.
The basic dishes, like penne pasta with
comfort-style homemade marinara sauce
or a simple piece of grilled salmon, are
perfect for when you've been on the road
too long and crave a healthy taste of home.
For those a bit more adventurous, game
meats make a strong presence, with dishes
like deer tenderloin or pasta with wild boar
meat sauce. House specialties include
smoked salmon and Parma ham. Parmesan
boasts some 5,000 colorful liquor
decanters in a variety of fun shapes—everything from a baby bottle to Mount
Rushmore. Rumor has it they're all full. A
serenading accordionist tops off the
evening. The Winter Carnival's dogsled
races usually run right past the restaurant's
front door.

Aux Anciens Canadiens

418-692-1627
www.auxancienscanadiens.qc.ca
34 Rue St-Louis, Québec, QC G1R 4P3
What's nearby: Musée des Ursulines
Price: $$$–$$$$

For traditional but upscale Quebecois cui-
sine that's appropriately situated in the
oldest house in Quebec—it dates to 1675
(just look for the bright red roof). The more
inexpensive way to go is the very affordable
lunch menu for about $15, which includes a
glass of wine or beer, soup, entrée, and
dessert. The menu suggestions include
meat pies and *grand-mère*'s meatball
ragout—you just can't get any more
Quebecois than that.

Café de la Paix

418-692-1430

www.cafedelapaix.restoquebec.com

44 Rue des Jardins, Québec, QC G1R 4L7

What's nearby: Clarendon Hotel, Musée des Ursulines

Price: $$–$$$

An Old Quebec staple since the 1950s. There's nothing trendy about Café de la Paix's understated décor, but the meal can't be beat. Phenomenal food choices include seafood, French cuisine, Italian fare, and wild game in season. The colorful avocado and shrimp appetizer, simple greens and vinaigrette, creamy seafood bisque, velvety spinach man-icotti, and pork with country bacon make for a memorable meal. Affordable table d'hôte lunches, too. You'll be served by a bevy of seasoned professionals.

L'Entrecôte St-Jean

418-694-0234

www.entrecotesaintjean.com

1011 Rue St-Jean, Québec, QC G1R 1S4

What's nearby: the St-Jean Gate

Price: $$

Satisfying from start to finish, L'Entrecôte St-Jean is the epitome of steak and fries. The word *entrecôte* means sirloin—so that's the specialty of the house (they serve upward of 350 steaks a day during summer). The basic formula starts with a hearty delicious potage and a simple salad of fresh greens, walnuts, and vinaigrette. Next is the steak, which is topped by their delectable secret sauce with hints of honey, curry, and mustard. The steak is served with a mound of shoestring fries accompanied by homemade mayon-naise—and it's perfectly cooked. The dessert specialty of the house is profiterole—puff pastry, vanilla ice cream, and chocolate sauce. The price is a bargain at about $20 for lunch or $30 for dinner. The staff is young and very professional—ask for Claudio when you're in town—and the atmosphere, day or night, is light and lively.

Les Frères de la Côte Restaurant

418-692-5445

1190 Rue St-Jean, Québec, QC G1R 1S6

What's nearby: Musée de l'Amérique Française, City Hall

Price: $–$$

A busy little bistro that shares the lobby entrance to the Hôtel du Vieux Québec. The open-style kitchen cooks up everything from pizzas to steaks. You can easily sneak a peek inside—it's almost all glass-enclosed—or simply scan the lobby's fun Polaroid snapshot collection of previously satisfied customers. May be too much of a tight squeeze for some during peak hours.

Le Pain Béni

418-694-9485

24 Rue Ste-Anne, Québec, QC G1R 3X3

What's nearby: Château Frontenac, Québec Expérience, Rue du Trésor outdoor art gallery

Price: $$–$$$

It takes a while to get through this ambi-tious French market-cuisine menu. Summertime selections include unique originals like grilled scallops with refresh-ing watermelon purée or blackened tuna with luscious fried polenta. The sincerely friendly staff won't rush you through any-thing. On busy pedestrian-only Rue Ste-Anne in front of the Château Frontenac. There's a small outdoor terrace and a color-fully modern-lit interior with cozy court-yard as well.

Le Patriarche

418-692-5488

www.lepatriarche.com

17 Rue St-Stanislas, Québec, QC G1R 4G7

What's nearby: St-Jean Gate, Rue St-Jean shopping

Price: $$–$$$

One of the most romantic spots in town. The table d'hôte dinner, while limited in selection, is a bargain at around $30. Selections include seafood risotto and grilled bison steak. The menu also includes pricier local game meats, steaks, and fish. The plates are beautifully presented and expertly prepared. It's quiet—though just off busy Rue St-Jean—and it's cozy, inside an old stone house, complete with fireplace, that dates to 1827. The service is professional and the staff is genuinely polite and attentive. The always impeccably dressed co-owner Guy Collins, who often works the front of the house dining area, is your most gracious host.

Paillard Café

418-692-1221
www.paillard.ca
1097 Rue St-Jean, Québec, QC G1R 1S3
What's nearby: Artillery Park National
   Historic Site of Canada
Price: $

Purely French in approach, this spacious, well-lit eatery features coffee, croissants, quick bites, sandwiches, fresh-baked bread, pastries, ice cream, fun communal seating, and most of all—lively atmosphere.

Portofino Bistro Italiano

418-692-8888
www.portofino.qc.ca
54 Rue Couillard, Québec, QC G1R3T3
What's nearby: Musée de l'Amérique
   Française, Hôtel du Vieux Québec
Price: $$–$$$

The best part about Portofino is that it's popular with the locals—that's always a good sign. And it seems co-owner James Monti knows and greets almost every one of them. The meal is hearty Italian fare made with fresh ingredients mostly imported from Italy. The thin-crust pizza—baked in a wood-fired brick oven—comes available in about two dozen varieties with your choice

Paillard Café is all about the atmosphere.

of white or wheat flour. The pizza *quattro stagioni* with ham, mushrooms, artichokes, and sun-dried tomatoes is a delectable hit. The pasta is homemade, the wine cellar impressive, and the staff gorgeous. In summer at night, Rue Couillard is closed to traffic and the party moves outdoors. Top your meal off with a Limoncello aperitif, and you're good to go.

Pub D'Orsay

418-694-1582
www.www.restaurantpubdorsay.com
65 Rue de Buade, Québec, QC G1R 4A2
What's nearby: Hôtel du Vieux Québec,
    Québec Expérience
Price: $–$$

A friendly bar/pub that offers menu basics like fajitas, burgers, and a very popular plate of barbecue ribs with fries and cole slaw. But Pub D'Orsay kicks it up a notch with affordable table d'hôte specialties that include a perfectly cooked chicken breast with blueberry honey for about $25. And how can you not like a place that has a full menu—for beer? They even have their own tasty D'Orsay brand house draft. Also features four televisions for the sports-fan fix and an outdoor summer terrace.

Le St. Amour

418-694-0667
www.saint-amour.com
48 Rue Ste-Ursule, Québec, QC G1R 4E2
What's nearby: Champlain Hotel
Price: $$$–$$$$

Ahhh, l'amour . . . love is in the air, and in their name, too. Le St. Amour is a Quebec dining institution. It's the place for a romantic dinner or a special occasion. The inventive French cuisine "inspiration" tasting menu will set you back at least $50, while the "discovery" menu tallies in at about $100. Flawless food presentation.

Tatum Café

418-692-3900
www.tatum.ca
1084 Rue St-Jean, Québec, QC G1R 1S4
What's nearby: Artillery Park National Historic Site of Canada

For serious coffee lovers. Features dozens of flavors from around the world. Teas, tisanes, hot chocolate, as well as a small breakfast and lunch menu.

Best Quick Bites: Poutine

Poutine is a real Quebecois original: fries, cheese curds (they have a squishy texture), and tangy brown gravy. Quebecers love it or hate it. Even McDonald's sells poutine in their Montreal and Quebec City restaurants. It's equal parts fast food and comfort food, and not for those counting calories. In Montreal try **La Banquise**, 976 Rue Rachel Est, 514-525-2415. In Quebec City at the **Chez Ashton** restaurant chain: in Old Quebec at 54 Côte du Palais, 418-692-3055, or 640 Grande Allée Est, 418-522-3449.

Lower Town: Old Port

Aviatic Club

418-522-3555
www.aviatic-club.com
450 Rue de la Gare-du-Palais, Québec, QC
    G1K 3X2
What's nearby: Train station, Hôtel le
    Saint-Paul
Price: $$–$$$

An inventive assortment that has something for everyone, from sushi and seafood starters, risotto with chicken, satisfying cuts of beef, and a flavorful variety of after-dinner cheese and salad selections like a grilled cheddar with caramelized onions or a warm goat cheese salad with caramelized pecans and pears. The décor features a soothing olive green interior complete with leaf-shaped ceiling fans and a stylish lighted wall behind the bar that colorfully changes from chic fuchsia to cool blue. Great for drinks, too. It's housed inside the train station.

Café Bistro du Cap

418-692-1326
67 Rue du Sault-au-Matelot, Québec, QC
  G1K 3Y9
What's nearby: Hôtel Dominion 1912, Old
  Port art galleries
Price: $–$$

A lovely little Old Port café that specializes in Breton-style stuffed crepes. Choose from about 16 varieties, including goat cheese, asparagus, and creamy béchamel sauce, or shrimp, curry, mushroom with béchamel as well. There's a small outdoor terrace along pedestrian-only (in summer) Sault-au-Matelot.

Café Riviera

418-694-4449
www.www.riviera-quebec.com
155 Rue Abraham-Martin, Québec, QC
  G1K 8N1
What's nearby: Train station, Old Port
  Market
Price: $–$$

Café Riviera is a seasonal spring and summer lunch, dinner, and weekend brunch spot that offers a basic hearty menu of omelets, burgers, salads, and mixed grill at prices that won't break the bank. A few seafood specialties, too, like lobster club sandwich or fish-and-chips. Café Riviera is owned by the affable Christian Bernier and Herminia De La Cruz, the same fine folks at the helm of Poisson d'Avril across the marina. And the view? One of the best in town. Quite popular with the local boaters, Café Riviera overlooks the Bassin Louise marina and showcases a Quebec City sky-

The Aviatic Restaurant bar inside the train station is an illuminating experience.

line that includes the train station (quite impressive), the Parliament Building, and Château Frontenac, among others. Wow!

Charbon Steakhouse
418-522-0133
www.charbonsteakhouse.com
450 de la Gare-du-Palais, Québec, QC G1K 3X2
What's nearby: It's inside the train station
Price: $$$

Charbon translates to coal. It was near this portion of the train station where coal was once loaded into steam engines way back when. Today the place still glows with bright red accent lighting, inviting deep-red upholstered booths, and an open grill concept for quality steaks, kebabs, ribs, and seafood.

Initiale
418-694-1818
www.restaurantinitiale.com

54 Rue St-Pierre, Québec, QC G1K 4A1
What's nearby: Hôtel St-Pierre, Old Port art galleries, Québec-Lévis ferry
Price: $$$–$$$$

I hate to admit it, but I haven't yet made it to Initiale. But I have to include it because it's always ranked as one of the best restaurants in town. I can tell you that you are in good hands. In the kitchen, chef Yvan Lebrun uses market cuisine and local products to create imaginative fine French fare that's expertly prepared. I have met restaurant partner Rolande Leclerc, who oversees the dining room and promises a flawless gastronomic experience.

Laurie Raphaël
418-692-4555
www.laurieraphael.com
117 Rue Dalhousie, Québec, QC G1K 8C8
What's nearby: Le Port-Royal Hotel, L'Inox Microbrewery, Musée de la Civilisation
Price: $$$–$$$$

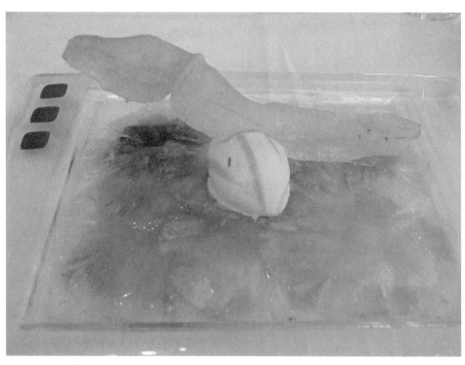

A Laurie Raphaël dessert tops off an exquisite meal.

Laurie Raphaël is the culinary brainchild of chef, cookbook author, and former television cooking show host Daniel Vézina. The menu features only simple explanations that suggest gastronomic hints of flavors to come. Rest assured you can put all of your palate's faith in Vézina's culinary creativity. It is indeed those little epicurean surprises that you remember most at a place like this—crunchy fried sliver of marine parsley, salmon with perfume of marjoram and coconut, vibrant sweet potato purée. For this particular entrée, the suggested Chandon sparkling rosé wine pairing was perfect. There's also a boutique full of gourmet gifts and an atelier/kitchen with classes taught by Vézina in the fall and winter months. The décor features a handful of coveted tables that offer window views of the kitchen as well as a stunning vibrant blue speckled bar top made of quartz from the nearby Thetford Mines. The service is ultra-professional and friendly. Try lunch if dinner is out of the budget. Most of all trust the chef's suggestions and treat yourself to a wonderful culinary experience.

Le 48 Saint-Paul
418-694-4448
www.le48st-paul.com
48 Rue St-Paul, Québec, QC G1K 3V7
What's nearby: Le Port-Royal Hotel, L'Inox Microbrewery, Espace 400e
Price: $–$$

A chic place in town to get a basic omelet for about $8. The décor is purely theatrical: Thick stone walls match comfy black upholstery, black tablecloths, and black-clad wait staff. Add to that vibrant red drapery and pillows, and Cirque du Soleil performances playing on two flat-screen TVs. The "48" stands not only for the address but also for the four dozen varieties of inexpensive delectable mouth-popping

Le Buffet de l'Antiquaire in the Old Port offers homespun Quebec-style cooking.

tapas that start at about $2 each. Burgers and sandwiches, too. If you get a bit chilly on their outdoor terrace, they'll loan you a blanket—in black, of course. Located in the same building as the Port-Royal Hotel.

Le Buffet de l'Antiquaire

418-692-2661
95 Rue St-Paul, Québec, QC G1K 3V8
What's nearby: Musée de la Civilisation, Le
    Port-Royal Hotel, Rue St-Paul antiquing
Price: $

A friendly family-run Quebec-style diner complete with counter service for six. Stick to the authentic Quebec specialties like pea soup, *cipaille*—a hearty stewlike concoction of meats (beef, pork, turkey) tenderly baked in a liberal deep-dish pie crust (vegetarians need not apply). Top it off with authentic sugar pie for dessert. Breakfast, sandwiches, and burgers, too, but tell the waitress your preferred cooking temperature or the burger may be too well done.

Le Café du Monde

418-692-4455
www.lecafedumonde.com
84 Rue Dalhousie, Québec, QC G1K 4B2
What's nearby: Québec-Lévis ferry, Louis
    Jolliet boat cruises, Espace 400e, Hôtel
    Dominion 1912
Price: $$

Café du Monde combines the right mix of everything you're looking for in a restaurant experience: quality French and international cuisine, friendly attentive service, lively bistro ambience, and great value for the meal—less than $20 for main entrées. The sweeping staircase builds suspense, and the open kitchen concept reinforces that you've picked a great place. The spacious dining area consists of high ceilings, black and white tile floor, and plenty of room between tables so you're not sitting atop your neighbor. There's an all-glass view of the St. Lawrence River adjacent to

where the ocean liners dock. The food is delicious: like a creamy thick bisque-style seafood gratin with mashed potatoes, as well as inventive: like fois gras crème brulée for desert. My preference was for the deep-fried ice cream.

L'Échaudé

418-692-1299
73 Rue du Sault-au-Matelot, Québec, QC
    G1K 3Y9
What's nearby: Rue St-Paul antiques shops,
    Museé de la Civilisation
Price: $$–$$$

L'Échaudé (say "le-show-day") is an Old Port staple for some two decades now. This small French bistro doesn't disappoint. It's a bit cozier than the area's counterparts, but there's a nice outdoor terrace along pedestrian-only Sault-au-Matelot during summertime. My experience was limited to some simple inventive appetizers (too many restaurants in town and so little time) like the beet salad with nuts and Parmesan cheese and the grilled shrimp with red pepper and artichoke bruschetta (about $20 for the two). Quite delicious—this means I'll soon be back for lunch or dinner. Although I could appetizer my way though this place and wouldn't be disappointed. Ambitious wine selection, also.

Le Cochon Dingue

418-692-2013
www.cochondingue.com
46 Blvd. Champlain, Québec, QC G1K 4H7
What's nearby: Centre d'Interpretation de
    Place Royale, Louis Jolliet boat cruises
Price: $

A cheerful and immensely popular bistro—especially if you have a budget or a family in mind. For breakfast, brunch, lunch, sandwiches, mixed grill, and dinner treats. Nice little extras, like the personal pitcher of real lemonade, homemade mayonnaise (the traditional condiment for fries here—not ketchup), a pot of pickles on every table, and the perfect cup of hot chocolate any time of year. Impressive service for such a young staff. Other locations in the city, too. Le Petite Cochon Dingue is just down the block at 6 Rue Cul de Sac.

Le Lapin Sauté

418-692-5325
www.lapinsaute.com
52 Rue du Petit-Champlain, Québec, QC
   G1K 4H4
What's nearby: Breakneck Stairs, Quebec
   Funicular
Price: $$–$$$

Lapin translates to rabbit and is the specialty of the house. The sampler picnic for two offers tasty fun and comes with pâté-like rabbit rillettes, grilled vegetables, focaccia bread, Migneron cheese, smoked salmon, and salad. The menu also offers French cuisine with a distinctive Quebecois flair. Try the generous pork chop stuffed with tangy goat cheese and locally produced maple syrup. For dessert, sample yummy apple cake drizzled with velvety caramel. Situated along touristy but charming Rue du Petit-Champlain. The outdoor terrace opens as soon as the weather warms up. Very popular for weekend breakfast. Young, friendly, attentive staff.

Le Marie Clarisse

418-692-0857
www.marieclarisse.qc.ca
12 Rue du Petit-Champlain, Québec, QC
   G1K 4H4
What's nearby: Breakneck Stairs
Price: $$$–$$$$

This Lower Town / Old Port bistro offers French fare and meat dishes but really specializes in high-end seafood. There are new menu items every night on their $38 four-course dinner table d'hôte—the affordable and satisfying way to go. Choose from succulent halibut and pistachios with orange and vanilla flavors or the almond and saffron scallops and shrimps. The building dates to the 1660s.

Le Petite Dana Thai

418-692-3848
311 Rue St-Paul, Québec, QC G1K 3W6
What's nearby: Old Port Market, the train
   station, Hôtel Le Saint-Paul
Price: $–$$
Le Petite Dana features Thai, Vietnamese, and Cambodian delicacies. Open for lunch and dinner. Located along a stretch of Rue St-Paul ethnic-style restaurants.

Les Artistes de la Table

418-694-1056
www.lesartistesdelatable.com
105 Rue St-Pierre, Québec, QC G1K 4A3
What's nearby: Hôtel le Priori, Old Port art
   galleries
Price: $$$$

Here's a fun activity for a group of 8 to 12 foodies—cooking school! The high-end modern kitchen is the stuff of glossy magazine pages and dream houses. The Old Port building dates to 1850 and was the former Quebec City head office of the Molson Bank. Your hosts are the very affable wife-and-husband team of Louise and Donald Martineau. Each participant has a job to do in the kitchen, but then the best part—everyone gets to eat. It's about $100 a person, and you can bring your own wine—but check what's on the menu first. Cooking classes and menu tastings last about four hours. On-site boutique as well.

Les Cafés du Soleil

418-692-1147
143 Rue St-Paul, Québec, QC G1K 3V8
What's nearby: Rue St-Paul antiques shops,
   Espace 400e
Price: $

A generous selection of coffees, teas, unique coffee machines and brewers, and affordable sandwiches for lunch.

Mistral Gagnant

418-692-4260

www.mistralgagnant.ca

160 Rue St-Paul, Québec, QC G1K 3W1

What's nearby: Rue St-Paul antiques shops, Espace 400e

Price: $$–$$$

Colorful blue and yellow Provençal décor highlights this quiet but genuinely cordial bistro. It's a place where they take their French food very seriously. Save room for sweetbreads with mushroom sauce, breast of duckling with peach sauce, hearty bouill-abaisse, or generous rack of lamb. Tables d'hôte range from $30 to $35. The thoughtful wine selection starts at $30 a bottle. Closed Sunday.

Piazza Mag

418-692-1910

www.pizzamag.com

363 Rue St-Paul, Québec, QC G1K 3X3

What's nearby: Old Port Market, the train station

Price: $–$$

It smells great and tastes even better. This superb pizza place offers 33 varieties, including the carbonara with crème fraiche, onions, Emmenthal cheese, and bacon, or the Stromboli with mushrooms, onions, and Calabrese sausage. The pies come available in a single-serving size to an extra-large pie enough to share. Taxes are included. Open daily.

Poisson d'Avril

418-692-1010

www.poissondavril.net

115 Quai St-André, Québec, QC G1K 3Y3

What's nearby: Train station, Old Port market, Espace 400e

Price: $$–$$$

Of just a few restaurants in town devoted to seafood, this is the more casual, complete with nautical décor and hearty fare. For starters, the deep-fried Caraquet oysters are a guilty pleasure. The main course surf and turf works well, too, with a surf choice of half lobster, shrimp, or prawns, added to a succulent cut of steak. The tasty all-you-can-eat mussels are served a dozen different ways, including lemon, pesto, or Provençal, with tomato sauce, white wine, and parsley—accompanied by a heaping helping of fries, of course. It's the same ownership of the seasonal Café Riviera across the marina. Incidentally, when you pull an April Fool's prank, in French that's a *poisson d'avril*.

Restaurant Allemand

418-691-2466

303 Rue St-Paul, Québec, QC G1K 3W6

What's nearby: Old Port Market, the train station, Hôtel Le Saint-Paul

Price: $–$$$

A small family-run restaurant that offers authentic German specialties like spaetzle, Wiener schnitzel, and knockwurst with sauerkraut. Wednesday through Friday for lunch. Tuesday through Sunday for dinner.

Restaurant L'Aubergine

428-692-5044

319 Rue St-Paul, Québec, QC G1K 3W8

What's nearby: Old Port Market, the train station, Hôtel Le Saint-Paul

Price: $–$$

Restaurant L'Aubergine (*aubergine* means eggplant) serves up tasty authentic Mediterranean cuisine in a simple atmosphere. Tasty takeout orders as well.

Toast!

418-692-1334

www.restauranttoast.com

17 Rue du Sault-au-Matelot, Québec, QC G1K 3Y7

What's nearby: Le Priori Hotel, Old Port art galleries

Price: $$$–$$$$

Toast! is one of Quebec City's top spots for lunch or dinner. For starters, the *mozzarella di buffala crostini* pops with wild mushroom flavor, while the "pizza" with crab and fennel combines soft textures served atop a crunchy, slightly salty black-eyed-pea cake—personally, one of my favorite appetizers in the entire city. The cassoulet proved hearty, but a glance at my neighbor's order of Asian scallops promises to be the next visit's treat. For dessert, the intoxicating *chocolat coeur coulant* cylinder cake oozes warm lemon cream when punctured, but requires a half-hour wait—so order at the beginning of your meal. The décor is vibrantly pleasant and stylish, combining stone walls and mod orange lighting. In summer the restaurant moves outdoors to a cozy courtyard. Toast! is run by chef Christian Lemelin and the very likable Stéphane D'Anjou, who's no stranger to the dining room. Sincere cheers to the staff of Toast!—one of the best in town.

Best Quick Bites: Smoked Meat

Smoked meat, or sandwich *à la viande fumée*, is a cured pastrami/brisketlike meat that's usually served up thick on thin slices of flavorful rye coated with tangy mustard. Don't ask for the lean—too dry. Instead, go for the fatty culinary high and book yourself an EKG upon your arrival home. In Montreal, **Schwartz's**, 3895 Blvd. St-Laurent, 514-842-4813, is the renowned house of smoked meat heaven. In Quebec City enjoy a smoked meat sandwich at **Pub Thomas Dunn**, 369 Rue St-Paul, 418-692-4693.

Lower Town: St-Roch

THE REBIRTH OF ST-ROCH—ALL IN GOOD TASTE

The rebirth of the St-Roch working-class neighborhood, located in the Lower Town

Toast! in the Old Port is an epicurean delight.

northwest of the Old Port near the train station and north of downtown and the St-Jean Faubourg city district, began during the mid-1990s. Improvements came in the form of the greening of small St-Roch Park, the addition of office space and new businesses, the elimination of an outdoor street mall, and the introduction of some very tasty places to eat—usually run by young, energetic restaurateurs who have carved out a unique gastronomic home for themselves. Most restaurants run along Rue St-Joseph and the short stretch of Avenue du Parvis, which is closed to traffic in the summertime. Save at least one lunch or dinner for the St-Roch neighborhood when you're visiting Quebec City—it really is worth the culinary trip. The following restaurant listings don't include a "what's nearby" section, as they are all quite close to one another. The entire Rue St-Joseph strip runs about three-quarters of a mile. Here are some suggestions. Bon appétit!

Bistro Les Bossus
418-522-5501
620 Rue St-Joseph Est, Québec, QC G1K 3B9
Price: $–$$

And then there's Maude. Les Bossus co-owner Maude Turgeon epitomizes the restaurateurs of the area: young, very hard-working, and sincerely likable. Her restaurant offers classic and inexpensive French bistro fare. The space opts for a roomy contemporary atmosphere, featuring black and white ceramic tile floor, large wood-framed mirrors, and the most inviting bar in the city: all wood and room for 12. The Toulouse sausage platter with sauerkraut, mashed potatoes, and spicy mustard dip is a delicious and satisfying dinner choice incredibly priced at about $12. The menu also features hearty pork chops, calf's liver, and green salad with duck confit selections. The crème caramel was smoothly spot on. Open

for breakfast, busy for lunch, and relaxed for dinner.

De Blanchet
418-525-9779
435 Rue St-Joseph Est, Québec, QC G1K 3B6

A neighborhood patisserie that offers baked snacks, fine spices, and select groceries.

Largo
418-529-3111
www.largorestoclub.com
643 Rue St-Joseph Est, Québec, QC G1K 3C1
Price: $$

Luscious Quebec digs. It's artsy—just look at the paintings on the walls. It's jazzy—there's often live music Thursday through Saturday. And it's comfy fun—just sink into that bright red banquette. The menu hovers between French and Mediterranean, combining culinary elements like pheasant with apricot sauce or salmon perfumed with saffron. The sweet and flaky house baklava is what's for dessert.

Le Café du Clocher Penché
418-640-0597
203 Rue St-Joseph Est, Québec, QC G1K 3B1
Price: $$

A classic French bistro with an open-style kitchen that uses local Quebec products. Specialties include blood sausage, salmon tartare, duck confit, and smooth café au lait. Popular weekend brunch.

Le Croquembouche
418-523-9009
235 Rue St-Joseph Est, Québec, QC G1K 3A9

This local patisserie features artisanal breads, chocolates, desserts, and colorful macaroons.

Piazzetta

418-523-7171

www.lapiazzetta.ca

357 Rue St-Joseph Est, Québec, QC G1K 3B3

Price: $–$$

Piazzetta is a provincial chain of two dozen Italian-style eateries. The St-Roch location employs a blue nautical theme that has nothing to do with pizza but somehow works for this Rue St-Joseph stretch of trendy bistros. Their signature thin-crust pizzas are a welcome diversion from typical Quebec pizza parlor takeout fare. Ample starters and salads, hearty focaccias and sandwiches, and Italian rolls like shrimp and curry powder or goat cheese and prosciutto. Also at 63 Rue St-Paul in the Old Port (with great outdoor seating).

Utopie

418-523-7878

www.restaurant-utopie.com

226 Rue St-Joseph Est, Québec, QC
    G1K 3A9

Price: $$$–$$$$

Utopie is an epicurean extravaganza presented by a very ambitious, talented, and dedicated team of young culinary engineers. The architecture is evident in the place—trunks of birch soar to the ceiling—and on the plate as dishes are presented with minimalist but appealing construction. The staff is professional and courteous, the sommeliers quite savvy. The inventive market cuisine menu costs about $70 for a seven-service meal without wine, while dinner tables d'hôte can start as low as about $29. The lunch table d'hôte at $19 is the absolute bargain way to enjoy the complete "U" experience.

Yuzu

418-521-7253

www.yuzu.ca

438 Rue du Parvis, Québec, QC G1K 6H8

Price: $$

Where St-Roch's young and beautiful go for Japanese fusion fare and fun. It's colorfully Zen in shades of orange and tan, while vibrant blocks of mood lighting leave the walls all aglow. The menu matches the youthful mood. Try the oyster shooters if you dare, like the Honey Moon with oysters, honey, vodka, and pistachio. Tempura and sushi, too—but be careful, those healthy delicious finger foods can add up.

Old Port Market

418-648-3640

160 Rue Dalhousie, Québec, QC G1K 7P7

What's nearby: Rue St-Paul antiques, the train station

Located east of the train station, near Bassin Louise in the Lower Town, the Old Port Market features dozens of vendors who sell local produce, flowers, pastries, and homemade packaged goods. The Quebec City skyline view is incredible, too. It's only a short walk from the train station and the perfect place to purchase healthy snacks for the train trip back to Montreal. Culinary souvenirs include fine gourmet spices at **La Route des Indes**, 418-933-2143; artisanal honey from **Miellerie Prince Leclerc**, 418-888-3323; tasty cheese snacks from **La Fromagerie**, 418-692-2517; and sweet dried cranberries flavored with hints of maple, apple, or orange—you can pop them like candy that's good for you—from **Saveurs Cultivées**, 418-802-9006.

Festival revelers dress up in their New France finest.

10

QUEBEC CITY CULTURE, SIGHTSEEING, AND SHOPPING—*S'AMUSER*

Get ready for some good old-time religion and the history lesson of your life. It's true that Quebec City's cultural scene boasts a decidedly historical and religious slant. But there's also fine art, festivals, and ferry rides as well. Listed are some of the city's best offerings when it comes to major attractions, museums, festivals, cruises, nightlife, and shopping. Activities are grouped according to neighborhood.

Price Guide
(for adult admission fees)
$ up to $10
$$$ 11 to $20
$$$$ 21+

Upper Town: Downtown / Outside the Wall / Grande Allée / Faubourg St-Jean

CULTURE / MAJOR ATTRACTIONS / ARCHITECTURE

Battlefields Park Discovery Pavilion of the Plains of Abraham
418-649-6157
www.ccbn-nbc.gc.ca
835 Ave. Wilfrid-Laurier, Québec, QC
What's nearby: Château Laurier, Grand Allée restaurants
Price: $

Battlefields Park, also known as the Plains of Abraham, celebrates its 100th birthday in 2008. It was created to mark Quebec City's 300th anniversary a century before. This long narrow stretch of green space overlooks the St. Lawrence River for about a mile and encompasses about 270 acres. The Plains of Abraham was witness to many military sieges, the most notable clash during 1759, when the British finally cracked the French stronghold in a battle that lasted less than half an hour. The Plains of Abraham was named after Martin Abraham, one of the first permanent settlers in the city. He didn't actually live there—he lived nearby, but used the land as a place to graze his cattle. The park is now home to a Discovery Pavilion, which offers Odyssey, an entertaining multimedia show that explores the park's history with a fun sense of humor. The pavilion also offers a museum space that explores the battles of Quebec and includes an impressive collection of re-created uniforms typical of those worn by British and French soldiers. Farther west in the park, you'll find Martello Tower 1, which offers three floors of exhibitions that tell about the daily life of a soldier, as well as the history of the towers. Still farther west, a 20-minute walk from the pavilion, you'll find the Edwin Bélanger Bandstand, which offers dozens of free summer concerts. At this point you're very close to the Musée National des Beaux-Arts du Québec. The park is Quebec City's four-season playground. In summer, take a stroll through the tranquil Joan of Arc Garden, which was created in 1938 and features about 150 varieties of flowers. During winter, many Quebecers take to snowshoes and cross-country skis along the park's many trails. In addition, the Plains of Abraham is home to the main site of the Quebec Winter Carnival. Abraham's Bus, which departs from the Discovery Pavilion, offers a guided bilingual half-hour tour of the park in season. Admission to the Plains of Abraham is free, but a day pass of about $10 offers admission to the bus tour, the Discovery Pavilion, and Martello Tower 1. From August 13–17, 2008, the site hosts the Plains of Abraham Epic, a large-scale reconstruction of 400 years of park history. About 500 costumed extras will be on hand. From August 6–9, 2009, the park commemorates the 250th anniversary of the Battle of the Plains of Abraham, which took place in 1759. More than 2,000 historical reenactors will be on hand, housed in actual camps, to bring the event to life.

Musée National des Beaux-Arts du Québec

418-643-2150
www.mnba.qc.ca
Battlefields Park, Ave. Wolfe-Montcalm, Québec, QC G1R 5H3
What's nearby: Located in the western portion of National Battlefields Park in the
    Montcalm district. A 20-minute walk from Parliament Hill along the Grande Allée, or
    take bus 11 to Grande Allée and Rue de Bourlemaque.
Price: $$ for visiting exhibitions, free for permanent collections

After a generous abundance of Old Quebec museums that cater to religion and history, here you'll find the provincial collection of fine art—which, of course, includes wonderful religious and historical artifacts. The museum includes two main historical buildings—alone worth the trip. The Gérard Morisset Pavilion, inaugurated as the sole museum space in 1931, offers grand neoclassical architectural features like ornate columns and high, sculpted ceilings. The Charles Baillairgé Pavilion is the former Quebec City prison, which opened in 1867 and was named after its architect. The prison, modeled after New York State's Auburn Penitentiary, contained 138 cells—97 for men and 41 for women, who were sometimes accompanied by their children. For four decades museum and prison stood almost side by side—about 300 feet away—until the prison became obsolete during the 1970s and was permanently shut down. The prison was transformed into museum space and was inaugurated in 1991. Two cell blocks were kept intact, and tours, led by a museum guide dressed as a prison guard, are available. The museum's permanent collection includes gallery space devoted to Quebec artists Jean-Paul Riopelle and Alfred Pellan. The gallery titled Tradition and Modernism in Quebec authentically re-creates the first European salons that displayed fine art. To commemorate the 400th anniversary of the city, the museum hosts the Louvre in Quebec City: Arts and Life, about 275 works of antiquity on loan from the Louvre Museum in Paris.

Observatoire de la Capitale—Capital Observatory
418-644 9841, 1-888-497-4322
www.observatoirecapitale.org
1037 Rue de la Chevrotière (the Marie Guyart Building), Québec, QC G1R 5E9
What's nearby: Parliament Hill, Grande Allée restaurants
Price: $

On a clear day you can see *pour toujours*—forever—or at least to Île d'Orléans, the sweep of the St. Lawrence River, and even the Appalachian Mountains along the Quebec-Maine border. The lobby entrance could use a tidy up (come on folks, you're the tallest point in town and you've got guests coming!), but once you're upstairs to the 31st floor, the panoramic view of Quebec City and its surroundings is unrivaled. Interpretive panels along the way point out neighborhood landmarks and buildings, and you can easily follow the line of the walled city and the star-shaped citadel. About $5 for admission, or use your museum card. Open daily June through October.

Parliament Building
418-643-7239
www.assnat.qc.ca
In the Parliament Hill neighborhood. Visitors' entrance at door No. 3 of the Parliament Building at the corner of the Grande Allée and Ave. Honoré-Mercier.

The Gérard Morisset Pavilion at Musée National des Beaux Arts du Québec.

Government is big business in Quebec City, the capital of the province. The center of the government is the Parliament Building, home to the 125 elected legislators of the National Assembly of Quebec. The building was constructed from 1877 to 1886 in the majestic Second Empire style. The façade is decorated with 22 bronze statues that commemorate important Quebec historical figures. It's quite impressive. Free guided tours and self-guided tours are available.

FESTIVALS / SPECIAL EVENTS / GUIDED TOURS

Edwin Bélanger Bandstand Outdoor Summer Concerts
418-648-4050
www.ccbn-nbc.gc.ca/_en/edwinbelanger
Where: Battlefields Park / The Plains of Abraham
Price: Free

The Plains of Abraham hosts three dozen free summer concerts every June, July, and August. The repertoire includes jazz, blues, world music, and local Quebec vocalists. Concerts are usually held Thursday through Sunday and start at 8 PM. The bandstand was named for Edwin Bélanger, a classical musician and conductor who co-founded the Cercle Philharmonique de Québec, was director of Orchestre Symphonique de Québec for 9 years, and was also the director of the Musique du Royal 22e Régiment for 24 years. The bandstand is accessed at Avenue Wolfe-Montcalm, opposite the Musée National des Beaux-Arts du Québec. Parking costs $5.

The Château Frontenac, the St. Lawrence River, and beyond, as viewed from the Observatoire de la Capitale

The façade of the Parliament Building.

The fountain in front of the Parliament Building.

Festival d'Été de Québec—Quebec City Summer Festival

418-523-4540, 1-888-992-5200

www.infofestival.com

Where: At various locations in the city

An annual bash since 1967 that offers music, arts, and fun in the summertime. The three main outdoors stages are at the Plains of Abraham, Parc de la Francophonie (known as Pigeonhole) near Parliament, and Place d'Youville just inside the wall. Indoor venues include the Grand Théâtre de Québec, the Imperial Theatre in St-Roch, and area bars and clubs. The event also features Arts de la Rue, where Rue St-Jean in Old Quebec is transformed into an outdoor art gallery. The 41st edition of the festival takes place July 3–13, 2008; the 42nd edition runs July 9–19, 2009.

Plein Art

418-694-0260

www.salonpleinart.com

Where: At Parc de la Francophonie (Pigeonhole) between Rue St-Amable and Grande Allée

Price: Free admission

Plein Art is a gathering of 100 artists who sell their one-of-a kind crafts, including jewelry, glass, ceramics, wood, and more. It's been presented since 1980 and is currently held the first two weeks of August every year. The year-round boutique Métiers d'Arts de Québec is in Place Royale.

THEATER/NIGHTLIFE/ENTERTAINMENT

Le Grand Théâtre de Québec

418-643-8131 (box office)

www.grandtheatre.qc.ca

269 Blvd. René-Lévesque Est, Québec, QC G1R 2B3

What's nearby: Delta Hotel, Parliament Hill

Price: Concert ticket prices vary

Le Grand Théâtre de Québec has been the city's repository for fine performance art since 1971. The repertoire includes invited dance companies, musical acts, and the resident Orchestre Symphonique de Québec and L'Opera de Québec. The theater offers two venues, the 1,875-seat Salle Louis Fréchette, named after the 19th-century Quebec writer, and the intimate 506-seat Salle Octave Crémazie, named for the Quebec poet.

ST-JEAN-BAPTISTE FAUBOURG BARS

Start near Boulevard Honoré-Mercier and walk west along Rue St-Jean (away from the wall and Old Quebec).

La Ninkasi du Faubourg

418-529-8538

www.ninkasi.ca

811 Rue St-Jean, Québec, QC G1R 1R2

For *biere et culture* (beer and culture)—it says so right on the sign. Young crowd, cold beer, live music by local bands. You can take a peek from the sidewalk. Open daily from noon to 3 AM.

Fou Bar
418-522-1987
525 Rue St-Jean, Québec, QC G1R 1P5
A popular St-Jean watering hole since 1983. Open daily from 3 PM to 3 AM.

Le Sacrilège
418-649-1985
447 Rue St-Jean, Québec, QC G1R 1P3

I love the fact that Le Sacrilège is just across the street from a church. A fun local bar since 1993 for draft beer, live music, and a nice outdoor terrace in back.

Nelligan's Pub Irlandais—Nelligan's Irish Pub
418-522-6504
275 Rue St-Jean, Québec, QC G1R 1N8
You'll hear Nelligan's before you see it—even though it's on the second floor.

Le Sacrilège Bar in the St-Jean neighborhood.

A stroll on Rue St-Jean inside the walled city.

SHOPPING: RUE ST-JEAN STROLL
Start near Boulevard Honoré-Mercier and walk west.

Boutique Hommes Mecs
418-525-5600
752 Rue St-Jean, Québec, QC G1R 1P9
Mecs offers quality men's wear.

Le Comptoir du Livre
418-524-5910
726 Rue St-Jean, Québec, QC G1R1P9
Used books mostly in French, but a generous collection of used vinyl, CDs, and DVDs as well.

Museovelo
418-523-9194
463 Rue St-Jean, Québec, QC G1R 1P3

The very affable Pierre Bernier has been a Rue St-Jean fixture for more than two decades. He knows everyone in the neighborhood, and they all know him. His store, Museovelo, is part bike shop and part museum. It's where Bernier custom-builds bikes from any spare part he can find and repairs them as well. The shop offers bike rentals for about $25 a day, and Bernier will even help you select an itinerary. During the slower winter season, the shop remains open to view the collection of bicycle memorabilia, which includes an authentic penny farthing.

L'Espace Contemporain
418-648-2002
www.lespacecontemporain.com
313 Rue St-Jean, Québec, QC G1R 1N8

An art gallery that features original works by local up-and-coming artists. Closed Monday and Tuesday.

Atelier de Luthier Moustache
418-529-6340
www.lutheriemoustache.com
249 Rue St-Jean, Québec, QC G1R 1N8

Moustache is an atelier/workshop run by Philippe Lemieux, Caroline Champagne, and Sebastien Dupuis—three young talented artisans who handcraft, sell, and repair fine stringed instruments, specializing in guitars, mandolins, and banjos. Closed Sunday.

Colisée du Livre
418-647-2594
175 Rue St-Jean, Québec, QC G1R 1N4

For used books, mostly in French, but check out the small English book section, actually two wooden bins, on the second floor. You never know what you'll find. Used CDs as well. There are two Colisée du Livres in Montreal as well.

Quebec City Museum Card

www.museocapitale.qc.ca

The museum card offers access to 20 local museums and attractions. The card costs $40, taxes included. It's valid for three consecutive days, and you're allowed one visit for each museum or attraction. The card includes a two-day unlimited pass for the city bus as well. The museum card is available at participating members and all Quebec City Tourism Information Bureaus, including at 835 Ave. Wilfrid-Laurier, 418-641-6290. The card is a very good deal.

Participating museums and attractions include:

Place Royale Interpretation Centre

Château Frontenac Guided Tours

Fortifications of Quebec National Historic Site

Artillery Park Heritage Site

Battlefields Park Discovery Pavilion

Musée Bon Pasteur

Musée de l'Amérique Française

Musée de la Civilisation

Musée des Ursulines de Québec
Royal 22nd Regiment Museum
Musée National des Beaux-Arts du Québec
Capitale Observatory
Martello Tower I
Québec-Lévis ferry

Upper Town: Old Quebec—Inside the Wall

CULTURE / MAJOR ATTRACTIONS / ARCHITECTURE

Artillery Park National Historic Site of Canada

418-648-4205, 1-888-773-8888
www.pc.gc.ca/lhn-nhs/qc/artiller
2 Rue d'Auteuil, Québec, QC G1K 7A1
What's nearby: Doll Economuseum, Fortifications of Quebec, St-Jean Gate
Price: $

Ready, aim, fire! Artillery Park is actually three visits in one: the Arsenal Foundry, the Dauphine Redoubt, and the Officers' Quarters. The Arsenal Foundry made ammunition for the Canadian Army from 1879 until the factory closed in 1964. It's now an interpretation center, and the centerpiece is an authentic model of Quebec City, used to plan defense against attacks, made by military engineers in 1808. Sensitive to light and heat, the large-scale model is displayed behind glass. The nearby Dauphine Redoubt is the striking four-story white structure. Built in 1712, it housed vaults, barracks, and an English officers' mess hall. And inside the Officers' Quarters, costumed guides offer impromptu tours of the house, with stops in the living room, bedroom, children's schoolroom, and kitchen, where the smell of fresh-baked bread often fills the air. Samples are free.

Basilica-Cathedral of Notre-Dame de Québec

418-692-2533 (rectory)
www.patrimoine-religieux.com
16 Rue de Buade, Québec, QC G1R 4Ai
What's nearby: Hôtel de Ville (City Hall), Musée de l'Amérique Française

Notre-Dame de Québec Cathedral has stood the test of time—at least in spirit. The building site dates to 1647, but the cathedral burned down on three occasions, most recently in 1922, when fire left only the foundation and walls standing. Each time the structure was rebuilt according to the original architectural plans. The current cathedral, completed in 1925, features a breathtakingly ornate, tentacled, golden-colored baldachin canopy above the altar.

Doll Economuseum

418-692-1516
www.damesdesoie.com
2 Rue d'Auteuil, Québec, QC G1K 7A1
What's nearby: Inside Artillery Park
Price: $

The Dauphine Redoubt at the Artillery Park National Historic Site.

Come here, my little *poupée*. Les Dames de Soie Economuseum combines a workshop and museum devoted to doll making (*poupée* means doll in French). Visitors can watch artisans at work creating dolls on site. A boutique features souvenir porcelain dolls dressed in traditional New France costumes of Quebec.

Fortifications of Quebec National Historic Site of Canada
418-648-7016
www.pc.gc.ca/fortifications
100 Rue St. Louis, Québec, QC G1K 7A1
What's nearby: the St-Louis Gate
Price: $ for guided tour

Quebec City stands as the only remaining fortified city in North America north of Mexico, and they've got 2.9 miles of walls to prove it. The Interpretation Center offers a thorough history of the city's unique defense system—the wall is in fact the third and last defense fortification, which was built by the French between 1745 and 1759. The recommended guided tour retraces city history, gets you out in the action, and offers great views of the city along the way. The tour meets near the Quebec Funicular and is led by the very likable Parks Canada tour guide Heather Moores, who comes supplied with maps showing the outlines of all three defense walls and adds important bits of historical trivia throughout the expedition. Out first stop was the nearby Dufferin Terrace, the wooden promenade that overlooks the St. Lawrence River. The terrace was named for Lord Dufferin, who was instrumental in preserving the fortified wall when others wanted to tear it down. In front of the Governor's Garden, the Dufferin Terrace features a row of cannons, mostly manufactured in Britain—you can tell by the lettering on the side of the barrel. But two of the cannons are Russian-made models, probably a souvenir from the Crimean War. The cannons had a range of about 1 kilometer, easily covering any potential threat well across the St. Lawrence River in Lévis a half kilometer away on the south shore. Moores says upward of 1,000 cannons remain throughout the city. The tour continued to the citadel—la Citadelle—with an impressive climb up the Cap Diamant hill, much like an enemy soldier might have attempted centuries ago. And boy, are you in for a surprise at the top of that hill: nowhere to run, nowhere to hide—simple but ingenious military technology of the day. Allow 90 minutes for the guided tour. Self-guided tours also available with information panels located all along the wall.

La Citadelle National Historic Site / Royal 22nd Regiment Museum
418-694-2815
www.lacitadelle.qc.ca
Côte de la Citadelle, Québec, QC G1R 4V7
What's nearby: Dufferin Terrace to the east, Battlefields Park to the west
Price: $

The Citadelle is the star-shaped fortress that's been dubbed the Gibraltar of America. It was built between 1820 and 1850 as part of the British fortifications of North America. While you can walk along the exterior of the Citadelle, accessible from the western end of Dufferin Terrace and Avenue St-Denis, visits inside are available only by guided tour, as the site remains an active military garrison, home to the Royal 22nd Regiment. The guided tour includes access to the Royal 22nd Regiment Museum, which houses uniforms, weapons, textiles, decorative arts, prints, maps, and miniature tin soldiers. During the summer, the regiment performs traditional changing of the guard ceremonies daily, accompanied by Batisse, the company's resident mascot goat. The Citadelle is also home to the official residence of the Governor General of Canada (it's actually the second official residence—the first is in Ottawa). Seasonal free guided tours of the Governor General's residence are available without paying the Citadelle admission fee. Call 1-866-936-4422 or visit www.gg.ca.

Musée Bon Pasteur

418-694-0243
14 Rue Couillard, Québec, QC G1R 3S9
What's nearby: Rue des Remparts (the street lined with authentic cannons)
Price: $

This small museum tells about the congregation of the Sisters of Bon Pasteur who oversaw a refuge for troubled women and abandoned children during the 19th and 20th centuries. Items include period furniture and artworks.

Musée de L'Amérique Française

418-692-2843
www.mcq.org
2 Côte de la Fabrique, Québec, QC G1R 4R7
What's nearby: Basilica-Cathedral of Notre-Dame de Québec
Price: $

Entrance to La Citadelle is by guided tour only—it's still a working army garrison.

Musée de l'Amérique Française has the distinction of being the oldest museum in Canada. It's located on the property of the Quebec Seminary, which was founded by François de Laval, first bishop of New France, in 1663 and is still a working school today. The permanent exhibit, the Settlement of French America, thoroughly explores the French language presence not only in Quebec and Montreal, but its influence in western Canada, Acadia, New England, and Louisiana. The exhibition also lets you research the history of your French family name. Other exhibit highlights include a variety of musicological artifacts collected by the seminary since its inception. Fine art, religious artifacts, and scientific instruments are all on display, as is Nen-Oun-Ef, a mummy and sarcophagus that dates to 1550–1350 B.C. that was purchased in Cairo in 1868 by a seminary priest. It is considered the first mummy to be brought to North America.

Musée des Augustines du Monastère de l'Hôtel-Dieu de Québec
418-692-2492
32 Rue Charlevoix, Québec, QC, G1R 5C4
What's nearby: Hôtel Manoir Victoria; Hôtel-Dieu de Québec Hospital
Price: $

The museum tells the story of the Augustine congregation from France, the nuns who founded the first hospital in North America in 1639. Objects include furniture, paintings, and a variety of medical instruments that date to the 17th century.

Musée des Ursulines de Québec
418-694-0694
www.museocapitale.qc.ca
12 Rue Donnaconna, Québec, QC G1R 3Y7
What's nearby: Café de la Paix
Price: $

The museum offers the history of the congregation of the Ursulines, which was founded by St. Angela of Merici of Brescia, Italy, in 1535. The congregation made its way to Quebec via France a century later, in 1639. The nuns originally followed a cloistered life and devoted their time to running a school for girls. The museum artifacts include period Quebec furnishings that date to the 1700s and ornate embroidery created by the nuns. The museum is housed in classrooms once used by Irish immigrant girls between the mid-1800s to 1955. The floors creak with history, and tall folks like me need to duck through certain doorways.

Musée du Fort
418-692-2175
www.museedufort.com
10 Rue Ste-Anne, Québec, QC G1R 4.7S
What's nearby: Château Frontenac, Quebec Funicular
Price: $

In this corner, the English. In that corner, the French. And in another corner, the Americans. Musée du Fort tells the account of six 18th-century military battles of Quebec City in a very low-tech but nostalgic manner—a half-hour diorama complete with model ships, miniature toy soldiers, and a 400-square-foot model of the city. The touristy admission price is best absorbed when using the museum card.

Old Quebec Funicular

418-692-4415
www.funiculaire-quebec.com
16 Rue du Petit-Champlain, Québec, QC G1K 4H4
What's nearby: Château Frontenac, Place Royale
Price: $

What's the easiest way to get from Lower Town to Upper Town? Hands down, take the funicular. Accessible from the Dufferin Terrace at the top and from Rue du Petit-Champlain at the bottom, the Funicular has been helping Quebecers and tourists up and down the 200-plus-foot cliff since 1879. Hey, it's either the funicular or the Breakneck Stairs, which you may want to avoid during winter. It's about $2 for the two-minute ride, so be quick with the camera. The Lower Town entrance is the house of Louis Jolliet, whose claim to fame was exploring and mapping the Mississippi River. Open every day.

Palais Montcalm

418-641-6040
www.palaismontcalm.ca
995 Place d'Youville, Québec, QC G1R 3P1
What's nearby: Place d'Youville

Palais Montcalm offers a contemporary repertoire of French performers and musical ensembles in a modern theater of 1,500 seats.

Architectural details at the Quebec Seminary/Musée de l'Amérique Française.

Basilica-Cathedral of Notre-Dame de Québec is worth a visit.

Québec Expérience

418-694-4000
www.quebecexperience.com
8 Rue du Trésor, Quebec City, Quebec G1R 4L9
What's nearby: Open-air art gallery along Rue du Trésor
Price: $

It's a 40-minute multimedia show about Quebec full of special effects and virtual images—any excuse to wear 3D glasses!

FESTIVALS / SPECIAL EVENTS / GUIDED TOURS

Dupont Tours

418-649-9226, 1-888-558-7668
www.tourdupont.com
Price: $$$

Dupont offers guided sightseeing tours of the city by bus. Options include a city tour that highlights all of Quebec's major attractions, and a country tour with stops at Montmorency Falls, Île d'Orléans, and Ste-Anne-de-Beaupré Basilica.

Les Tours du Vieux-Québec

418-664-0460, 1-800-267-8687
www.toursvieuxquebec.com
Price: $$$

The Quebec funicular is the easiest way to get from Lower Town to Upper Town.

Tours du Vieux-Québec offers the usual city tours, as well as Quebec City by Land and by Sea, a combination city trip by bus with a boat excursion on the St. Lawrence aboard the *Louis Jolliet*. All-day whale-watching and fjord cruises also available.

Quebec City Tours
418-836-8687, 1-800-672-5232
www.quebeccitytours.com
Another well-known tour operator that offers city and country excursions.

Calèche Horse-Drawn Carriage Rides
Price: $$$

Horse-drawn carriage rides are readily available in Old Quebec—it's almost like hailing a cab. The carriages can always be found in front of the Château Frontenac.

Les Calèches de la Nouvelle-France
418-692-0068
www.calechesquebec.com
1440 Chemin Jean-Gauvin, Québec, QC G3K 1X2

Les Calèches de la Nouvelle-France operates 12 carriages in the city. They are also available for weddings.

Palais Montcalm offers music and theater performances.

Hail a cab or a calèche on Rue des Jardins.

Calèches du Vieux-Québec

418 683-9222
www.calecheduvieuxquebec.com
2575 Rue Lahaye, Québec, QC G1P 2N8

Calèches du Vieux-Québec offers 45-minute tours throughout the city, highlighting Château Frontenac, Parliament Hill, and the Plains of Abraham. Tours cost $80 for a maximum of four people, taxes included.

Château Frontenac Guided Tour

418-691-2166
www.fairmont.com/frontenac
1 Rue des Carrières, Québec, QC G1R 4P5
What's nearby: Musée du Fort, Pub D'Orsay, Dufferin Terrace
Price: $

If you don't have the pocket to stay at the Château Frontenac, you can still take a tour of the facility. Led by a costumed guide, the hour-long tour offers an intriguing insight into the workings of one of the world's most beautiful hotels and Quebec's most recognizable landmark. Entertaining topics include history (the Château opened its doors December 20, 1893, with 170 rooms, 93 with private bath, which was a pretty big deal for the day); famous guests (Queen Elizabeth, Grace Kelly, and Charles Lindbergh, among others); and fun trivia (the corridor carpeting, all 8.4 miles of it, is changed every 15 years). Bring your camera, as

A view from inside the Château Frontenac.

The archaeological dig at Dufferin Terrace has uncovered artifacts that date to the 1620s.

the view is magnificent inside and out. Daily May through mid-October; weekends during the rest of the year. Reservations required.

Dufferin Terrace / St-Louis Forts and Châteaux National Historic Site of Canada
418-648-7016
www.pc.gc.ca/lhn-nhs/qc/saintlouisforts
2 Rue d'Auteuil, Québec, QC G1K 7A1 (mailing address)

The Dufferin Terrace is the landmark promenade at the foot of the Château Frontenac that overlooks the St. Lawrence River. It has been a people-watching place since 1879. The terrace was named for Lord Dufferin, who advocated the preservation of Quebec City's walled fortifications. In recent years the terrace has become an active archaeological site, as workers unearth the remnants of Fort St-Louis, the home where Samuel de Champlain lived until his death in 1635. Artifacts found on the dig site date to the 1620s. In August 2007 archaeologists discovered the actual site of Champlain's living quarters. The archaeological digs, supervised by Parks Canada, will continue to 2008.

Festival International de Musiques Militaires de Québec—Quebec City International Festival of Military Bands
418-694-5757, 1-888-693-5757
www.fimmq.com
Where: Locations throughout the city
Price: A mix of free and paid events

Tattoo you. The Quebec City International Festival of Military Bands is a colorful and historical celebration saluting the art of the military band and its music. The festival plays hosts to dozens of ensembles from Quebec and from elsewhere in Canada and around the world in a five-day fete every August. The free parade usually takes place the Saturday afternoon of the event and runs along the Grande Allée, past the St-Louis Gate, and along Rue St-Louis to City Hall. The Quebec City Military Tattoo features more than 1,800 musicians at a ticketed event at the Colisée Pepsi. Upcoming Festival dates are August 14–24, 2008, and August 26–30, 2009.

WALKING TOURS

Les Tours Voir Québec
418-694-2001
www.toursvoirquebec.com
12 Rue Ste-Anne, Québec, QC G1R 3X2
Price: $$
A two-hour guided walking tour of Quebec City by licensed guides.

Witchcraft on Trial
418-692-9770
www.ghosttoursofquebec.com
Price: $$

An hour-long re-created Quebec witch trial, circa 1661, complete with costumed actors. Court is held at 71 Rue Ste-Ursule in Old Quebec near Rue St-Louis. The company also hosts **Ghost Tours of Quebec**, a walking tour in search of some Old Port ghosts. Departs from 98 Rue du Petit-Champlain.

THEATER/NIGHTLIFE/ENTERTAINMENT

Capitole Theatre
418-694-4444, 1-800-261-9903
www.lecapitole.com
972 Rue St-Jean, Québec, QC G1R 1R5
What's nearby: Place d'Youville, St-Jean Gate
Price: Depends on performance

The Capitole, part dinner-theater, concert hall, and cabaret, offers a variety of musical performances and shows. The most popular production is Elvis Story, a long-running tribute to Elvis Presley. The show returns to the Capitole every summer. The complex features the recommended Il Teatro restaurant.

St-Alexandre Pub
418-694-0015
www.pubstalexandre.com
1087 Rue St-Jean, Québec, QC G1R 1S3

A Quebec City park.

A fun and friendly Rue St-Jean pub that features live music, full menu for burgers, ribs, and nachos, and a very relaxed atmosphere.

SHOPPING: OLD QUEBEC
From the St-Jean Gate walk east along Rue St-Jean and turn right on Côte de la Fabrique.

Logo Sport
418-692-1351
1047 Rue St-Jean, Québec, QC G1R 1R9

Logo Sport offers a full line of professional team sportswear. And even though they haven't been an NHL franchise since moving to Colorado in 1995, the Quebec Nordiques are still a favorite, with their T-shirts, jerseys, and caps among the best sellers in the store.

Archambault
418-694-2088
www.archambault.ca
1095 Rue St-Jean, Québec, QC G1R 1S3
The place for CDs, books, and a small selection of instruments.

Librarie Pantoute
418-694-9748

Old Quebec shopping along Côte de la Fabrique has something for everyone, including the venerable Simons department store.

www.librairiepantoute.com
1100 Rue St-Jean, Québec, QC G1R 1S5

A store for new books, mostly in French, with English bestsellers as well. Also in St-Roch
at 286 Rue St-Joseph Est, 418-692-1175.

Simons
418-692-3630
www.simons.ca
20 Côte de la Fabrique, Québec, QC, G1R 3V

The Simons department store chain dates to 1840. This location, which doubles as company headquarters, dates to 1870. There are currently seven Simons stores in the province
that offer contemporary men's and women's fashions.

Harricana par Mariouche
418-204-5340
www.harricana.qc.ca
44 Côte de la Fabrique, Québec, QC G1R 3V7

It is a hot August day, and the handwritten sign on the window of Harricana states: *air cli-
matisée*—air conditioned. But why would you want to try on winter fur in the middle of
summer? Because it's Harricana high-end clothing made entirely with recycled fur.
Harricana is the brainchild of designer Mariouche Gagné, whose recycled fur collection

Rue du Trésor offers unique souvenirs.

includes hats, scarves, boots, bags, jackets, and coats. The line is now available at retailers in 16 countries around the world. Also in Montreal at 3000 St-Antoine Ouest, 514-287-6517.

Lower Town / Old Port

CULTURE / MAJOR ATTRACTIONS / ARCHITECTURE

Musée de la Civilisation
418-643-2158, 1-866-710-8031
www.mcq.org
85 Rue Dalhousie, Québec, QC G1K 7A6
What's nearby: Café du Monde, Le Priori Hotel, *Louis Jolliet* Cruises
Price: $

The museum space of the human race. Musée de la Civilisation explores a variety of world cultures through a number of diverse exhibits. There's a little something for everyone. Permanent exhibitions include People of Quebec . . . Then and Now, a fascinating and thorough history from New France to the present. Artifacts on display run the gamut from coins that date to 1643 to treasures from Expo 67 and the 1976 Montreal Summer Olympics. Another permanent exhibit, Encounter with the First Nations, offers a modern glimpse into the lives of 11 native nations of the province. Past exhibits have explored the Inca civilization in a unique adventure called In Peru with Tin Tin, which combined Peruvian treasures and the artwork of two Tin Tin books. Another recent exhibit offered a colorful look at dragons, mythical creatures, and folklore from around the world. The museum boasts 10 exhibition spaces in all, so you could spend all day—or at least come back; admission allows for re-entry during the same day. The museum celebrates two decades in 2008.

Notre-Dame-des-Victoires Church / Place Royale
418-692-1650
32 Rue Sous-le-Fort, Québec, QC G1K 4G7
What's nearby: Place Royale Interpretation Centre, Quartier Petit-Champlain

Notre-Dame-des-Victoires dates to 1688 and stands as the oldest stone church in North America. The interior features the suspended scale-model of the ship *Le Brézé*, which arrived in New France with contingents of soldiers in 1664. While a popular tourist spot, the church remains an active place of worship. In the front courtyard, you'll find yourself in Place Royale, once the center of New France commerce. It wasn't until 1686 that the public market square was officially called Place Royale, after public official Jean Bochart de Champigny installed a bust of Louis XIV, a version of which remains today.

Place Royale Interpretation Centre
418-646-9072
www.mcq.org
27 Rue Notre Dame, Québec, QC G1K 4E9
What's nearby: Notre-Dame-des-Victoires Church, Musée de la Civilisation
Price: $

Place Royale mural and musician.

Place Royale Interpretation Centre gets down to business—New France style. The museum explores the area's importance as a hub of trade from the 17th to 19th centuries. The collection of 14,000 items offers an intricate glimpse into the lives of merchants who lived, worked, and thrived in the area. The artifacts are displayed in a beautifully designed space that combines old and new. Fun topics about the art of these New France deals explore the area as a center for lodging—those visiting fur traders needed to stay somewhere, didn't they? The first inn in the area, which was owned by Sieur Boidon, dates to 1648. The space also explores how to set a proper New France table, complete with hundreds of pieces of porcelain, pottery, and tin-glazed earthenware on display. Finally, all these goods had to get to New France from Europe somehow, and the best way to store these delicate items for a treacherous cross-Atlantic journey—roll out the barrel. The sturdy, multipurpose, easy-to-use barrel gets its proper due.

Quartier Petit-Champlain / Breakneck Stairs
www.quartierpetitchamplain.com

At the bottom of the funicular you'll find yourself in the Quartier Petit-Champlain and Rue du Petit-Champlain, one of the oldest sections and streets in the city. Some of the historical houses that line the street date to the late 1600s. Today, the quarter is lined with dozens of restaurants and shops and attracts about 1.5 million visitors a year. Before there was a funicular to help Quebecers up and down the side of the cliff, there was the *escalier casse-cou*, or the Breakneck Stairs. A stairway dates to the location as early as 1660. The current staircase received upgrades in the 1960s and 1990s.

FESTIVALS / SPECIAL EVENTS / GUIDED TOURS

Les Fêtes de la Nouvelle-France—New France Festival
www.nouvellefrance.qc.ca
Where: Old Quebec, the Old Port

The city celebrates colorful costumes, Old World customs, and pure Quebec camaraderie during the New France Festival, a five-day summer bash held every August. And the locals come out in droves for this New France fashion show—it attracts about 30,000 costumed participants every year. Everywhere you turn, these local Quebecers proudly walk about the city in full dress—sometimes during very hot weather. The town really deserves a nod for its infectious New France spirit. The event is not limited to locals, as everyone is invited to dress in costume. The Web site offers beautifully detailed ideas for New France styles of attire. Other festival activities include musical acts, military parades, and storytelling. The highlight of the fest is the Meeting of the Giants, a parade of giant effigies in the style of European street fairs. The parade usually features about 30 effigies every season, but about 50 of the big-headed heroes and heroines will be on hand for the 400th anniversary celebrations. A festival pass, good for access to all venues, costs about $10. Where to buy one—don't worry, they'll find you. These costumed New France salespersons are on every street corner come festival time. A word to drivers: Côte de la Montagne is closed to car traffic during the fest. Upcoming festival dates are August 5–10, in 2008 and 2009.

Rue du Petit-Champlain is one of the oldest streets in Quebec City.

FERRY AND BOAT CRUISES

Québec-Lévis Ferry
418-643-8420, 1-877-787-7483
www.traversiers.gouv.qc.ca
10 Rue des Traversiers, Québec, QC G1K 8L8
What's nearby: Rue du Petit-Champlain, Musée de la Civilisation
Price: $

The Québec-Lévis ferry is operated by Société des Traversiers du Québec. The ferry operates year-round and takes only 10 minutes to travel the half-mile or so to the south shore. The boat departs from the Old Port where Boulevard Champlain and Rue Dalhousie meet—you can't miss it. Departures are every 30 minutes during the day and every hour at night. It's the perfect mini-cruise. Don't forget to bring the camera for great Quebec City skyline photo opportunities. The round-trip ferry admission is part of your museum card. Extra fees apply if you're traveling with your bicycle or car.

Louis Jolliet / AML Cruises
1-800-563-4643
www.croisieresaml.com
124 Rue St-Pierre, Québec, QC G1K 4A7
Price: $$$

Quebec's iconic *Louis Jolliet* is synonymous with St. Lawrence River cruises. Day cruises visit Montmorency Falls and Île d'Orléans; night cruises offer the best view of the annual fireworks show at Montmorency Falls. Food-themed cruises include a Sunday brunch buffet, a four-course evening dinner cruise, and a tropical dinner buffet. Departs from the Chouinard Pier in front of Place Royale along Rue Dalhousie.

THEATER/NIGHTLIFE/ENTERTAINMENT

L'Inox Microbrewery
418-692-2877
www.inox.qc.ca
37 Quai St-André, Quebec, QC G1K8T3
What's nearby: It's adjacent to Le Port-Royal Hotel

Beer *ici*. L'Inox produces 11 of their own brews. Five ales are available year-round, like the Transat extra-blonde. There are six seasonal tastes, like Kermesse, a barley and wheat concoction infused with cardamom, orange bock, and coriander available from St-Jean-Baptiste Day (June 24) to harvest time. Montagnaise, which is available in autumn, is flavored with honey, Labrador tea, and cloud berries, a tiny fruit cousin of the raspberry or blackberry found along the northern St. Lawrence coast. Pool table, live music, nice outdoor summer patio. Open noon to 3 AM.

L'Oncle Antoine
418-694-9176
29 Rue St-Pierre, Québec, QC G1K 3Z3

This New France Festival effigy honors Samuel de Champlain

Uncle Antoine offers beer and bar food. The building dates to 1754 and was home to Marie-Anne Barbel, considered one of Quebec's first businesswomen—she took over her husband's trading business after his death to provide for their seven children. The bar includes an arched-ceiling room that once stored furs and pottery. Outdoor terrace spring and summer.

Pub Thomas Dunn
418-692-4693
369 Rue St-Paul, Québec, QC G1K 3X3

A wonderful, busy Old Port pub great for drinks or dinner. Thomas Dunn features 150 brands of beer, 11 varieties on tap, and a generous selection of Scotches. Just across from the train station.

SHOPPING

Boutique la Dentellière Lace
418-692-2807
56 Blvd. Champlain, Québec, QC G1K 4H7
A place for lace in the Old Port.

Dugal Ebiniste
418-692-1564
15 Rue Notre Dame, Québec, QC G1K 4E9

This Place Royale boutique offers the wood crafts of 20 local artisans. Furniture, sculptures, jewelry, and decorative objects.

Librairie du Nouveau Monde
418-694-9475
www.total.net/~linomond
103 Rue St-Pierre, Québec, QC G1K 7A1

A little bookstore with mostly French titles that boasts an ample selection of nautical maps, charts, and navigational guides in both French and English. A number of English titles are devoted to specialty antiques and antiques price guides, which may come in handy when strolling the nearby antiques shops along Rue St-Paul.

Lush
418-694-9559
www.lush.com
102 Rue du Petit-Champlain, Québec, QC G1K 4H4

Living the Lush life means treating yourself to cosmetics and bath and skin-care products that are all handmade and never tested on animals. The British-based chain of Lush stores now numbers 32 in Canada, with one shop in Quebec City and two in Montreal. The place resembles a colorful culinary gourmet boutique with soaps that mimic chunks of chocolate, scoops of sorbet, and wheels of cheese. The soaps are cut, wrapped, and sold by the pound. It's near Cochon Dingue restaurant.

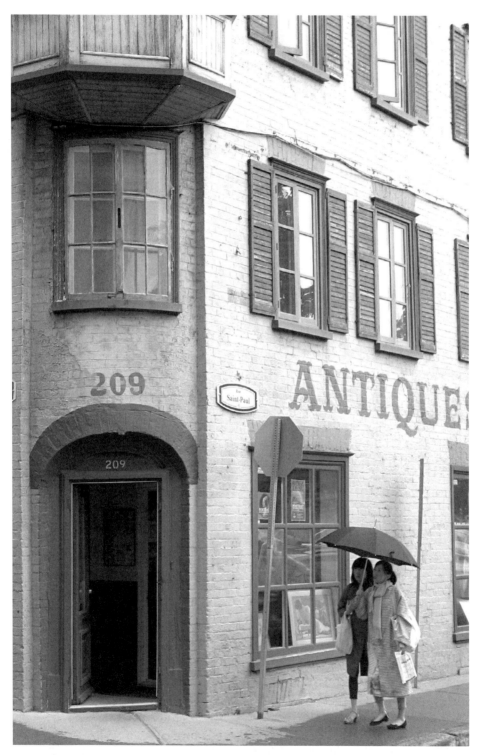

Antiques shopping abounds along Rue St-Paul in the Old Port.

Mer Mode
418-692-0163
55 Rue St-Paul, Québec, QC G1K 9G9

Mer means sea. Mode means fashion. This small men's and women's clothing boutique features colorful nautical-themed attire.

Verrerie la Mailloche
418-694-0445
www.lamailloche.com
58 Rue Sous-le-Fort, Québec, QC G1K 4G8
Shop and gallery entrance at the Escalier Casse-Cou—the Breakneck Stairs

Shopping in the Petit-Champlain / Place Royal area ranges from tacky souvenir shops to high-end crafts. Verrerie la Mailloche glassblower falls into the latter category. You'll find exquisite glass objects including vases, pitchers, lamps, dishes, bowls, and objets d'art that are all handcrafted on the premises by master glassblower Jean Vallieres. You can browse the store or watch glassblowing demonstrations for a nominal fee. Custom-made orders are accepted.

ANTIQUES SHOPPING ALONG RUE ST-PAUL IN THE OLD PORT
Start at the corner of Rue St-Paul and Sault-au-Matelot and walk north.

Vitrail Original
418-522-5888
79 Rue St-Paul, Québec, QC G1K 3V8

Original and ornamental painted stained-glass lamps and night-lights made on-site by craftsman Vasile "Mike" Obretin. Small items can be shipped.

Les Antiquités Marcel Bolduc
418-694-9558
www.marcelbolduc.com
74 Rue St-Paul, Québec, QC G1K 3V9

A well-stocked and well-kept antiques store that defines the phrase "a place for everything and everything in its place." The antiques run the gamut and include high-quality antique furniture, collectibles, religious artifacts, vintage postcards, fun folk art, gramophones, and Quebec license plates.

La Nouvelle-France Antiquités
418-694-1807
110 Rue St-Paul, Québec, QC G1K 3V9
For antique furniture, objets d'art, and decorative pieces as well.

Candeur Savonnerie
418-353-1683
www.candeur.com
113 Rue St-Paul, Québec, QC G1K 3V8

OK, this one's not an antiques shop, but it's worth a stop. For artisanal handmade soaps and beauty products. The place smells great!

Charme Antique
418-694-9313
133 Rue St-Paul, Québec, QC G1K 3V8

Owner Elizabeth Godin can't resist an antique linen when she sees one. She brings many pieces back from her travels to Europe and offers them to you in her boutique. For table-cloths, runners, bed linens, as well as a collection of fine antique prints.

Boutique à la Capucine
418-692-5318
145 Rue St-Paul, Québec, QC G1K 3V8

One of the more fanciful antiques shops along the street. The emphasis here: whimsical Quebecois folk art. Fun to browse.

Librarie Argus
418-694-2122
160 Rue St-Paul, Québec, QC G1K 3W1
A small boutique that specializes in rare antique books, engravings, and postcards.

De Retour
418-692-5501
273 Rue St-Paul, Québec, QC G1K 3W6

Everything not-so-old is new again. De Retour specializes in 20th-century retro furniture and lighting with an emphasis on Scandinavian, European, American, and Canadian designers. Lots of teak, chrome, and Plexiglas. It's a bit farther down the block, but close to almost a dozen nearby restaurants.

Lower Town / St-Roch

PARKS AND PUBLIC GARDENS

Jardin de St-Roch
Where: Bordered by Rues de la Couronne, St-Vallier, du Parvis, and Ste-Hélène

Nothing more than a vacant lot 15 years ago, the space was inaugurated in 1993 as the St-Roch Garden, a small urban green space that has become the symbol of the neighborhood's revitalization. The park is surrounded by light industry and office space and is two blocks from the bustle of Rue St-Joseph.

SHOPPING

Le Comptoir Emmaüs
418-692-0385
915 Rue St-Vallier, Québec, QC G1K 3P9

Located along the border between Upper Town and St-Roch, Emmaüs offers four floors of secondhand bargains. If you prefer your thrift stores with a little dust, then this is the place for you. You'll find vintage appliances and spare parts, glassware, china, souvenirs, books, clothing, furniture, bric-a-brac, and knickknacks. All proceeds go to charity.

ST-ROCH—RUE ST-JOSEPH SHOPPING TOUR
Start at the corner of Rue Monsignor Gauvreau and walk west on Rue St-Joseph.

Villa Import
418-524-2666
www.villaimport.com
600 Rue St-Joseph Est, Québec, QC G1K 3B9
Fine furniture and accessories.

Laliberté Department Store
418-525-4841
595 Rue St-Joseph Est, Québec, QC G1K 3B7
For men's and women's clothes. In business since 1867.

Benjo
418-640-0001
www.benjo.ca
543 Rue St-Joseph Est, Québec, QC G1K 3H4
A fun colorful shop that offers clothing, toys, and candy for kids.

Jardin St-Roch helped revitalize a neighborhood.

Hugo Boss
418-522-5444
505 Rue St-Joseph Est, Québec, QC G1K 3B7

What else can I say? It's a Hugo Boss boutique for men's and women's fashions in lil' old St-Roch!

Baltazar
418-524-1991
461 Rue St-Joseph Est, Québec, QC G1K 3B6
For whimsical modern housewares and furniture.

Mountain Equipment Co-op
418-522-8884
www.mec.ca
405 Rue St-Joseph Est, Québec, QC G1K 3B6

Everything for the great outdoors: clothing, camping gear, and canoes. There are 11 MEC sports gear cooperatives throughout Canada.

Kaverna-Oggi
418-522-3805
277 Rue St-Joseph Est, Québec, QC G1K 3B1

In business for 40 years, Kaverna recently moved to the St-Roch district. You'll find rugs, lamps, and imports from India, Morocco, and Indonesia.

St-Roch district architecture.

Trouvailles et Trésors

418-554-4243
275 Rue St-Joseph Est, Québec, QC G1K 3B1

This small antiques shop features fine china as well as a generous collection of vintage cuff links and tie clasps.

X20

418-529-0174
www.x20.com
200 Rue St-Joseph Est, Québec, QC G1K 3A9

Goth kids to the front of the line. For clothing and accessories, mainly in black, Dr. Martens boots, and every color and style of Converse sneaker under the sun. Also in Montreal at 3456 Rue St-Denis, 514-281-0986.

THEATER/NIGHTLIFE/ENTERTAINMENT

Boudoir Lounge

418-524-2777
www.boudoirlounge.com
441 Rue du Parvis, Québec, QC G1K 9L6

A lively inviting lounge, nightclub, and restaurant on pedestrian-only Rue du Parvis. Open daily until 3 AM.

L'Impérial de Québec

418-523-3131
www.imperialdequebec.com
252 Rue St-Joseph Est, Québec, QC G1K 3A9

The Imperial Theatre has stood the test of time in the St-Roch neighborhood, with origins dating back to the early 1900s. Recently restored, the venue now features a variety of French acts in a cabaret setting.

Suburbs

CULTURE / MAJOR ATTRACTIONS / ARCHITECTURE

Parc Aquarium du Québec

418-659-5264, 1-866-659-5264
www/sepaq.com/aquarium
1675 Ave. des Hôtels, Québec, QC G1W 4S3—Located just under the Pierre Laporte Bridge
Price: $$

Operated by Parcs Québec, the Aquarium offers 10,000 specimens large and small, including resident walruses, seals, and two polar bears. The site is home to 300 species in all, both fresh- and salt-water creatures. The main tank is appropriately called Awesome Ocean—it holds almost 100,000 gallons of water. You can get a great close-up view in the glass tunnel that runs underneath the tank. The park also features wetlands complete with marsh and footbridge, and a coastal zone where you can reach out and touch the likes of starfish and sea urchins. The park reopened in 2002 after two years of renovations. The aquarium celebrates its 50th anniversary in 2009.

Parks and Public Gardens

Montmorency Falls
418-663-3330, 1-800-665-6527
www.sepaq.com
2490 Ave. Royale, Quebéc, QC G1C 1S1
Located about 7.5 miles east of downtown Quebec in Beauport. Take Autoroute 40 west or
    Blvd. Ste-Anne, Highway 138 west.
Price: $ for cable car access; $$ for general admission to the fireworks

Montmorency Falls cascades about 240 feet to the St. Lawrence River below—it's a longer drop than the Niagara Falls by about 100 feet. The park features hiking trails, walkways, a pedestrian suspension bridge that hovers directly above the falls, and cable car rides. The site also includes Manoir Montmorency, which offers a boutique, an interpretation center, and a terrace restaurant—buffet brunch is offered Sunday for about $22. During summer, Montmorency Falls becomes the perfect backdrop for six spectacular fireworks shows every July and August. Buses depart from Place d'Youville terminal in Old Quebec. Visit www.lesgrandsfeux.com. Snowshoeing, ice climbing, and sledding are available at Montmorency Park during winter. There is a parking fee in addition to cable car admission.

Sports/Biking/Activities

ExpoCité
418-691-7110
www.expocite.qc.ca
250 Blvd. Wilfrid-Hamel, Québec, QC G1L 5A7

ExpoCité is a multi-complex venue that includes the Exhibition Centre, which hosts trade shows, the Colisée Pepsi, and the Hippodrome de Québec, which offers horse racing and agricultural shows.

Quebec Remparts / Colisée Pepsi
418-525-1212
www.remparts.qc.ca
250 Blvd. Wilfrid-Hamel, Québec, QC G1L 5A7

Colisée Pepsi is a 15,000-seat arena that was the former home to the Quebec Nordiques. Today the arena is the home ice of the Quebec Remparts hockey team, members of the Quebec Major Junior Hockey League. The site also hosts musical concerts and ice shows.

Shopping

Les Galeries de la Capitale
418-627-5800
www.galeriesdelacapitale.com
5401 Blvd. des Galeries, Québec, QC G2K 1N4

This shopping mall features 280 stores, including Zellers, Sears, Simons, the Bay, Aldo Shoes, Baby Gap, and Future Shop Electronics. But here's the best part—they also have an amusement park inside. Mega Park features 18 rides and attractions, including a merry-go-round, bumper cars, a climbing wall, an ice-skating rink, and a Ferris wheel.

Quebec City 400th Anniversary Celebration 1608–2008
www.MyQuebec2008.com
The party has begun. Quebec City 400th anniversary celebrations continue through 2008—and beyond! Not confirmed, but U2 and the Pope are scheduled to appear. Cirque du Soleil has already signed on. So has Celine Dion—she'll share the stage in a free concert on the Plains of Abraham Aug. 22, 2008. Celebrations take place all over the city and are centered at Espace 400e in the Old Port. Everyone in town is joining the fun. Here are some event highlights.

Espace 400e
Location: Bassin Louise (Louise Marina) along Rue St-André
Espace 400e hosts many 400th-anniversary events. The centerpiece is the Ephemeral Gardens, a connecting promenade on the Louise Marina. After the official parties have ended, Espace 400e, which is owned by Parks Canada, will become an interpretation center that will offer a permanent exhibit about immigration.

Passengers Exhibition
Espace 400e
June 3–October 19, 2008
A tribute—to the tourist! This exhibit pays tribute to the millions of people who have visited the city from day one.

The Image Mill
Espace 400e
June 20–July 29, 2008
www.exmachina.qc.ca
A multimedia show created by visionary artist Robert Lepage.

Urbanopolis
Musée de la Civilisation
Until April 19, 2009
An exhibit that explores an urban vision of the future accompanied by talks, performances, and cinema.

Official Commemorations
The big day is July 3, 2008
Location: Basilica-Cathedral of Notre-Dame de Québec; Plains of Abraham; Bassin Louise
The Basilica of Québec hosts formal High Mass and a salute to Champlain. Next is the Freedom of the City Ceremony, as well as all the pomp and circumstance of the traditional official ceremonies.

The day includes a military parade and afternoon song and dance. The 2008 edition of the Festival International d'Été de Québec (summer festival) opens that night on the Plains of Abraham, and the evening concludes with a torch-lit parade from the Plains of Abraham to the Louise Marina.

Family Snapshot
This is one big happy family. And if you're in town on July 6, 2008, make your way to the Plains of

Abraham, where you and as many people who show up will be photographed from the air. The photo will be preserved for future generations who will celebrate Quebec City's 500th anniversary!

Québec Vue par Kedl: 400 Ans de Passion
Capitale Observatory
Until October 31, 2008
Quebec City captured in photographs by artist Eugen Kedl in an exhibit titled 400 Years of Passion.

Quebec: A City and Its Artists, 1670–1970
Musée National des Beaux-Arts du Québec
Until April 27, 2009
An exhibition that highlights past and present artists associated with Quebec City.

Quebec City Forever: Champlain's Mark
Centre d'Interpretation de Place-Royale
Until December 31, 2009
Follow Samuel de Champlain on his journey to Quebec.

The Life and Work of François de Laval
Musée de l'Amérique Française
Until March 22, 2009
An exhibit dedicated to New France's first bishop.

The City: Outdoor Installations by Franco Dragone
Musée de la Civilisation
May 1–October 31, 2008
Producer and stage-show creator Franco Dragone, who has worked with Cirque du Soleil and Celine Dion, transforms the exterior of the Musée de la Civilisation's stairways, terraces, and walls into architectural works of art.

400th Anniversary Souvenir Tree
The Quebec Forest Industry Council will distribute 400,000 trees to the citizens of Quebec City.

Urban Forests: Meeting Place
Until October 31, 2008
The greening continues. Guided tours of Quebec City's urban parks.

Magic Nights of the 400th
July 30–August 3
Quebec City and Lévis
This uplifting event features 80 hot-air balloons in full flight on both shores of the St. Lawrence River.

The Louvre in Quebec City: Arts and Life
Musée National des Beaux-Arts du Québec
June 5–October 26, 2008
Musée National des Beaux-Arts du Québec presents an exhibition of the collections of the Louvre Museum. Artifacts will include Oriental, Egyptian, Greek, and Roman antiquities.

Golf Revival
Plains of Abraham
August 21–31, 2008
Quaaaatre! I mean fore! The Plains of Abraham were once the site of the Quebec Golf Club, the second-oldest golf club in North America, founded in 1874. To commemorate the sport, a nine-hole

course will be set up for four days in August. Invited golfers will come dressed in period golf attire and get a chance to use equipment of the time as well.

The Quebec Bridge—Meet Me in the Middle

August 16 and 17, 2008

The Quebec Bridge (next to the Pierre Laporte Bridge) will be closed to cars and open to visitors, musicians, and circus performers. Activities include a parade, a picnic, guided visits, and fireworks.

Mois Multi Productions Recto-Verso

September 11–20, 2008

St-Roch District

St-Roch gets a chance to celebrate with art installations throughout the neighborhood. The finale is Under Scan Quebec, an installation by artist Raphaël Lozano-Hemmer.

Bike Ride

October 5, 2008

Beauport and Côte-de-Beaupré Districts

A cycling tour along the St. Lawrence River. Cyclists can choose from a 15-, 30-, or 60-kilometer circuit.

Sommet de la Francophonie

October 17–19, 2008

The 12th conference of government heads of state from French-speaking nations.

Closing Event by Cirque du Soleil

October 19, 2008

An original Cirque du Soleil production to take place at the end of the Sommet de la Francophonie.

Château Frontenac winter scene.

11

Quebec City Side Trips

Charlevoix Region

Culture / Major Attractions / Architecture

Charlevoix Casino
418-665-5300, 1-800-665-2274
www.casino-de-charlevoix.com
183 Rue Richelieu, La Malbaie, QC G5A 1X8

Run by Loto Québec, the Charlevoix Casino offers all the gambling staples that you'll need to hit it big, including baccarat, poker, roulette, blackjack, and more than 800 slot machines. The casino is about 95 miles northeast of Quebec City. Bus transportation to the region from Quebec City is available on Intercar, 418-525-3000 or www.intercar.qc.ca.

Lodging

Le Manoir Richelieu
418-665-3703, 1-800-257-7544
www.fairmont.com
595 Côte Bellevue, La Malbaie, QC G5A 1C7

Adjacent to the Charlevoix Casino, Le Manoir Richelieu is a Fairmont property that offers golf, health club and spa, fine dining, accommodations, and spectacular views of the St. Lawrence River.

Sports/Activities/Skiing

Le Massif
418-632-5876, 1-877-536-2774
www.lemassif.com
1350 Rue Principale, Petite-Rivière-St-François, QC G0A 2L0

Le Massif ski resort is about 45 miles east of Quebec City or about 45 miles west from La Malbaie and the Charlevoix Casino—it's right in the middle. The mountain offers 43 trails, 5 lifts, and 9 miles of cross-country ski and snowshoe trails. The views of the St. Lawrence River don't get any better than this.

There's always a rainbow at Canyon Ste-Anne.

Île d'Orléans

Île d'Orléans Tourist Information Center
418-828-9411, 1-866-941-9411
www.iledorleans.com
490, Côte du Pont, St-Pierre-de-l'Île-d'Orléans, QC G0A 4E0

The earliest of New France settlers established themselves at Île d'Orléans beginning in the 1630s. Some 300 French family names can trace their ancestral roots to the island. The island's pastoral farmland provides Quebec with many good things to eat. It also provides foodies with a feast for body and soul. The island's food producers include cheese makers, a chocolate factory, vineyards, cider producers, sugar shacks, a microbrewery, and pick-your-own farms that offer a bounty of apples, strawberries, and raspberries, to name a few. Île d'Orléans also boasts dozens of boutiques and art galleries, two golf courses, and about two dozen inns and bed-and-breakfast establishments. Access to the island is by the Île d'Orléans Bridge, or Pont de l'Île, about 8 miles from Quebec City on Autoroute 440 or Route 138 east.

Chemin du Roy
www.lecheminduroy.com
The adventure is all in the journey. The Chemin du Roy (which translates to the King's Road) was the first carriage road that connected Montreal to Quebec City. A New France decree at the turn of the 18th century stated that a road be built to accommodate the settlements along the St. Lawrence River. When completed in 1737, the road measured 175 miles long and 24 feet wide. The road remained active for a century and a half and was the main mail route of the time, with 29 relay stations along the way. Mail between Montreal and Quebec City could be delivered in a brisk two days' time. Today the route hugs the northern shores of the St. Lawrence, mostly following along Route 138. There are dozens of parks, panoramic views of the river, picnic sites, historical buildings, churches, and accommodations through two dozen municipalities along the way, as well as clearly marked Chemin du Roy signs. The Route Verte bicycle path follows most of the Chemin du Roy as well. Informational brochures are available through the Web site and at Bonjour Québec at 1-877-266-5687.

Lévis

CULTURE / MAJOR ATTRACTIONS / ARCHITECTURE

Lévis Forts National Historic Site of Canada

418-835-5182, 1-888-773-8888
www.pq.gc.ca/levis
41 Chemin du Gouvernement, Lévis, QC G1K 7A1
Price: $

Lévis Fort No. 1 is the last of three forts built by the British between 1865 and 1872. It was intended to further protect the British from any future American invasions. The Brits were nervous for two reasons: The United States was in the middle of a Civil War, with relations tense between London and Washington—and a railway linked Lévis to Maine. To ensure their safety in defending the country, the British decided to build the fort, even though the impending threat died down just as construction got under way. The fort sits atop Point Lévy, the highest point in the area. The site features a multimedia program and spectacular views of Quebec City across the river. Open from mid-May to the end of September.

Parcs Québec

LODGING

Ice Hotel

418-875-4522, 1-877-505-0423
www.icehotel-canada.com
143 Route Duchesnay, Ste-Catherine-de-la-Jacques-Cartier, QC G0A 3M0

Can someone crank up the heat? Uh, no. Things would get a little messy. The Ice Hotel is made of 4-foot-thick walls and boasts an average indoor temperature of about 25 degrees Fahrenheit. The site features ice sculptures and a bar where drinks are served in glasses made of hollowed ice. Accommodations don't come cheap—midweek rates start at about $300 a night, while a Saturday night stay in a room with a fireplace costs $575. You don't have to stay overnight. A visit with cocktail and transportation from Quebec City costs about $47. The Ice Hotel is open the beginning of January until the beginning of April. It is located on the grounds of Station Touristique Duchesnay of Parcs Québec, about 30 miles from Quebec City. Take Autoroute 40 west to Highway 367 / Route de Fossambault north.

Station Touristique Duchesnay

418-875-2122, 1-877-511-5885
www.sepaq.com
143 Route Duchesnay, Ste-Catherine-de-la-Jacques-Cartier, QC G0A 3M0

About 30 miles west of Quebec City, Station Touristique Duchesnay offers four seasons of outdoor adventures and a variety of accommodations including an auberge, 10-room log cabins, villa rentals on the shores of Lake St-Joseph, and a Scandinavian Spa. Winter activities include dogsledding ($78 for an hour and a half), a cross-country skiing and skating package ($35 for the day), and ice-fishing ($35 for three hours). Take Autoroute 40 west to Highway 367 / Route de Fossambault north.

Ste-Anne-de-Beaupré Region

CULTURE / MAJOR ATTRACTIONS / ARCHITECTURE

Musée de l'Abeille—Honey Economuseum
418-824-4411
www.musee-abeille.com
8862 Blvd. Ste-Anne, Château Richer, QC GoA 1No

How sweet it is. The Honey Economuseum is part exhibition space about bees, part production center for honey. And if you like honey the way I like honey, oh honey are you in for a treat. They've got flavors like clover and sweet summer honey reasonably priced—about $8 for a 2.2-pound (1 kg) jar. You can sample a variety of the flavors, but no double dipping. Other products include jelly, pollen, honey candy, mead honey wine, beeswax candles, and bee propolis, which is known for its healing properties. It's just off Route 138 on the way to Ste-Anne-de-Beaupré.

Ste-Anne-de-Beaupré Shrine
418-827-3781
www.ssadb.qc.ca
Ste-Anne-de-Beaupré, QC GoA 3Co

Ste-Anne-de-Beaupré celebrates its 350th anniversary in 2008. The shrine dates to 1658 and is considered the oldest pilgrimage site in North America. The site has been home to five churches in its history; the first two, made of stone and wood, lasted only two decades. The third church, built of stone, lasted for an entire two centuries, from 1676 to 1876. The first larger basilica lasted almost half a decade, until it was ravaged by fire in 1922. The present basilica, built in 1923, features architectural details like hand-carved pews, a mosaic about the life of Ste. Anne, and a statue of Ste. Anne with her daughter Mary, the mother of Jesus. In the small glass-enclosed blessing office near the monastery and church store, a priest is always on hand to offer visitors a benediction. Separating the parking lot from the church is a rail line that until the mid-1990s carried pilgrims from Montreal and Quebec City to the shrine. The rail line now only accommodates freight cars, and you occasionally have to wait until the train passes to get back to your car.

SPORTS/ACTIVITIES/SKIING

Canyon Ste-Anne
418-827-4057
www.canyonste-anne.qc.ca
206 Route 138 East, Beaupré, QC GoA 1Eo

Canyon Ste-Anne offers an exhilarating morning or afternoon outdoor excursion just 20 minutes from Quebec City. The site features a 240-foot waterfall and a 200-foot pedestrian bridge above the canyon. It's a thrilling view and was enough to inspire a number of famous visitors, including Henry David Thoreau, who visited in 1850, and artist Cornelius Krieghoff, who painted the falls in 1855. The basic visit requires a bit of hiking on your part, but everything is well-marked and completely safe. If you're really the adventurous type, you can explore the canyon by *via ferrata*, which means the mountain-

Climbers navigate Canyon Ste-Anne.

side includes built-in safety cables for your harness. Admission costs about $10; equipment rentals extra.

Mont Ste-Anne
418-827-4561, 1-888-827-4579
www.mont-sainte-anne.com
2000 Blvd. du Beau Pré, Beaupré, QC G0A 1E0

In winter the mountain offers 65 trails of skiing. Spring through fall the mountain offers panoramic gondola rides for about $15 round-trip.

St. Lawrence River

CULTURE / MAJOR ATTRACTIONS / ARCHITECTURE

Grosse Île and the Irish Memorial National Historic Site of Canada
418-234-8841, 1-888-773-8888
www.pc.gc.ca/grosseile
2 Rue d'Auteuil, Québec, QC G1K 7A1 (mailing address—at Fortifications National Historic Site of Canada)

Some 30 miles east of Quebec City on the St. Lawrence River, a majestic Celtic cross monument welcomes visitors to Grosse Île and the Irish Memorial National Historic Site. The site commemorates Quebec's role in Canadian immigration as well as Grosse Île's role as a quarantine station for the Port of Quebec from 1832 to 1937. The site also tells the tragedy of thousands of immigrants fleeing Ireland during the Great Famine who died at sea in an 1847 typhus epidemic. Usually, arriving vessels underwent quarantine for six days, but several ships remained in isolation for more than three weeks due to the typhus outbreak. About 5,000 people died while waiting for medical attention. In all, about 7,500 people are buried at Grosse Île. The site offers visits to a memorial and the Irish cemetery, and trolley tours of the village. Les Croisières le Coudrier offers Grosse Île cruises from mid-May through mid-October. Allow a full day for the visit. The ferry departs from Quebec City at 9:30 AM and stops in Lévis and Île d'Orléans. The Grosse Île visit lasts for about five hours. The boat returns to Quebec City at 5 PM. The cost is about $17.

GUIDED TOURS / WHALE-WATCHING TOURS

AML Cruises
418-692-1159, 1-800-563-4643
www.croisieresaml.com

AML Cruises offers a 10-hour whale and fjord cruise that departs from Tadoussac. The price includes hotel pick-up and bus transportation from Quebec City. The season lasts from the end of May to early October. About $105 for adults.

Dufour Cruises
418-692-0222, 1-800-463-5250
www.dufour.ca

Dufour offers whale-watching cruises that depart from Tadoussac and Baie Ste-Catherine, about 125 miles east of Quebec City. Season runs May through October. About $57 for adults.

Cruise Ships
Montreal and Quebec City are popular ports of call. Here are a few cruise lines that visit the region.

Celebrity Cruises
1-877-202-4345
www.celebritycruises.com
Celebrity offers 12-night Canada and New England cruises on board the *Constellation*, with round-trip service from Cape Liberty in Bayonne, New Jersey. Stops include Portland, Maine; Charlottetown, Prince Edward Island; Quebec City; Halifax; and Bar Harbor, Maine.

Crystal Cruises
1-866-446-6625
www.crystalcruises.com
The *Crystal Symphony* embarks on four cruises to the region every fall. Thematic cruises include an 11-day Northeast Discovery golf-themed cruise from Montreal to New York in late September 2008 and a 10-day New World Explorer wine and food festival cruise from Montreal to New York in mid-October 2008.

Holland America
www.hollandamerica.com
The MS *Eurodam* offers two Canada New England Atlantic Coast cruises every fall. The 10-day September departure sets sail from Quebec City to New York. The 14-day October departure continues to Fort Lauderdale. The MS *Maasdam* sets sail from Montreal to Boston, with stops including

Quebec City, on a seven-day Canada New England Discovery Cruise in June, July, and September of 2008. The October 2008 cruise continues to Fort Lauderdale.

Norwegian Cruise Lines
www.ncl.com

1-866-625-1166

Norwegian Cruise Lines offers a 12-day Canada and New England cruise round-trip from New York, with a stop in Quebec City aboard the *Norwegian Dawn* in fall.

Princess Cruises
1-800-774-6237

www.princess.com

The *Grand Princess* and the *Sea Princess* both use Quebec City as an embarkation point for five fall cruises that range between 10 and 19 days.

Royal Caribbean
1-866-562-7625

www.royalcaribbean.com

Explorer of the Seas offers a nine-night Atlantic Canada and Quebec Cruise. The cruise originates in New Jersey and stops at Sydney, Nova Scotia; Charlottetown, Prince Edward Island; Quebec City; and Halifax, Nova Scotia. Cruises run from late August to early October.

Seabourne Cruises
1-800-929-9391

www.seabourn.com

Seabourne offers 10-day luxury yacht cruises aboard the 208-passenger *Seabourne Pride*, with itineraries that include Montreal and Quebec City.

St. Lawrence River cruises come large and small.

General Index

Palais de Congrès, 111
Palais Montcalm, 248
Parc Aquarium du Québec, 271–72
Parcs Québec, 181
Parcs Québec (Quebec City), 279
Parking, 124–25
parking and signage, 51–52, 196
parks and public gardens (Montreal): down-
   town, 113; Eastern Townships, 167–68;
   Hochelaga/Maisonneuve, 129–30;
   Hudson/Oka, 181; Jean Drapeau Park, 136;
   Lachine, 156; Lachine Canal/Little Burgundy
   and St-Henri, 156–57; The Plateau, 147–49
parks and public gardens (Quebec City): St-
   Roch, 268; suburbs, 272
Parliament Building, 235–36
Passengers Exhibition, 273
Passion des Fruits, 100
passports, 23–24
Pâtes à Tout, 100
Petits Gâteaux, 100
pets, traveling with, 26
pharmacies, 54, 198
Piazza Mag, 228
Piazzetta, 231
Piccolo Diavolo, 87
Pierre du Calvet/Les Filles du Roy, 92
Place d'Armes, 143
Place de la Cité, 213
Place des Arts, 116
Place Jacques Cartier, 143
Place Jean-Paul-Riopelle, 76, 113
Place Laurier, 213
Place Montreal Trust, 115
Place Royale Interpretation Centre, 259, 261
Place Ste-Foy, 213
Plateau, The (Montreal): dining, 98–99, 101–5;
   lodging, 70–73; map of, 40; overview of, 45;
   parks and public gardens, 147–49; shopping,
   150–52; sports/biking/activities, 153; the-
   ater/nightlife/entertainment, 153–54
Plaza St-Hubert, 154
Plein Art, 239
Pointe à Callière, the Montreal Museum of
   Archaeology and History, 143–44
Pointe-du-Buisson Archaeological Park, 177–78
Poisson d'Avril, 228
police, 52, 196
Ponte St-Charles (Montreal) culture/major
   attractions/architecture, 158–59
population, 35, 185

Portofino Bistro Italiano, 221–22
post offices, 54, 198
poutine, 222
Premiere Moisson Boulangerie, 131
Priape, 124
Pride Quebec, 208
Princess Cruises, 283
professional sports, 117
Pub Claddagh, 116
Pub D'Orsay, 222
Pub Thomas Dunn, 229, 265
public gardens. See parks and public gardens
   (Montreal); parks and public gardens
   (Quebec City)
public transit, 50–51, 195
Pullman, 103
Pulsations, 178–79

Q

Quadricycle, 144–45
Quai Des Brumes, 153
Quartier Petit-Champlain/Breakneck Stairs, 261
Quebec: A City and Its Artists, 1670-1970, 274
Quebec Bridge, TheMeet Me in the Middle, 275
Quebec City. See also Charlevoix Region (Quebec
   City); Île d'Orléans (Quebec City); Lévis
   (Quebec City); Parcs Québec (Quebec City);
   St. Lawrence River (Quebec City); Ste-Anne-
   de-Beaupré Region (Quebec City): air travel
   and shuttles, 189; area codes, 199; bus travel,
   191, 195; car rentals, 192; carpooling, 191–92;
   culture/major attractions/architecture,
   233–36, 243–50, 259–61, 271–72; dental
   emergencies, 197; dining, 215–31; downtown
   overview, 187; emergency services, 196; ferry
   and boat cruises, 263; festivals/special
   events/guided tours, 236–39, 250–56, 261,
   282–83; geography and general orientation,
   183, 185; grocery stores, 198; hospitals, 197;
   lodging, 201–13; map of downtown/St-
   Jean/Old Quebec, 186; map of metropolitan
   area, 184; map of Old Port, 190; map of Old
   Quebec fortifications, 188; map of St-Roch,
   194; Montcalm overview, 189; museum card,
   242–43; news media, 199; Old Port overview,
   187; Old Quebec overview, 187; park-
   ing/signage, 196; parks and public gardens,
   268, 272; pharmacies, 198; population, 185;
   post offices, 198; public transit, 195; Quebec
   City 400th Anniversary, 273–75; roads and
   highways/bridges/ferry/rush hour, 196; safety

Lodging by Price—Montreal

$	up to $75
$$$	76 to $150
$$$$	151 to $250
$$$$$	251+

$–$$
Anne ma soeur Anne Hôtel-Studio, 70
Château de l'Argoat, 67
La Loggia, 64

$$
All Suite VIP Loft Montreal, 66
Aubergell, 64
Dauphin Hotel, 59
La Concierge Guest House, 67
Le Roberval, 67
Turquoise B&B, 66

$$–$$$
Alexandre Logan (1870), 63
Auberge de la Fontaine, 70
Best Western Europa, 57
Best Western Ville Marie Hotels and Suites, 57,
   59
Candlewood Suites Montréal, 66–67
Cantlie Suites Hotel, 59
Gouverneur Hotel Place Dupuis, 64
Holiday Inn Express, 67
Hôtel de l'Institut de Tourisme et d'Hôtellerie du
   Québec, 73
Le Relais Lyonnais, 67
Lord Berri, 67
Marriott Courtyard, 61
Novotel Montréal Centre, 61
Sir Montcalm Bed and Breakfast, 64
Square Phillips, 62

$$$
Delta Hotel, 59–60
DoubleTree Hilton, 70, 73
Meridian Versailles Montréal, 59

$$$–$$$$
Auberge Bonaparte, 68
Château Versailles, 59
Hilton Bonaventure, 60
Hotel Gault, 68
Hotel Nelligan, 69
Hôtel XIXe Siècle, 69
Hyatt Regency, 60
InterContinental Hotel, 69–70
Le Saint-Sulpice Hotel, 70
Marriott Château Champlain, 61
Marriott SpringHill Suites, 61
Opus Hotel, 61–62
Queen Elizabeth Hotel, 62
Ritz Carleton, 62
Sofitel Montreal, 62
W Montréal, 62

$$$$
Hostellerie Pierre du Calvet, 68
Hôtel Le St-James, 68
Hotel Place d'Armes, 69
Le Germain Hotel, 60
Loews Hotel Vogue, 60–61

Dining by Price—Montreal

(For a dinner entrée)
$$ 1 to $15
$$$ 16 to $30
$$$$ 31 to $40
$$$$$ 41+

$
Arahova, 80
Boulangerie les Co'pains d'Abord, 98–99
Byblos Le Petit Café, 99
Café Santropol, 99
Chez Cora, 84
de Gascogne, 97
Euro Polonia, 86
Juliette & Chocolat, 97
La Banquise, 101
La Paryse, 86
Quoi de N'Oeuf, 89
Restaurant Mont-Royal, 103
Rôtisserie Laurier, 97–98
Saloon, 87–88
Schwartz's, 104
SoupeSoupe, 104
St-Hubert, 88
Wilensky Light Lunch, 95

$–$$
Berlin, 93
Café Rococo, 80
Cuba Saveur Tropicale, 86
MBCo, 82
Olive et Gourmando, 91
Soy, 95
Wok du Chef, 105

$$
Bistro le Porto, 84
Chao Phraya, 96
Chez le Portugais, 99
Chez Lévêque, 98
Chu Chai, 99
Cluny ArtBar, 90
Dans La Bouches, 101
Élla Grill, 86

Grand Comptoir, 81
Jardin Nelson, 90–91
La Iguana, 101
La Petite Ardoise, 97
La Raclette, 101–2
Le Limón, 88–89
L'Entrecôte St-Jean, 82
L'Express, 102
Mazurka, 102
Piccolo Diavolo, 87
Pullman, 103
Senzala, 104
Thursdays, 83
Zen Ya, 83–84

$$–$$$
Au Petit Extra, 84
Bazaar Anise, 96–97
Bu, 93–94
Carte Blanche, 84
Cuisine et Dépendance, 94
Gandhi, 90
Il Cortile, 81
La Capannina, 81–82
La Loïe, 86
Laloux, 101
L'Atelier, 94–95
Nuevo, 103
Resto Robin de Bois, 103–4
Stash Café, 92–93
Truffert Bistro de Christophe, 104–5

$$–$$$$
Decca 77, 80–81

$$$
Med Bar & Grill, 103
O Thym, 87

$$$–$$$$
Aix Cuisine du Terroir, 89
Aszú, 89
Au Pied du Cochon, 98
Brontë, 80

Lodging by Price—Quebec City

Dining by Price—Quebec City

(For a dinner entrée)
$1 to $15 $
$16 to $30 $$
$31 to $45 $$$
$46+ $$$$

$
Chez Victor, 215
Commensal, 216
Diana, 216
Le Buffet de l'Antiquaire, 226
Le Cochon Dingue, 226–27
Les Cafés du Soleil, 227
Paillard Café, 221

$–$$
Bistro Les Bossus, 230
Café Bistro du Cap, 223
Café Riviera, 223–24
Le 48 Saint-Paul, 225–26
Le Petite Dana Thai, 227
Le Sultan Café, 218
Les Frères de la Côte Restaurant, 220
Piazza Mag, 228
Piazzetta, 231
Pub D'Orsay, 222
Restaurant L'Aubergine, 228

$–$$$
Restaurant Allemand, 228

$$
Blu Bar & Grill, 215
Cosmos Café, 216
Il Teatro, 217
Largo, 230
Le Café du Clocher Penché, 230
Le Café du Monde, 226
Le Hobbit, 218
Le Veau d'Or, 218
L'Entrecôte St-Jean, 220
Yuzu, 231

$$–$$$
Au Parmesan, 219
Aviatic Club, 221–22
Café de la Paix, 220
Ginko, 216
Le 47ième Parallèle, 218
Le Lapin Sauté, 227
Le Pain Béni, 220
Le Patriarche, 220–21
L'Échaudé, 226
Mistral Gagnant, 228
Poisson d'Avril, 228
Portofino Bistro Italiano, 221–22
Voo Doo Grill, 219

$$$
Charbon Steakhouse, 224

$$$–$$$$
Aux Anciens Canadiens, 219
Initiale, 224
L'Astral, 217–18
Laurie Raphaël, 224–25
Le Marie Clarisse, 227
Le St. Amour, 222
Toast!, 228–29
Utopie, 231

$$$$
Les Artistes de la Table, 227